VCs

OF THE FIRST WORLD WAR

SPRING
OFFENSIVE 1918

VCs

OF THE FIRST WORLD WAR

SPRING OFFENSIVE 1918

GERALD GLIDDON

First published 2004
This new edition first published 2013

The History Press
The Mill, Brimscombe Port
Stroud, Gloucestershire, GL5 2QG
www.thehistorypress.co.uk

ISBN 978 0 7524 8730 4

Typesetting and origination by The History Press
Printed in Great Britain

CONTENTS

CONTENTS

ACKNOWLEDGEMENTS

I would like to thank once again the staff of the following institutions for their assistance during the research for this book: the Commonwealth War Graves Commission, the Imperial War Museum, the National Army Museum and the National Archives at Kew. In addition, I would also like to thank the archivists and curators of the many regimental museums who responded to my requests for information.

Where recently taken photographs have been included, their owners have been acknowledged with each individual illustration.

As was the case with my two earlier books in the *VCs of the First World War* series, Donald C. Jennings of Florida has been immensely kind in supplying me with pictures of the majority of graves or memorials included here.

Most of the maps reproduced in this book first appeared in *Military Operations France and Belgium*, edited by J.E. Edmonds, Macmillan/ HMSO, 1922–49.

Maurice Johnson once again spent many hours in the National Archives on my behalf, searching out and reading the appropriate War Diaries. It was hardly surprising to learn that material for the beginning of the Spring Offensive was in short supply. So many units, especially in the forward forces, were simply overwhelmed in the first part of the battle.

Other individuals who also gave assistance include Peter Batchelor, who also compiled the index, for which I am grateful, John Cameron, Jack Cavanagh, Colonel Terry Cave CBE, David Cohen, Peter Harris, Dennis Pillinger and Steve Snelling. Other people who provided material but whose names are not listed here have been acknowledged in the Sources section at the end of the book.

PREFACE TO THE 2013 EDITION

The History Press have decided to re-issue the *VCs of the First World War* series in new editions and I have taken advantage of this decision by revising and updating the texts of the current volume.

Since the initial research for this book was carried out nearly ten years ago, there has been an increasing interest in and awareness of the stories and lives of the men who were awarded the nation's and the Commonwealth's highest military honour. Evidence of this can be found in the amount of new books being published on the subject; the re-issuing of servicemen's records by the National Archives and the accessibility of other records of family history, which are now available via *Ancestry*, the family history magazine. The internet has also played a major part in the increase in the availability of information. Finally, the founding of the *Victoria Cross Society* in 2002 by Bran Best has encouraged further research and publication of informative articles on the holders of the Victoria Cross.

One of the heartening consequences of this new interest in the subject is in the erection of new or replacement headstones on some of the graves of these brave men, and it is hoped that, in time, every man who has a grave will have it properly marked.

Gerald Gliddon, October 2012

INTRODUCTION

At the end of 1917, after three years of trench warfare on the Western Front, the two main Allied Armies, the British Expeditionary Force (BEF) and the French, and their main opponent, the German Army, had reached a point of exhaustion and hibernation. At the same time various changes had been made which led to a re-alignment of the two sides.

Firstly, the revolution in Russia had led to the collapse of their military involvement in the war, which in turn released a great number of extra men and equipment, and the German Army was no longer obliged to conduct a major campaign on two fronts. In addition, Italy had collapsed and Rumania had sued for peace.

On the Allied side, the French Army in 1917 had endured the failure of the Nivelle Offensive on the Aisne and had also had to cope with a series of mutinies within its ranks. Although the French Army, with over a hundred divisions to draw upon, was far bigger than the British could hope to put into the field, its morale was extremely low and in early 1918 the French handed over an extra 25 miles of line to the British. In the Allies' favour, the German submarine campaign to prevent supplies getting through from the USA to Britain had been a failure in 1917. However, the trump card for the Allies was the announcement of the involvement of America in the war. With the USA's seemingly inexhaustible supply of both men and supplies, it was felt that, whatever the Germans might achieve, in the long term their efforts would inevitably end in defeat, probably in 1919. However, General (Gen.) J. J. Pershing, in command of the American Army, was not intending to throw the lives of his men away piecemeal and was planning to enter the conflict only when his army was equipped and ready to be used to fight as an individual force.

Discontent was not confined to the French Army, however, and the BEF was riddled with rumours that Field Marshal (FM) Sir Douglas Haig was to be replaced, as David Lloyd George, the British prime minister, considered him to be a squanderer of men's lives, and the high casualties of the Passchendaele offensive in the autumn of 1917 reinforced this view. However, although in his diary Haig indicates that he was prepared to step down, he knew that his position was pretty safe as there was simply no better commander, either British or Dominion, who could take his place. Lloyd George therefore adopted another tactic in order to prevent Haig from seeking yet another costly offensive. He simply starved him of manpower.

The period from January to mid-March 1918 was one of the quietest of the whole war and the Allied line was now 126 miles long. To the south of the Allied lines was General Sir Hubert Gough's Fifth Army of twelve infantry divisions and three cavalry divisions. They were responsible for about 42 miles of front, with the southernmost section of about 10 miles thought to be unsuitable for fighting. Overall, they were responsible for about a third of the British sector of the Western Front. Gough was convinced that it was his thinly held line which was going to have to bear the full brunt of the German offensive, which was known to be in preparation. To his left was Gen. Byng's Third Army of fourteen divisions; two more than Gough had and yet with a line of only 28 miles to look after. This included the Flesquières (Cambrai) Salient and a position on the left of the Fifth Army at Gavrelle, about 6 miles to the north-east of Arras. To the left or north of the Third Army were the British First and Second Armies, covering 33 miles and 23 miles respectively. The Flesquières Salient was to be held as a false front.

The build-up to the German offensive over the first three months of 1918 was all too obvious to the British; even the date of 21 March could be guessed at as a result of interviewing German prisoners. The Germans sometimes called their offensive Operation Michael, after the German patron saint, and sometimes *Kaiserschlacht*, the Kaiser's battle. When it began in the early hours of 21 March, it consisted of a bombardment which lasted for several hours. A great stroke of good fortune for the German Army was the presence of a thick mist, especially in the area where the attack was planned, namely the line held by the Fifth Army. However, the mist, which was much less dense on the Third Army front, turned out to be a mixed blessing for both sides, as neither always had the visibility that it required. The attackers, when they began to break through the Allied lines, operated on a front of 50 miles and the total number of divisions that were involved in the initial fighting came to sixty. Despite Gough's warnings about the vulnerability of his line, his orders were not altered and his troops had little choice other than to fight and then retreat in good order. In fact, at many points, the Fifth Army simply collapsed under the overwhelming German onslaught, in which the enemy used a mixture of gas, rifle and machine-gun fire, accompanied by artillery. Despite the swiftness of the German advance, Gough was still to hold the lines of the River Somme at all costs; there was to be no withdrawal from this position. On the 26th, Gough was 'to delay the enemy as long as possible without being so involved as to make retirement impossible'.

On the left of the Fifth Army, Gen. Byng's Third Army was hanging on despite its right flank being exposed. The holding of the Flesquières Salient had not been a good plan to follow and made the situation even more confusing than it might have been.

An Allied conference took place at Doullens on 26 March to discuss the serious situation on the British Fifth Army front (Gen. Gough had not been invited) and also the possibility of a united Allied command structure. FMl Haig was quite willing to serve under Gen. Foch, the chief of staff of the French Army, to co-ordinate the Allied command. Sir William Robertson was to cease being the Chief of the Imperial General Staff (CIGS), and Foch told Haig that the decision would give Gen. Pétain a morale boost after the French Army mutinies of 1917. Despite this increase in co-operation, however, the French seemed in no hurry to assist the British Army defend the River Somme line and, indeed, were much more preoccupied in defending Paris, which was now being threatened by German long-range guns.

In his memoir of the Fifth Army, Gough writes of a visit by Gen. Foch to his headquarters (HQ), whereby the Frenchman harangues his British colleague for his inadequate handling of the Fifth Army. Naturally, Gough was unhappy about this incident and at not being invited to the Doullens conference in the first place. He must then have realised that his days as commander of the Fifth Army were numbered.

On 3 April, a week after the Doullens conference, Lloyd George told Haig that Gough must go and this was confirmed in a cable sent by Lord Derby the next day. History has not really made up its mind about the career of Sir Hubert Gough and to give him his 'bowler hat' for the poor performance of the Fifth Army during the March Somme battles does seem a trifle unfair. If anything, he should perhaps have been given the sack for 'underachieving' in earlier campaigns in the Salient, or at Bullecourt in 1917, or on the Somme in 1916. As on most occasions when the careers of his colleagues were threatened, Haig stood by his friend when the news came through from London that he was to go. However, if Haig complained too much then the spotlight would inevitably be turned upon his own performance. So loyal was Haig to Gough after he had been sent home in early April, that it was not until 16 June that one reads the following note of exasperation in his published diary:

> I am sorry that he is talking so stupidly but I don't think it would be any use writing to him. Some of his friends are advising him to keep quiet. I am doing all I can do to help him, but, as a matter of fact, some orders he issued and things he did were stupid – and anything of the nature of enquiry would not do him any good.

By 5 April the Allied line had been severely dented but, despite the collapse of the British Fifth Army, the German Army had overstretched itself and was running out of supplies. Gough had been replaced by Sir Henry Rawlinson and the Fifth Army was made the Reserve Army.

The German commander, Gen. Ludendorff, decided on a change of plan and on 9 April his army mounted an attack, under the name 'Georgette', between Ypres and La Bassée. The German Fourth Army were to take on the British Second Army under General Plumer and the German Sixth Army was to be pitched against General Horne's First Army. After progressing for 10 miles and beginning to threaten the Channel ports, Ludendorff decided to call off the assault at the end of April as he was unable to make a strategic gain. Meanwhile, on 9 April, Lloyd George stated in the House of Commons that the fighting strength in France and Flanders was greater on 1 January 1918 than a year before. In fact, it was 41,000 men less. Three days later, Haig issued his famous 'backs to the wall' order in which he called upon the BEF to fight it out: 'Every position must be held to the last man: there must be no retirement. With our backs to the wall, and in believing in the justice of our cause, each one of us must fight on to the end.'

From early May, the Germans moved southwards with their plans of attack and decided to take on the French from 27 May in a campaign which lasted until 6 June. The British were still involved, under the French command with their British IX Corps. Later the British were also involved in the Marne fighting from 20 July–2 August as, once again, Paris was threatened with enemy occupation.

This book does not pretend to be a full-blown military history of the 1918 German Spring Offensive, a subject on which there are already a good many volumes. It is one of a series covering the lives and deeds of the men who won the VC in the First World War, and is a collective or group biography of the fifty-seven men – 60 per cent of them officers – who won the VC in the period from March to the end of July 1918 while serving in the British Army on the Western Front.

Despite the poor showing of the British Fifth Army in March 1918, this book ends on a note of optimism for the Allies as they prepared their great counter-blow against the German Army which would, in turn, lead to the end of the war within a hundred days.

C.G. ROBERTSON

*West of Polderhoek Château,
Belgium, 8/9 March*

In the first months of 1918, only one Victoria Cross was awarded to a British soldier on the Western Front: G58769 Lance Corporal (L. Cpl) Charles Graham Robertson of 10th (S) Royal Fusiliers, on 8 March. This was thirteen days before the start of the German Spring Offensive, codenamed Operation Michael. The fighting in this part of 1918 hardly receives any attention in the history books and the importance of the attempted German breakthrough overshadowed what had gone on in the period between the closedown of Third Ypres at the end of October 1917, followed by the Cambrai battle, and the famous 21 March date.

The Allied line in the Ypres Salient bent round the easterly side of Polygon Wood and ran southwards to the west of Polderhoek Château before crossing the Menin Road and bending in a south-westerly direction.

At 6.30 a.m. on 8 March 1918, the enemy began a bombardment which grew fiercer and continued for ten and a half hours, with only a brief pause. The shelling was particularly heavy to the north of the Menin Road. On the front of the 13th (S) Royal Fusiliers (11th Brigade (Bde), 37th Division (Div.)), no attack was carried out by the enemy but the bombardment had resulted in casualties. To the left of the 13th, the 10th Royal Fusiliers, who had been in support at the commencement of the shelling, were, by the afternoon, providing reinforcements for the 13th (S) King's Royal Rifle Corps who had been attacked. They had sent up D Company (Coy), which included L. Cpl Charles Robertson MM (Military Medal). The *History of the Royal Fusiliers* states that the situation provided him 'with an opportunity for an action calling as much on his skill as his heroism'.

His citation in the *London Gazette* of 9 April 1918 stated:

For most conspicuous bravery and devotion to duty in repelling a strong attack by the enemy on our position. On realising that he was being cut off, L.-Corpl Robertson sent back two men to get reinforcements, and remained at his post (with only one other man) firing his Lewis gun and killing large numbers of the enemy, who were in range on his right. No reinforcements came up, and, realising that he was being completely cut off, he withdrew, with the only survivor of the garrison of the post, to a point about ten yards further back, where he successfully held his position. Here he again stayed for some considerable time, firing his Lewis gun and inflicting casualties on the enemy. The position was, however, made impossible for him by the heavy hostile bombing and machine-gun fire, so he was forced again to withdraw and arrived at a defended post. At this post he got on top of the parapet with a comrade, mounted his gun in a shell-hole and continued firing at the enemy, who were pouring across the top and down an adjacent trench. He had not been firing long when his comrade was killed and he himself severely wounded. He managed to crawl back, bringing his gun with him, but could no longer fire it, as he had exhausted all his ammunition. L.-Corpl. Robertson was alone throughout these operations, except for the presence of one other man, who was later killed, and the most determined resistance and the fine fight which he put up undoubted prevented the enemy from making a more rapid advance. His initiative, resource and the magnificent fighting spirit are worthy of the highest praise.

Although Robertson's was the first military VC to be gained in 1918, he had to wait, probably owing to his severe wounds, until two days before the Armistice before he was decorated by King George V in the Ballroom at Buckingham Palace on 9 November 1918. He was discharged from the Army a few weeks later on 19 December and was given the Silver War Badge.

Charles Graham Robertson was born in Penrith, Cumberland, on 4 July 1879, the only son of James and Catherine Robertson. James was a gardener and, later, the family moved to Dorking in Surrey, living on the north-eastern edge of the town in a road named Riverside. Today, this road consists of terraced cottages and is a cul-de-sac ending in a railway embankment.

As a boy Robertson sang in Pixham Church choir and the church is around the corner from Riverside at the point where Leslie Road meets Pixham Lane. He attended the local National School (later St Martin's) and then moved on to Dorking High School.

After finishing his education Robertson took part in the Boer War as a trooper in the 34th Coy (Middlesex) Imperial Yeomanry. During the Great War he transferred from the cavalry to the infantry and became a member of the Royal Fusiliers, arriving in France on 19 November 1915. His MM was gazetted on 2 November 1917. In March 1918, he was severely wounded in the stomach during his VC action and returned to England, spending some time in a hospital in Ipswich; he was not expected to survive. However, a surgeon from Guy's Hospital took an interest in Robertson's case and, after two intricate operations, he began to recover. He returned to Dorking for a few days' leave from hospital in December 1918 and the townspeople turned out in their thousands to welcome him home at a special presentation.

A procession was formed which included Boy Scouts, Girl Guides, boys from schools that he had attended, the National and St Paul's, local volunteers and the town band. Robertson was taken by brougham to the High Street, where the two horses were unharnessed and the carriage was then pulled to the Red Lion Hotel by soldiers who had been wounded and later discharged, called the Silver Badge men. The presentation took place in front of the decorated inn and Mr J.B. Wilson, chairman of the local council, made a speech, as did Lord Ashcombe and the MP for Reigate.

Robertson was subsequently presented with an award by the population of Dorking. At first he was unwilling to accept any gifts, but eventually he gave way and was duly presented with a gold watch and chain, along with a gift of cash which he directed to a deserving charity. He resumed work for the railway as a booking clerk and, for the rest of his life, served as a clerk in the London offices of the LNER. He was very active in local affairs and served with many organisations. At one time he was a member of the Dorking Football Club and was a keen cricketer and strong swimmer. However, his wounds curbed his sporting activities, although he loved to watch sports at Pixham, his local parish, or at Westcott, a village to which he often walked. He took an active part in the work of the local British Legion, who elected him vice-president. He liked nothing better than to walk over Box Hill, a well-known beauty spot outside Dorking, and at one time he used to swim in the River Mole near Castle Mill.

He served as a sergeant in the Home Guard during the Second World War and, after the war, although he had been a very active sportsman, he became increasingly unwell. In the period 1951–1954 he was to suffer a stroke and became chairbound. His wife Doreen Madeline looked after him devotedly during his final years at their home at 5 Longfield Road, Dorking. He died in the Garth Nursing Home, where he had been a patient for several weeks, on 10 May 1954. He did not wish for a military funeral and was buried from the cemetery chapel at Pixham, across the road from the church he used to attend. He is buried in the town cemetery, Plot 36, Grave 360.

In his home town Robertson was very highly thought of, not just as a war hero, a subject of which he rarely spoke, but also for his warmth and friendliness. He was always at his happiest watching sport or playing a game of snooker. In 1977, Robertson's widow presented his medals to the Royal Fusiliers for their museum in the Tower of London, and she outlived her husband by thirty-three years, dying in 1987. Apart from the VC, MM, 1914–15 Star, BWM (British War Medal), VM (Victory Medal), his decorations included those from the Boer War and the Coronation in 1937 and 1953. As Robertson later ceased to believe in the justification or legality of the South African War, he no longer wore the appropriate awards which he had been awarded, including the Queen's South African Medal with Clasps, Cape Colony, Orange Free State and Transvaal. As a result they became separate from his Great War decorations and were sold in 1977 by C.J. & A.J.Dixon of Bridlington.

E.F. BEAL
St Léger, France, 21/22 March

In mid-March the 121st Bde of the 40th Div. was sent to reserve positions at Hendecourt, a village about 8 miles to the south-west of Arras. The brigade was to be ready to move at three hours' notice. On the eve of 20 March, enemy gunfire could be heard targetting the next, and thsis continued into the next day. At 6.00 a.m., the 13th (S) Battalion (Bn) The Yorkshire Regiment (Regt) (Alexandra, Princess of Wales's Own) 'stood to' and at 1.15 p.m. marched off to the village of Hamelincourt, about 3 miles to the south-east. Their orders were to take over front trenches of the third line of defence in a position from the Mory-Ecoust road to St Léger, together with the 12th Suffolks. Brigade HQ was in a sunken road to the south of Mory.

It was already known that the villages of Croisilles and Ecoust to the north-east had fallen and the enemy had broken through other parts of the British line, but the depth of penetration was uncertain. At midnight, A and C companies of the 13th Yorkshires moved up to a communication trench in order to take up their positions. However, a patrol reported that the enemy were in occupation already. In addition, it was discovered there was a 400 yard gap between them and the adjacent unit, and that several enemy machine-guns had been set up there. Progress was halted while 2nd Lieutenant (2nd Lt) E.F. Beal of the supporting D Coy worked his way up the communication trench with a Lewis gun team and a supply of bombs. He succeeded in disabling no fewer than four enemy machine-gun teams and captured their guns, in addition to one prisoner.

By dawn, A Coy was occupying the German frontline positions from the south-east corner of St Léger Wood. Later in the morning,

Beal went out to collect one of his men who had been wounded, but tragically was himself then mortally wounded by a shell.

Beal's VC was published in the *London Gazette* of 4 June 1918:

> For most conspicuous bravery and determined leading when in command of a company detailed to occupy a certain section of trench. When the company was established, it was found that a considerable gap of about 400 yards existed between the left flank of the company and the neighbouring unit, and that this gap was strongly held by the enemy. It was of vital importance that the gap should be closed, but no troops were then available. Organising a small party of less than a dozen men, he led them against the enemy. On reaching an enemy machine gun, Second Lieut. Beal immediately sprang forward, and with his revolver killed the team and captured the gun. Continuing along the trench he encountered and dealt with another machine gun in the same manner and in all captured four enemy guns, and inflicted severe casualties. Later in the evening, when a wounded man had been left in the open under heavy enemy fire, he, regardless of danger, walked up close to an enemy machine gun and brought in the wounded man on his back. Second Lieut. Beal was killed by a shell on the following morning.

Ernest Frederick Beal, son of J. J. W. Beal and Jane Sturman Beal was born in Brighton on 27 January 1883, and his home address at the time was 55 East Gate. He had two brothers, Harold Robert and John James, who were also to serve in the Great War. Ernest was educated at Brighton Grammar School and later worked in his father's stationery shop. When he enlisted in the 2/1 Sussex Yeomanry on 24 September 1914, he gave his address as the family home at 148 Lewes Road, Brighton. By 11 June 1915 he was promoted to sergeant and, on 15 September, was posted to the 1/1 Sussex Yeomanry, serving with them in the Balkans. On 16 December 1916 he moved to the 16th Royal Sussex Regt and was recommended for a commission with the 13th (S) Bn The Yorkshire Regt (Alexandra, Princess of Wales's Own) on 26 October 1917, joining D Coy.

A few months after Beal died from wounds while winning his VC, the posthumous award was presented to his parents in the Quadrangle of Buckingham Palace on 3 July. The couple were accompanied by Miss May F. Bundy, Ernest's fiancée, of 37 Crescent Road, Brighton.

Ernest Beal was later commemorated in a number of ways; as a former member of the Boys Brigade, an annual award in his memory was presented to the member of the Brighton Boys Brigade who had been the most most proficient during the year. In their turn, Brighton Corporation presented his parents with an Illuminated Address, which conveyed the town's congratulations and also sympathy at their loss. On this occasion it was pointed out that Beal was the first Brighton man to win the Victoria Cross. His name is also listed on Bay 5 of the Arras Memorial to the Missing in France.

On the death of J. Beal senior, Ernest's VC was inherited by his brother Harold who, in 1964, wrote to the Green Howards Regimental Museum (formerly the Yorkshire Regt) and indicated that they could have it on permanent loan, which they did from 1966. Apart from the VC, the other service medals included the 1914–15 Star, BWM and VM which had been bequeathed to May Bundy, who also lent them to the Green Howards. Later the loan arrangements were converted to outright gifts.

J.C. BUCHAN

East of Marteville, France, 21 March

 On 21 March, 2nd Lt John Crawford Buchan of the 1/7th Argyll and Sutherland Highlanders (A & SH) was attached to the 1/8th A & SH of the 183rd Bde, 61st (2nd South Midland) Div. The division was about 4 miles to the east of the pre-21 March British line which ran around the west side of St Quentin. The area was in the Fifth Army sector. Buchan had been wounded early in the day, but despite this he insisted on remaining with his men and encouraging them when visiting their positions, even when under the most intense shellfire. His platoon suffered many casualties.

His posthumous VC was published in the *London Gazette* of 2 May 1918 and tells the story as follows:

> When fighting with his platoon in the forward position of the battle zone, Second Lieut. Buchan, although wounded early in the day, insisted on remaining with his men, and continually visited all his posts, encouraging and cheering his men, in spite of most severe shell fire, from which his platoon was suffering heavy casualties. Later, when the enemy were creeping closer and heavy machine-gun fire was raking his position, Second Lieut Buchan, with utter disregard of his personal safety, continued to visit his posts, and though still further injured accidentally, he continued to encourage his men and visit his posts. Eventually, when he saw the enemy had practically surrounded his command, he collected his men and prepared to fight his way back to the supporting line.
>
> At this point the enemy, who had crept round his right flank, rushed towards him, shouting out 'Surrender'. 'To hell with surrender,' he replied and shooting the foremost of the enemy, he finally repelled this advance with his platoon. He then fought

his way back up the supporting line of the forward position, where he held out to dusk. At dusk he fell back as ordered, but in spite of his injuries again refused to go to the aid post, saying his place was beside his men. Owing to the unexpected withdrawal of troops on the left flank, it was impossible to send orders to Second Lieut. Buchan to withdraw, as he was already cut off, and he was last seen holding out against overwhelming odds. The gallantry, self-sacrifice and utter disregard of personal safety displayed by this officer during these two days of most severe fighting is in keeping with the best traditions of the British Army.

Buchan died near Marteville on 22 March 1918 having won his VC the day before to the east of the village. When he was killed his body was taken 7 miles northwards to be buried in Roisel Community Cemetery Extension which had been begun by the Germans to the north of the Communal Cemetery. The village of Roisel is 7 miles to the east of Péronne and had been an important CCS Centre. Buchan's grave is in Plot II, Row 1, Grave 6.

John Crawford Buchan was born in Alloa, Clackmannan, Scotland on 10 October 1892, and was the third son of David and Margaret Buchan. His father was the editor of the local paper, the *Alloa Advertiser*. Before the war John was educated at the Alloa Academy and later became a reporter at his father's newspaper. He also worked in the Scottish camps of the YMCA. He was a keen mountaineer and, at the outbreak of war, was on holiday in Switzerland, later returning home and enlisting with the RAMC. He was commissioned into the 7th Argyll and Sutherland Highlanders on 25 January 1917 and was later attached to the 8th Bn. He went to France on 4 October 1917.

Two of his four brothers were also killed in the war, his eldest brother, Lieutenant (Lt) David Buchan, on 9 April 1917 when serving with the Gordon Highlanders, and his younger brother, 2nd Lt Francis Hall Buchan, who died of wounds on 7 August 1918 when struck by a shell fragment near Béthune while serving with the 11th Rifle Bde. At one time a portrait of John Buchan used to hang at the A & SH Club in Glasgow.

Buchan's mother, Margaret, had died in 1907, which was the first tragedy in the Buchan family history, so John's VC was presented to his father at Buckingham Palace on 3 March 1920. The *Times Weekly Edition* carried a photograph of the occasion, which was later presented to the Alloa Public Library. A memorial plaque was, at one time, in the possession of the regimental archivist to the A & SH at Stirling Castle. In addition, a second plaque was to be found in the Alloa Museum, along with a copy of a picture which recreates 'To Hell with Surrender'. Buchan's name is also included on the Alloa War Memorial.

Buchan's father's health gradually broke down and he died in 1926, having lost three members of his family within a fairly short time.

John Buchan had been a good friend of Lt William Bissett, another winner of the VC, who was a member of the 1/6 A & SH and won his VC in October 1918. He survived the war, living until May 1971.

John Buchan's VC and service medals are not publically held.

E. DE WIND

*Racecourse Redoubt near
Grugies, France, 21 March*

2nd Lt Edmund de Wind was one of seven
men to win the VC on 21 March 1918, which
he earned when in charge of the defence of a
position called Racecourse Redoubt, south-
east of Grugies. He was a member of the 15th
(S) Bn, North Belfast Royal Irish Rifles (RIR)
(107th Bde, 36th (Ulster) Div.). 108th Bde
was to their right and 109th Bde to their left.
The Ulster Div. was to the south-west of the
German-held town of St Quentin, where, by
17 March, it was obvious to the Ulstermen
that there was a huge increase in German activity. The much-anticipated
German offensive was surely close at hand.

Racecourse Redoubt straddled a railway line that led into St Quentin
and was one of fourteen redoubts in the area. They had been established
because of the thinness of the defensive line; in fact, there was a group
of three in this forward zone, each held by one of the three divisional
brigades. Racecourse Redoubt was in the middle of the three and the
15th RIR occupied it, together with the 1st RIR.

At 4.35 a.m. on 21 March the German artillery opened fire and the
enemy assault on the Ulster Div. began at 9.40 a.m. The attackers were
helped by a thick mist and they quickly reached the line of redoubts,
which were immediately surrounded and cut off. The one known as
Jeanne d'Arc was overrun first as it was the most easterly. The mist
then began to clear, which helped the defence of the two remaining
redoubts to hold out; however, as each trench line was fought for and
eventually overrun, it was only a question of time before the inevitable
surrender. Finally only a small part of the redoubt around the railway
cutting remained and this fell soon after de Wind had collapsed,
mortally wounded. The time was just before 6.00 p.m. and he had

gained a posthumous VC for his bravery and self-sacrifice. Immediately after he was killed the remaining men in the garrison surrendered. De Wind's citation published in the *London Gazette* of 15 May 1919 tells the story:

> For seven hours he held this most important post, and, though twice wounded and practically single-handed, he maintained his position until another section could be got to his help. On two occasions with two N.C.O.s [non-commissioned officers] only he got out on top under heavy machine-gun and rifle fire, and cleared the enemy out of the trench, killing many. He continued to repel attack after attack, until he was mortally wounded and collapsed. His valour, self-sacrifice and example were of the highest order.

Thirty or so survivors (including HQ staff) were ordered by the Germans to remove their boots and were marched off barefoot into captivity.

De Wind was officially listed as missing and a cable dated 19 April 1918 was sent to his mother by the War Office, who remained reluctant to authorise a death certificate despite his death becoming increasingly obvious as the months went by. Then, in September, a report from a rifleman arrived at the War Office via the German Red Cross Society; it was given by Rifleman A. Wright of D Coy, supported by an unnamed officer in de Wind's battalion, who confirmed that de Wind had been killed. According to Wright, a trench mortar shell landed close to de Wind at about noon on 21 March 1918 and killed him outright.

Edmund de Wind was born in 'Kinvara', Comber, County Down in Northern Ireland on 11 December 1883. He was the youngest son of Arthur Hughes de Wind, chief engineer of the Belfast and County Down Railway, who died in 1917, and Margaret Jane de Wind. In 1900 the family lived at 32 and 32a Bridge Street, Comber, and then they moved to 31 Castle Street, which was later demolished. In 1908/9 Arthur de Wind built a house which he called 'Kinvara' in Killinchy Road, and the family took up residence there in 1909. Arthur de Wind worshipped at the St Mary's Church for more than forty years and was organist and choirmaster there. Edmund began school at Campbell College in Belfast in May 1895 and left five years later in December 1900 when he was 17. He joined the Bank of Ireland and worked in Belfast and Cavan. In 1911 he left for Canada, working in the Bank of Commerce and holding positions in several of its branches, including Toronto. He had served as a private for five months in 1912 with the 2nd Regt of Queen's Own Rifles of Canada, and on 16 November 1914 he enlisted in the 31st Bn (Calgary Regt) in Edmonton, Alberta. The 31st Bn was in 6th Bde, 2nd Canadian Div., which was part of the Canadian Corps under First, Second, Fourth and Reserve (Fifth) Armies. According to his attestation papers, he was 5ft 6in foot, with dark blue eyes, and dark brown hair which was going slightly grey. He sailed for England with his battalion on 29 May 1915 and, after training, left for France on 15 September in the same year.

Between September 1915 and April 1917 he served in the machine-gun section of his battalion. During his frontline service he was at Thiepval, on 1 July 1916, at Courcelette in September 1916 and at Vimy Ridge, Messines Ridge and Cambrai in 1917. After Vimy Ridge he was sent to an officer cadet school, and on 26 September he was commissioned in the 15th Bn RIR. He had first applied for a commission with this regiment when still in Canada. In December he returned to the front with them, before being involved in the German offensive of 21 March 1918, when he became one of three soldiers from his regiment to win a VC in the Great War. At the time of his death he was engaged and played hockey and cricket when at home in Ireland. He was also keen on sailing, shooting, fishing and tennis.

De Wind's VC was not gazetted until the much later, on 15 May 1919, because details of his extreme bravery were only revealed after the Armistice, when former occupants of Racecourse Redoubt returned from prisoner-of-war (POW) camps. It was presented to his mother, Mrs Margaret J. de Wind, in the Quadrangle at Buckingham Palace on 21 June 1919; although over eighty years of age she travelled from Belfast with her daughter to accept the award. While waiting in the Palace ante-room, the King noticed Mrs de Wind and gave instructions to an equerry to arrange for a private audience, which took place and saved the elderly woman from a long wait. Mrs de Wind died in 1922. After de Wind's death the gross value of his will was £1020 15s 7d and his executor was his siter, Catherine Anne.

De Wind's name is listed on the Pozières Memorial to the Missing, as he has no known grave, and after the war a captured German field gun was presented to the town of Comber as a memorial to him. It was placed in the town square, and details of his action in winning the VC were included on a commemorative plate. The gun disappeared in the Second World War in the drive for scrap metal towards the war effort, but the plate was saved and is now in the porch of the St Mary's Church in Comber. A memorial plaque to de Wind is also in the church itself.

In 1948, Mount de Wind was named after him in Jasper National Park, Alberta. One of the entrance pillars in St Anne's Cathedral, Belfast is dedicated to de Wind's memory with an inscription. A road in Comber is called de Wind Drive and is part of a housing estate built in 1961. His name is also remembered with a blue plaque in Bridge Street, Comber, which was unveiled on 14 September 2007, on the local war memorial, and a photograph hangs in the central hall of Campbell College, Belfast, which also contains a photograph of his memorial plaque. A school building is also named after him and his name is listed on the school war memorial. In 1985, de Wind's name was also included in the stone memorial to Ulster VCs in the approach to the Ulster Tower at Thiepval.

Keith Haines, a head of history at Campbell College, de Wind's old college has privately published a short biography of de Wind.

His decorations, apart from the VC, include the 1914–15 Star, BWM and VM, but they are not publically held.

W. ELSTOB

Manchester Redoubt, near St Quentin, France, 21 March

Temporary Lieutenant Colonel (T/Lt Col) Wilfrith Elstob was in command of the 16th (S) Bn (1st City) Manchesters (90th Bde, 30th Div.) when they took up positions opposite St Quentin on 18 March, three days before the great German Offensive. The position was called Manchester Hill, which consisted of a very well-defended, featureless hill position. Behind the hill was a quarry, which was used to provide cover and dug-outs, and served as a battalion HQ until 21 March, when the HQ moved forward to the battle HQ position. In this area of the Fifth Army, the plan of setting up fifteen redoubts was made because of the acute shortage of manpower. Defences were organised in depth and were sited to give the best field of fire for the Lewis and Vickers guns, together with rifle fire. Elstob had just written to a friend saying: 'If I die, do not grieve for me, for it is with the Sixteenth that I would gladly lay down my life.'

In the forward zone and facing east, A Coy of the Manchesters was to the right and B Coy to the left. In addition, a chain of sentries was set up and their orders were to withdraw should an enemy attack develop. The redoubt itself was made up of deep dug-outs and was set up for all-round defence; it was stocked with ammunition and protected by wire in its approaches. D Coy, together with battalion HQ, was actually in the redoubt itself, and C Coy was in reserve for use in counter-attack: two platoons positioned north of the redoubt in Francilly-Selency and two platoons to the south of the railway line. All told, the battalion frontage stretched for about 2,000 yards and the purpose of the garrison was to hold on as long as they could after the expected attack finally began, and to disorganise the enemy as much as possible. This plan, in advance of an expected German artillery bombardment, must have seemed hopeless in the eyes of the defenders, as retirement was not an option to be considered despite the redoubt having planned artillery support.

Manchester Redoubt was to the south of Francilly-Selency, a village where Major (Maj.) F.W. Lumsden had won a VC in early April 1917, following its capture by the 2nd Manchesters together with a section of the line which they named Manchester Hill.

Elstob's HQ was in Brown Quarry, to the rear of the actual hill, and on 21 March at 2.00 a.m. a patrol reported that there was no enemy activity. At about 4.30 a.m. a German barrage mixed with gas shells began in a thick mist and, at around this time, Elstob was reported to have announced that: 'Here we fight and here we die'. At 6.30 a.m. Elstob was still in a position to telephone 90th Bde, whose HQ was in Vaux, and this connection remained intact for much of the day. At the same time a box barrage was concentrated on the area of Etreillers to the rear by enemy artillery. The first sign of trouble for the garrison was the scream of a sentry who had been bayoneted. The first troops to be engaged with the enemy soon after at 10.30 a.m. were those in Manchester Redoubt, and the German bombardment continued until 11.00 a.m. The flanks were overrun and Germans were seen actually by-passing the redoubt on their way to the battle zone to the left. Elstob asked the artillery for a barrage, which was slow to arrive, and when it did it caught some of the British positions. Meanwhile he had left his HQ in the quarry and moved to a position on the redoubt. The enemy artillery was then moving down the road from St Quentin towards the redoubt. By midday the situation for the garrison was looking hopeless, although Elstob informed his brigadier that he would hang on until the end. In the fighting, Elstob himself was using a mixture of weapons: rifle, revolver and grenade.

The mist began to clear and 90th Bde was busy taking on the enemy to the rear of the position. All this time the heavy mist had given the attackers an advantage and they were quickly able to reach within bombing range of the redoubt. For a time the Vickers gun set up in the redoubt was out of action and the enemy had to be repelled by rifle fire, which could not sustain a defence for very long. By this time the redoubt had become surrounded, all battle positions were manned and any papers deemed to be of use to the enemy were destroyed. The redoubt fell to the enemy after a very stout defence by the Manchesters and, according to the war diary written up by a 2nd lieutenant on 2 April 1918, no frontal attack had been carried out by the enemy: the British frontline had been attacked from the rear. Elstob was twice wounded, his Vickers guns was put out of action and many of the garrison had been wounded; in addition, the trench mortars were out of ammunition. Elstob's final message was received at 3.22 p.m., in which he was reported to have said 'Goodbye'. The redoubt fell very soon after Elstob was shot in the head and killed. Later his body was apparently stripped, probably for souvenirs. The remaining defenders of the garrison surrendered almost immediately. At the start of the siege the redoubt was occupied by eight officers and 160 men, and about three-quarters of them surrendered after Elstob's death.

Of the three redoubts in this immediate area, the author considers that Manchester is the one that still boasts the most visible remains; in March 1995 one could still find slabs and sections of concrete together with baulks of timber, which were clearly part of the original defensive position. To the rear of the hill is the site of Brown Quarry, near which is a field used for motor coursing. Almost twenty years earlier, in 1976, the historian Martin Middlebrook had come across the remains of an artillery observation post (OP) on the top of the hill.

Fifteen months after his death, Elstob's posthumous VC was published in the *London Gazette* of 9 June 1919 as follows:

During the preliminary bombardment he encouraged his men in the posts in the Redoubt by frequent visits, and when repeated attacks developed controlled the defence at the point threatened, giving personal support with revolver, rifle and bombs. Single-handed he repulsed one bombing assault, driving back the enemy and inflicting severe casualties. Later, when ammunition was required, he made several journeys under severe fire in order to replenish the supply. Throughout the day Lieut.-Colonel Elstob, although twice wounded, showed the most fearless disregard of his own safety, and by encouragement and noble example inspired his command to the fullest degree. The Manchester Redoubt was surrounded in the first wave of the enemy attack, but by means of the buried cable Lieut.-Colonel Elstob was able to assured Brigade Commander that 'The Manchester Regiment will defend Manchester Hill to the last'. Some time after this post was overcome by vastly superior forces, and this very gallant officer was killed in the final assault, having maintained to the end the duty which he had impressed on his men-namely, 'Here we fight and here we die'. He set the highest example of valour, determination, endurance and fine soldierly baring.

As with 2nd Lt Edmund De Wind, details of Elstob's award were not officially published until the summer of 1919 due to a delay in trying to establish the actual circumstances of his death. The findings were not helped by various conflicting reports made by different witnesses who claimed to see Elstob's dead body lying out in the open. These included a report by Private (Pte) J. Franklin, who claimed to have buried the commander at a point about 200 yards in front of battalion HQ on the east side of the redoubt where a Vickers Gun had been set up. A Corporal (Cpl) Bamber also claims to have seen the body on 21 March, as did a Sergeant (Sgt) Banks. Three POWS also reported to have buried Elstob on Good Friday, and added that he was by the side of a dead brother officer of the Manchester Regt. The author suggests that the brother officer might have been Captain (Capt.) Norman Sharples, an adjutant who was attached to the 16th Manchesters. Like Elstob he was also reported missing and his name is similarly listed on the Pozieres Memorial. After the war, at the instigation of Hubert Worthington, a boyhood friend of Wilfrith's attempted to identify the burial place of his remains at Manchester Redoubt but without success.

Wilfrith Elstob, the third son of Canon John George Elstob and his wife Frances Alice Elstob, was born in Chichester, Sussex, on 8 September 1888. The canon held a position in the cathedral, but he was later appointed vicar of Capesthorne with Siddington in Cheshire where the family moved. At first Wilfrith was educated at Ryleys Preparatory School in Alderly Edge and at the age of 10 moved to Christ's Hospital School near Horsham in Sussex, where, apart from his school work, he joined the school Cadet Corps and became a lance corporal. In 1905 he left for Manchester University where he took a degree and diploma in education, gaining a BA four years later. His ambition had always been to be a schoolmaster and, after a brief period in Paris, he took up a position in Edinburgh as a master in the Merchiston Castle School. When war broke out he enlisted on 11 September 1914 as a private in a Public Schools Battalion, but accepted a commission on 30 October 1914 in the newly formed 1st Manchester Pals Battalion, which later became the 16th Manchesters. He was a member of A Coy and his promotion up the military ladder was rapid. He was a striking and imposing individual, and, in addition to being 6ft 1in tall and a superb athlete, he was also a big, burly man of splendid physique and bearing who was to become very much respected in the Army. He was simply one of those seemingly born to be a leader of men.

After initial training in England, the Manchesters went overseas in early November 1915 and Elstob was soon promoted to captain and commander of D Coy. At the beginning of July 1916 he was a company commander in the successful capture of Montauban on the Somme, during which action he was slightly wounded. He was again in charge of his company when wounded a second time in the fighting in Trônes Wood during the period 8–11 July 1916. Three months later, on the death of his battalion commander, Elstob, already a major, became battalion CO.

In 1917 the 16th Manchsters were in reserve for the Arras offensive in the spring, and at the beginning of the Third Battle of Ypres at the end of July Elstob took part in the fighting at Sanctuary Wood when his men were involved in 'mopping up' under machine-gun and sniper fire. At the end of 1917 he was temporarily in charge of 90th Bde, and in early 1918 was back in England for a brief leave when he managed to play some rugby which he had always been proficient at.

After Wilfrith's death in March 1918, his father was presented with his son's VC at Buckingham Palace by the King on 24 July 1919, accompanied by Hubert Worthington. Canon Elstob had been rural dean of Macclesfield between 1904 and 1912, and from 1911 an honorary canon of Chester Cathedral. He died in 1926.

Before winning his VC, Wilfrith Elstob had already won the MC (Military Cross) (*London Gazette*, 1 January 1917) and DSO (Distinguished Service Order) (*London Gazette*, 1 January 1918) and at one time Elstob's VC was kept in the library of Christ's Hospital School, but is now part of the collection of the Manchester Regt at their museum at Ashton-under-Lyne, to whom it is on loan. However, in November 2010 it was lent to the Imperial War Museum for display in the new Ashcroft Gallery. Elstob's name is included on the Macclesfield War Memorial in Cheshire and there is also a window and plaque to him in All Saints' Church, Siddington, Cheshire, where Canon Elstob, his father, had been the vicar. Another memorial, a small library in the 'Toc H' HQ in Victoria Park, Manchester was dedicated by his father on 31 January 1923 and was also a tribute to the 16th Manchesters. The plaque and framed photograph of Wilfrith were later transferred to the HQ of The Manchesters Coy of the 5th/8th Bn, The King's Regt in Ardwick Green where they are displayed. Wilfrith also has a school house named after him at Ryleys School where Worthington was a fellow pupil, and his name is also included on the Memorial to the Missing at Pozières, together with the names of those officers and men who fell with him at Manchester Redoubt and have no known grave. Finally, there is a memorial to the Manchester Regt in Francilly-Selency between the Maire and the church, which was unveiled at a special ceremony on 30 June 1996, adjacent to the village's own memorial.

R.F.J. HAYWARD
Near Fremicourt, France, 21/22 March

Acting Captain (A/Capt.) Reginald Hayward was in command of a company of the 1st Wiltshire Bn (The Duke of Edinburgh's) (7th Bde, 25th Div.) when he won his VC in the period 21–2 March 1918. Other brigades of this division, which was part of IV Corps, were the 74th and 75th. On 21 March at 4.40 a.m., divisional camps were woken up by the sound of heavy artillery gunfire which was being directed against the whole of IV Corps' front. The enemy was targeting the back areas and the Wiltshires were in the village of Achiet le Grand, which was being hit by high-velocity shells. At 11. 30 a.m. the Wiltshires moved forward to positions north-west of Fremicourt, south of the Bapaume–Cambrai road. The village was about 1½ miles north-east of Bapaume. The battalion became part of corps reserve, and worked hard on improving their defences and in establishing a new line.

The corps' defence line had two German lodgements, at Vaulx and Maricourt Woods, and the night of 21–2 March was spent in preparation for the inevitable fight with the enemy which would take place the next day. By 7.30 a.m. enemy shelling was continuous and the first enemy infantry attacks were being made. Vaulx Wood soon fell and sections of the 75th Bde were surrounded on three sides in the Vaulx–Morchies line. By dusk the 8th (S) Bn The Border Regt had fallen back to join the 1st Wiltshires in reserve and were subsequently reorganised.

On 23 March the Germans began a further attack on the Wiltshires' positions; they were twice repulsed in the morning and a third time in the afternoon. Hayward, the commander of the Wiltshires, was wounded by shellfire but still insisted on taking his company into action. Two days later he was badly wounded in the arm, but again remained in charge of his unit, encouraging his men and setting up defensive positions until he was wounded again, this time more seriously and in the head; he subsequently collapsed with exhaustion and was evacuated with the other casualties on the night of 25 March. He had displayed considerable powers of endurance and courage, earning himself a Victoria Cross. The citation for the award was published in the *London Gazette* of 24 April and continues the story:

> This officer while in command of a company displayed almost superhuman powers of endurance and consistent courage of the rarest nature. In spite of the fact that he was buried, wounded in the head, and rendered deaf on the first day of the operations, and had his arm shattered two days later, he refused to leave his men (even though he received a third serious injury to his head) until he collapsed from sheer physical exhaustion. Throughout the whole of this period the enemy were attacking his company's front without cessation; but Capt. Hayward continued to move across the open from one trench to another with absolute disregard of his own personal safety, concentrating entirely on reorganising his defences and encouraging his men. It was almost entirely due to the magnificent example of ceaseless energy of this officer that many most determined attacks upon his portion of the trench system failed entirely.

On 24 March the 1st Wiltshires suffered heavily from German shelling when the battalion was withdrawing and the enemy delivered a third attack. After dark the remaining men were collected up at Bihucourt and marched to a position on the Achiet–Bucquoy road where they camped. By this time all of the company commanders had become casualties, including Hayward.

Reginald Frederick Johnson Hayward was the eldest son of Frederick Johnson of Limpley Stoke, Bath and Gertrude Hayward and was born in Beersheba, East Griqualand, South Africa on 17 June 1891. His father was at one time a well-known stock breeder in South Africa. Reginald was educated at Hilton College where he excelled at sports, including football and cricket, and especially at rugby. He was also a keen shot and horse rider. Serving with the cadets he became regimental sergeant major (RSM) and, after leaving school, attended business college in Durban from 1909–10, and represented Natal against English rugby teams in 1911.

In May 1912 he travelled to England and began studying at the Royal College of Veterinary Surgeons and captained their rugby XV in 1913. He also played for Rosslyn Park Club and for Middlesex.

He was commissioned in the 6th (S) Wiltshire Regt on 29 September 1914 and was promoted to temporary lieutenant on 24 December in the same year. In March 1915 he was made a full lieutenant and transferred to the 1st Wiltshires. In 1916 he won the MC at Stuff Redoubt for conspicuous gallantry and initiative, which was gazetted on 8 October 1916. On 19 December he was promoted to acting captain. He won a bar to his MC at Messines Ridge on 7 June 1917, which was gazetted on 18 September 1917. He was presented with the VC and MC at Buckingham Palace by King George V on 24 October 1918.

After the war he became adjutant of the 1st Wiltshires (1919–21) and served in Dublin, Egypt and Palestine. He was promoted to lieutenant and later to captain with the 1st Wiltshires on 21 September 1927.

In 1935 he retired from the Army and, in 1938, married Linda, daughter of Charles Brice Bowen. In the same year, he was recalled and he served in the Anti-Aircraft Command (CRASC) during the Second World War. From 1945 to 1947 he was Commandant, Prisoner of War Camps. For the next five years he worked in the publications department of the BBC and from 1952 to 1967 was games manager of The Hurlingham Club. He died at 7 Ormonde Gate, Chelsea, London SW3 on 17 January 1970 and his wife died a few months later, in August. Hayward was cremated at Putney Vale on 23 January and one of the avenues in the cemetery was named after him. His VC, together with his other medals, were bequeathed to his former regiment, then the Duke of Edinburgh's Royal Regt (now Royal Gloucestershire, Berkshire and Wiltshire Regt) whose collection is part of Salisbury Museum. The medals included the MC and Bar, 1914–15 Star, BWM, VM and 1939–45 Defence and War Medals, together with a silver presentation sword and a portrait by Cowan Dobson. Finally he is remembered with a memorial in St Mary's Church, Limply Stoke, Avon.

M.A. JAMES

Near Vélu Wood, France, 21 March

The 8th (S) Bn The Gloucestershire Regt were part of 57th Bde, 19th (Western) Div., which was part of V Corps reserve before it was transferred to IV Corps on 21 March 1918. The other brigades in the division were the 56th and 58th.

On 21 March the 51st (Highland) Div. occupied positions that straddled the Bapaume–Cambrai road between the villages of Louverval and the northern edge of Hermies. Divisional orders were to retain the high ground between Hermies and Lebucquière to the west of the 51st's front. The 19th Div. were in reserve to the east of Bapaume.

During the day the village of Doignies, north-west of Hermies, was overrun and the 57th Bde was brought up to try and recapture it in the evening. In this counter-attack, two battalions of the 57th Bde were assisted by twelve tanks of 8th Tank Bn. Owing to mist and failing light, the tanks were unable to proceed and therefore the counter-attack was only partially successful. As a consequence, the 8th Gloucesters suffered heavy losses when they became caught in a trap. After a battalion company commanders' conference the battalion withdrew to a position a few hundred yards up a slope, where they were to be overwhelmed about thirty-six hours later.

The 19th Div. was responsible for covering the withdrawal of the 51st (Highland) Div. and their rear lines were then defended by 56th and 58th brigades. The 8th Gloucesters of the 57th Bde withdrew to positions to the north of Vélu Wood.

On 23 March, after a heavy bombardment, the enemy tried to break the British line near Chaufours, to the north of Beaumetz and across the Bapaume–Cambrai road, but they were repulsed. They then concentrated on a valley to the south of the main road, at the head of which was Beaumetz. By 10.00 a.m. the Germans had reached the western side of Lebucquière, a village to the south of Beaumetz. To the immediate south of Lebucquière was the village of Vélu, which had an east–west railway line running along its northern edge, with a second line running southwards. Vélu Wood was near to where the Gloucesters had taken up positions after their previous mauling.

152nd Bde of the 51st Div. was ordered to retire through Vélu Wood around the western side of Lebucquière and, despite the enemy having already occupied Vélu and Vélu Wood, the brigade managed to complete its retirement and reach the rendezvous at Bancourt, just outside Bapaume.

154th Bde was not attacked until 9.30 a.m. and the fighting was beginning to spread in a south-westerly direction. By mid-morning the enemy had fought its way to Beaumetz and succeeded in getting to the rear of the 8th Gloucesters, who were in a salient. The 10th Royal Warwicks fell back on the Lebucquière–Vélu railway line, where they formed a defensive flank facing the northern edge of Vélu Wood. By 1.00 p.m. the wood was rapidly becoming full of Germans, who suffered many casualties when they became visible. However, 57th Bde's left flank was threatened and, after about half an hour, its defenders were overwhelmed by sheer numbers. They had failed to receive messages to retire and continued fighting the enemy, thus preventing the Germans from emerging from the village of Vélu or its wood.

In covering the retirement of 57th Bde, together with its supporting artillery, Capt. M.A. James (A Coy, 8th Gloucesters) was left behind with a machine-gun, and it was assumed that he had been killed; in fact he had been seriously wounded and taken prisoner.

At 2.50 p.m. the brigade finally received news that it was to retire and it 'fell back in good order', reaching Bancourt at about 7.00 p.m.

It was for his covering in this retirement, and for his work in the previous two days, that Capt. James was awarded his VC.

A survivor of James' company later wrote:

I was the only man left of my Lewis gun section and Captain James came up a few minutes before we were surrounded by the Germans and took my rifle and bayonet as I was filling belts in a Vickers gun, my gun being out of action. Captain James said to us few who were left, 'we are surrounded boys, every man for himself'. He then got on the fire step and started firing at the advancing enemy telling us to run for it if we could possibly get away. . . . After that I saw nothing more of the Captain or other officers nor have I seen them since. I am certain that none got away from that trench after I left as I looked back some minutes after and saw the Germans getting into the trench at the back. I would just like to say that Captain James' action that day certainly saved the remainder of our company.

Another witness wrote:

Captain James was shot in the head by a bullet and died instantly; I saw it happen; it was near Hermies in the open ground, in the morning, during a rearguard action as we were retreating.

It was hardly surprising that James was thought to be dead after all these reports had been received.

The announcement of his VC was made in the *London Gazette* of 28 June 1918 and the citation was as follows:

For most conspicuous bravery and devotion to duty in attack at Vélu Wood. Capt. James led his company forward with magnificent determination and courage, inflicting severe losses on the enemy and capturing twenty-seven prisoners and two machine guns. He was wounded, but refused to leave his company, and repulsed three hostile onslaughts the next day. Two days later, although the enemy had broken through on his right flank, he refused to withdraw, and made a most determined stand, inflicting very heavy losses on the enemy and gaining valuable time for the withdrawal of guns. He was ordered by the senior officer on the spot to hold on 'to the last', in order to enable the brigade to be extricated. He then led his company forward in a local counter-attack on his own initiative, and was again wounded. He was last seen working a machine gun single-handed, after having been wounded a third time. No praise can be too high for the gallant stand made by this company, and Capt. James, by his dauntless courage and magnificent example, which undoubtedly enabled the battalion to be withdrawn before being completely cut off.

As for Manley James, taken prisoner on 23 March, he ended up on the Polish border in Stralkowo Camp, close to Posen, and when released he returned home via Rastatt and Schweidnitz in Silesia.

Before the March offensive, Vélu and its wood were sleepy places, untouched by shell-fire, but in 1917 it had been evacuated when the Hindenburg Line was built. A year later, all the villages in the area were flattened and the Germans used a long-range gun based at Cambrai to add to the destruction of the Allied positions. In Vélu Wood is a château and the adjacent road takes its name from this building, which in the war served as a hospital where no less than Adolf Hitler was treated when wounded. This château was destroyed in the war and later rebuilt, and is now a farm. Close by lives a farmer whose farm was rebuilt in 1926. He has a private collection of weapons and ammunition found on the battlefields and is an authority on the history of Vélu in the Great War.

Manley Angell James was born in Odiham, Hampshire on 12 July 1896. He was the son of Dr John Angell James MRCS, LRCP, a medical practitioner, and Emily Cormel James of 43 Nevil Road, Bishopston, Bristol. The family moved to the city when Manley was a child. He went to Bristol Grammar School in 1906 and joined the Officer Training Corps (OTC), rising to the rank of sergeant. He was good at cricket, hockey and, as with Hayward, especially rugby, a sport that he played at club level. For a career, he intended to follow his father into the medical profession and was entered for a medical course at Bristol University in the autumn of 1914.

After war began he was gazetted as temporary 2nd leiutenant on 1 December 1914 in the 8th Bn The Gloucestershire Regt and was promoted lieutenant on 28 June 1915 and became commander of the battalion's Lewis gun detachment. In 1915 he went to France with his battalion, which was in the 19th Div. (known as the 'Butterfly' division because of its insignia) and took part in the fighting for the capture of the village of La Boisselle in July 1916. His commanding officer was Lt Col Adrian Carton de Wiart, who won a VC in the action, and in his autobiography *Happy Odyssey* de Wiart wrote the following:

> We were allowed only twenty officers in an attack, which meant careful choosing and elimination, and countless heart breaks for those who had to be left behind. Lieutenant James prevailed on me to let him take part, and I regretted my weakness, as he was very badly wounded in the leg, but he recovered. Later in the war he was awarded the V.C.

Other accounts confirm that James was badly wounded in the thigh during the La Boiselle fighting and invalided home to England for five months. He was Mentioned in Despatches (MID) for the way that he handled his guns in the Somme fighting and was fit enough to return to France on 19 December 1916 as a member of the 57th Bde HQ staff. He was keen to return to his regiment, which he soon did, but was wounded again in February, this time by shrapnel. He was later Mentioned in Despatches again in April 1917.

On 22 February he was promoted to acting captain and, in July, he was present during the fierce fighting at Wytschaete and Messines Ridge, where he was slightly wounded and won the MC. On the night of 9–10 July he was commanding officer of A Coy, which was mainly responsible for the capture of a position called Druid's Farm. Prior to a British advance he took up a forward position, when under heavy enemy artillery fire, so that he could gauge the progress of the advance. He later assisted in the capture of a strong point. During a counter-attack on 27–8 July, A Coy was again in the thick of the action and on 2 August the divisional commander, Maj. Gen. Tom Bridges, issued a special order awarding a badge of Honour to A Coy. The badge was to be worn on the right sleeve of every member of the company.

James was held in the greatest esteem by the men who served under him and a piece entitled 'Our Captain' was specially written for a trench journal:

> However 'A' Coy are unanimous in their opinion that his best feat was on Sept. 20th when showing amazing coolness under heavy fire and a keen and ready recognition of military tactics he succeeded in getting the Company in contact with the Regiment on their right at a time when the attack was very disorganised . . .
>
> The Capt. had established himself firmly in the esteem of all men from the latest recruit to the oldest member of the Company and we all look forward to the time when Capt. James will receive the further honours that we are confident he will gain.

After James won the VC in March 1918, there were different reports as to whether he had been killed, captured or missing. The confusion probably arose from James becoming unconscious from his wounds and assumed to be dead. However, in May, James sent a field postcard to his father from a prisoner-of-war camp, informing him that he had been wounded in the neck, shoulder, jaw and stomach. He finally returned to England on Christmas Day 1918. He was decorated with his VC by the King in the Ballroom at Buckingham Palace on 22 February 1919. A week before, he received a gold watch together with an Illuminated Address at Colston Hall, Bristol where he attended a ceremony with other Bristol VCs – four

Bristol men won this high honour during the war. At the end of the war he was demobilised, although he wanted to stay in the Army and make it his career. He was commissioned as a lieutenant on 8 December 1920 and became one of only two Glosters' officers with wartime commissions allowed to transfer to the Regular Army.

Between the wars he served in a series of staff and battalion appointments, including serving in Kanturk with the Army of Occupation, Silesia (1922) and Cologne (1923).

In 1925 he was made substantive captain and served as the adjutant in the 1st Gloucestershires for three years between 1925 and 1928.

In 1926 he became engaged to Miss Noreen Cooper of Clifton, Bristol, whom he subsequently married in 1928 and they had one son. From 1928–30 Manley was with the 1st Gloucestershires in Egypt and was posted home to the regimental depot in Bristol. On 14 June 1930 he passed for entrance to Staff College, Camberley, and was there until the following year. He became company commander in 1933, was promoted to major in 1936, and took command of 2nd Bn Royal Sussex Regt in 1939 when he was gazetted as brevet lieutenant colonel. He served with this battalion in Belfast, and in June 1939 inspected a Bristol Grammar School OTC parade. He became brigadier in 1941 and he was then appointed general staff officer (grade 1) (GSO 1) in 54th Div., and in February 1941 took command of 128th Bde, 43rd (Western) Div., which consisted of three Hampshire battalions. After a long period of training for desert warfare he took the brigade to North Africa with the First Army. During the next few months he served in the African campaign as brigade commander and was gazetted for a DSO for his work at Beja, Tunisia in 1942. He was described as: 'Personally as brave as a lion, he was at the same time careful and solicitous about how he committed his troops.'

When the war in Africa finished, the Italian war began and James' brigade was at the forefront of the 46th Div. landing at Salerno in September 1943. After four days of battle, James was badly wounded in the leg and, after a visit by Gen. Alexander to the front, James allowed himself to be evacuated in a hospital ship to Egypt in order to recover. In 1944 James was back in England in command of 140th Bde, who were in training for D-Day, but he was no longer fit for active service and was appointed Brigadier Training Home Forces until October 1945. He then transferred to the RAF Regt and went to Germany as the regiment's senior officer with 2nd Tactical Air Force (TAF). For the next three years he was in command of the Army of Occupation in Germany, and in 1948 he was appointed Director of Ground Defence at the Air Ministry.

He finally retired in March 1951 with the rank of brigadier and then took up a post as Works Defence Officer with the Bristol Aeroplane Company at Filton, just outside Bristol. He was deputy lieutenant for Gloucestershire in 1957 and was made MBE (Civil) in 1958, finally retiring a second time in 1961. James was a well-known Bristol figure and took an active role in the affairs of his former school, Bristol Grammar, and of his old regiment, being instrumental in keeping its 8th Battalion Old Comrades' Association going. He lived for twenty-five years in the same house in Pasten Road in Westbury-on-Trym, a north Bristol suburb.

In 1970 his medals were stolen from his home and in October 1971 he offered a reward of £100 for their recovery. The thief was apprehended and sentenced to six years' imprisonment. James died on 23 September 1975 in his Bristol home, and his body was cremated at Canford Crematorium, Bristol and his ashes spread in ' The Shrubbery'. During his life his main recreations had been fishing, shooting, cricket and gardening. In his will he left £29,335 gross (£29,044 net). His decorations, apart from the VC, included the MC, 1914–15 Star, BWM, VM and for the Second World War, the DSO, 1939–45 Star, and Africa Star and Clasp. He also qualified for Coronation Medals for 1937 and 1953, and the Civil Defence Long Service Medal. His decorations were offered for sale by Christie's in October 1991 when they were expected to fetch a price between £25,000 and £30,000, before finally reaching a price of £37,400. They are displayed in the Ashcroft Gallery in the Imperial War Museum. Prior to his death, James had told his only son Peter that he would have no objection to his medals being sold. Peter followed his father into the Gloucestershire Regt, but as a result of a knee injury had to resign his commission.

A.E. KER

Near St Quentin, France, 21 March

On 21 March 1918, Lt Allan Ker was a member of the 3rd (Reserve) Bn The Gordon Highlanders, attached to the 61st Bn Machine Gun Corps (61st Div.) of the Fifth Army, and their position was to the west of the German-held town of St Quentin.

After a heavy enemy bombardment, the flank of the division became exposed and Ker, with a single Vickers gun and the assistance of his sergeant and some of the wounded, managed to delay progress of a large enemy force. The gun team inflicted many casualties and Ker sent a message to his battalion HQ, indicating that, with the help of his sergeant and some of his other men, they were going to hold on until a counterattack was carried out which would relieve their perilous position. However, at about the time that their ammunition ran out, a party of Germans had worked around the rear of the group and began to attack them with bombs, bayonets and a machine-gun. The defenders then began to drive back these attacks with the use of their revolvers as their Vickers machine-gun had been put out of action. Helpfully they also managed to get hold of a German rifle with ammunition, which was used to good effect. The wounded had been moved into a small shelter and Ker decided to defend the position and the wounded to the last.

Inevitably, there could only be one outcome to this uneven struggle and, after holding out for three hours, Ker's party were finally overwhelmed and taken prisoner. Nevertheless, they had managed to hold up 500 of the enemy for over three hours.

Not surprisingly Ker's action was to earn him a VC, but it wasn't officially published in the *London Gazette* until 4 September 1919. The eighteen-month delay was once again due to the recipient being subsequently made a POW. The decoration was to be one of four such awards earned by members of the Gordon Highlanders during the Great War.

On 21st March, 1918, near St Quentin, after a heavy bombardment, the enemy penetrated our line, and the flank of the 61st Division became exposed. Lieut. Ker, with one Vickers gun, succeeded in engaging the enemy's infantry, approaching under cover of dead ground, and held up the attack, inflicting many casualties. He then sent back word to his Battalion Headquarters that he had determined to stop with his Sergeant and several men who had been badly wounded, and fight until a counter-attack could be launched to relieve him. Just as ammunition failed, his party were attacked from behind with bombs, machine guns, and with the bayonet. Several bayonet attacks were delivered, but each time they were repulsed by Lieut. Ker and his companions with their revolvers, the Vickers gun having by this time been destroyed. The wounded were collected into a small shelter, and it was decided to defend them to the last and to hold the enemy as long as possible In many of the hand-to-hand encounters a German rifle and bayonet and a small supply of ammunition was secured, and subsequently used with good effect against the enemy. Although Lieut. Ker was very exhausted from want of food and gas poisoning, and from the supreme exertions he had made during ten hours of the most severe bombardment, fighting and attending to the wounded, he refused to surrender until all his ammunition was exhausted and his position was rushed by large numbers of the enemy. His behaviour throughout the day was absolutely cool and fearless, and by his determination he was materially instrumental in engaging and holding up for three hours more than 500 of the enemy.

Allan Ebenezer Ker was the eldest son of Robert Darling Ker and was born in Edinburgh on 5 March 1883. He was educated at the Edinburgh Academy and studied law between 1903 and 1908 at Edinburgh University. He became a writer on the *Signet* in 1908 and joined the Queen's Edinburgh Mounted Infantry. Towards the end of 1914 he had to travel to Aberdeen and had the sad task of winding up the affairs of his cousin Capt. Melford Ker, who had been killed within a couple of weeks of taking the first detachment of Gordon Highlanders across the English Channel to France.

At that time Ker was planning to join the Scots Greys, but at the Gordons' barracks he was persuaded to join the famous Highland Regt. He was told that the 'cavalry had no future'. He began service with the 3rd Gordon Highlanders as a 2nd lieutenant in June 1915 and went to France in October, then to Salonika in July 1916, where he was involved in the Battle of Muchkovo near the Vardar River. In December 1916 he was invalided home and was promoted to full lieutenant in January 1917. In May he returned to the Western Front and took part in the fighting at Passchendaele, Arras, Ypres, Cambrai and lastly St Quentin, where he won his VC when attached to the 61st Bn Machine Gun Corps and was taken prisoner. While in captivity he was Secretary and Food Controller for British Officers at Karlsruhe and Beeskow until December 1918.

Ker received his VC from the King at Buckingham Palace on 26 November 1919, more than a year after the Armistice and twenty months after he won the medal.

After the war Ker had originally intended to work in legal partnership with his father in Edinburgh, but when the King invested him with his VC he asked him to consider staying on in the Army and offered him the chance of a commission in the Scots Guards. Ker indicated that he would prefer to stay with the Highlanders, so he was sent back to the Army until he 'tired of the quiet life', becoming a captain in 1920 (staff capt. at the Judge-Advocate General's Dept). He married Vera Irene Gordon-Skinner and went to India to practise as a solicitor.

In February 1925, Capt. Ker defended Pte Dick Wright of the West Yorkshire Regt, who was accused of killing a British soldier and a German girl named Maria Stasiak. It appears that Maria was at one time in love with Wright but changed her mind. Wright was sentenced to death but this sentence was later commuted to life imprisonment. In the same year Ker laid a wreath at the Machine-Gunner's Memorial at Hyde Park Corner.

In 1937, as a practising solicitor, Ker was suspended from acting in the High Court because of a minor infringement of the rules. In the Second World War he was re-employed with the rank of major with the Department of the Chief of the Imperial Staff at the War Office as GSO 2. From 1946 he worked as chief clerk of the Rents Tribunal for Paddington and Marylebone, a job in which he had to sort out the problems and complaints of tenants and landlords alike.

During his lifetime he attended several of the VC functions, including the centenary at Hyde Park on 26 June 1956. At this time he was living at 24 Fordwych Road, London NW2. In a newspaper article he was described as being 'broad shouldered, mentally as alert as a man half his age'. He was chairman of the Fifth Army Comrades' Association.

He died on 12 September 1958 at New Garden Hospital, Hampstead, NW London at the age of 75, and was buried five days later in West Hampstead Cemetry, Fortune Green Road, Hampstead and the grave reference is Section Q/4.

In June 1991 Ker's medals were offered for sale by Buckland, Dix and Wood with a price guide of between £16,000 and £18,000. Apart from the VC, his decorations included the BWM, VM, King George V Silver Jubilee Medal, Defence Medal (1939–45), Order of Military Merit, and lastly the George VI and Queen Elizabeth II Coronation Medals. At present the collection is part of Lord Ashcroft's collection on display in the Imperial War Museum.

J.W. SAYER

Le Verguier, France, 21 March

L. Cpl J.W. Sayer of the 8th (S) Bn Queen's (Royal West Surrey Regt) won his VC on 21 March 1918 at Le Verguier. The 8th Queen's were part of 17th Bde of the 24th Div., and on 21 March were in positions to the north-east of the village, about 5 miles to the north-west of St Quentin and east of Jeancourt. To their right was the 3rd Bn The Rifle Bde (The Prince of Consort's Own); in reserve were the 1st Royal Fusiliers, while behind them were the 72nd and 73rd brigades which formed the rest of the 24th Div.

The enemy had already targeted the village with artillery fire on the previous day, and followed this up with a very severe bombardment with high explosives and shrapnel, which lasted until 10 a.m. The Allied positions at Le Verguier came under attack from the north, east and the south. The attack from the east was easily detected and quickly dealt with, but after the enemy had progressed to the north, the situation became desperate and it looked as though the village would quickly fall. However, the 8th Queen's, north-east of the village, managed to hold out together with the 3rd Rifle Bde. The latter battalion was in Cooker Quarry on the left of the Bihécourt–Vadencourt road, numbered the D33.

The enemy advance was held up by the incredible bravery of machine gunner John Sayer when the 24th Machine Gun Bn and the 8th Queen's defended their positions desperately. It was during the fighting for the village that L. Cpl J.W. Sayer of C Coy won his VC at a position known as Shepherds Copse to the north-east, close to the Hindenberg Line, which he managed to capture single-handed. In fact, this position was really three separate posts connected by trenches and was at a bend on the road in a valley which runs to Villeret from Le Verguier. It is likely that the enemy may have based their plans for advance on using this valley.

Sayer hung on to the post for two hours. Although the enemy was extremely close to his position, he was protected by a thick mist which reduced visibility down to 30 yards as well as an earth mound. He somehow managed to repel a series of attacks and, at the same time, inflict heavy casualties. During this defence, Sayer also had to use his rifle and bayonet a great deal, as for some reason there was no supply of grenades. He killed at least six Germans with his bayonet and probably killed three more with his rifle. He managed to hold on to the positions until most members of his garrison of twenty-two men were either dead or wounded, and he too had been badly wounded. After the enemy finally overwhelmed his positions, he was taken prisoner with four other wounded men.

Four weeks later, on 18 April, Sayer died of his wounds when still in German captivity, having had a leg amputated which led to complications. He was buried at Le Cateau Military Cemetery, Plot 1, Row B, Grave 59B. The cemetery is to the west of Le Cateau and close to the crossing of the road to Caudry. It was laid out by the Germans in early 1916, and they made separate plots for the British and for their own dead. Most of the British graves are in the plots on the north-east side.

The citation for Sayer's posthumous VC was published fifteen months later in the *London Gazette* of 9 June 1919 as follows:

> For most conspicuous bravery, determination, and ability displayed on 31 March 1918, at Le Verguier, when holding for two hours, in face of incessant attacks, the flank of a small isolated post. Owing to mist the enemy approached the post from both sides to within thirty yards before being discovered. L.-Corpl. Sayer, however, on his own initiative and without assistance, beat off a succession of flank attacks and inflicted heavy casualties on the enemy. Though attacked by rifle and machine-gun fire, bayonet, and bombs, he repulsed all attacks, killing many and wounding others. During the whole time he was continuously exposed to rifle and machine-gun fire, but he showed the utmost contempt of danger, and his conduct was an inspiration to all. His skilful use of all descriptions enabled the post to hold out until nearly and all the garrison had been killed and himself wounded and captured. He subsequently died as a result of wounds at Le Cateau.

John William Sayer, the eldest son of Samuel and Martha Margaret Sayer, was born at 50 Wellington Road, Islington on 12 April 1879 (the building was demolished in the 1960s). His father was a farmer and the family home where John was brought up was at Wangye Hall Farm in Chadwell Heath. The Sayers had been farmers in the area for several generations, but this link came to an end when the building was demolished in 1936.

John was educated in Ilford but later lived in Cricklelwood where he ran a corn and seed merchant's business, although at that time his parents still farmed in Chadwell Heath and expected him to take it over. When he was 25 years old, John married Edith Louise Maynard on 15 August 1904 in Ilford. Her address was 8 Empress Avenue, Ilford. The couple met when John was a chorister at St Mary's Church and Edith's older brother was occasionally a preacher there. The couple then moved to Middlesex. Over the next fourteen years, Edith gave birth to six children – four girls and two boys – and, with so many mouths to feed, Sayer was eligible for exemption from joining up when the war began. Although he delayed his decision, he finally decided to join up and attested under the Derby Scheme in Cricklewood on 10 December 1915. When he reached France he served as a machine gunner and was promoted to lance corporal the following year. In August 1917 he was paraded by the colonel of the battalion for exceptional bravery, but details of the circumstances have proved illusive, although it might have centered on 'Jobs Post' on 1 August. His VC was gazetted on 9 June 1919, seven months after the war ended, and Edith was presented with her late husband's posthumous award by the King at Buckingham Palace on 26 July.

After the war, Edith and her six children, still all under 14, including an 8-month-old baby, left for Hastings as their home in Cricklewood had been condemned. When in Hastings their address was a small terraced house at 35 Norman Terrace, Old London Road, although it was later renumbered 105. Edith had very, very little income and it was mainly friends clubbing together who bought her the house in early 1919 as a public subscription, due to war fatigue, did little to ease her financial plight. Also, despite approaches to Sir James Craig at the Ministry of Pensions, no further pension was provided by the government. Even £50 a year would have helped enormously and this financial burden only began to ease when the children became old enough to go to work. To give an example of the times, Edith was even criticised when she first wore her husband's VC in public for the first time in 1919.

Her husband's headstone used to state his age incorrectly as 38, but this error has since been corrected and now shows the proper age of 39. According to family papers, she paid 6s 8d to have an inscription added to his headstone at Le Cateau: 'Never Shall His Memory Fade'.

Possibly owing to the late publication of his VC citation, it would appear that Sayer's role in helping to win the war, on what history has deemed to be a pivotal day in the campaign, and the one when the enemy had lost their last real chance of winning, is unrecognised in the historial records. Also, by June 1919 the country had grown tired of heroic stories about brave soldiers and had other things on its mind as it struggled to find the road to economic recovery. Another reason for a seeming gap in the archives is that the standard files dealing with the events at Le Verguier contain very little information in them which is correct. Col Harold Wylly, the battalion historian, doesn't even mention Sayer's great deeds.

To go back to the events themselves, the 8th Queen's Bn made a smooth withdrawal on the 22nd, and Claude Lorraine Piesse, the Australian commander of Sayer's platoon, was taken into German captivity for nine months. David Baker, a grandson of Sayer, has gone into the background in great detail and the following information owes much to him uncovering it. It is his thesis that Claude Lorraine Piesse's award of the DSO for his role in the defence of Le Verguier virtually 'airbrushed out' Sayer's far more pivotal role in the defence of the village and a possible holding up the inevitable enemy advance by several hours. The battalion commander, Hugh Chevalier Peirs, also seems to have gone along with the idea of leaving the situation as it was, as bringing Sayer's actions to the fore would make 'things complicated' for posterity. It has to be said that Piesse was aware of the role of Sayers and, indeed, in a letter of 24 February 1919, he produces a report in which he recommends Sayer for a VC.

Sayer's VC, BWM and VM are not publically held.

C.E. STONE

Caponne Farm, France, 21 March

Between 3 and 4 miles south of St Quentin, the 18th (Eastern) Div., with its 53rd, 54th and 55th brigades, was preparing to face the long-awaited German advance on the misty early morning of 21 March 1918. The 53rd Bde in the divisional frontline was sandwiched between the Oise Canal to the front and the Crozat Canal to the rear. The infantry brigade consisted of 7th (S) Bn The Queen's Own (Royal West Kent Regt), the 8th (S) Bn The Princess of Charlotte of Wales's (Royal Berkshire Regt) and the 10th (S) Bn The Essex Regt. On the 21st the West Kents and the Berkshires were virtually wiped out in the German advance, and this left the 10th Essex in the rear holding on to two positions, Caponne Farm and Moulin Farm, which were a short distance apart.

Two artillery batteries from 83rd Artillery Bde, RFA, were commanded by Capt. Leslie McGowan Haybittel (C Battery), whose usual role was Divisional Trench Mortar Officer, and Lt Ellis (D Battery). They were supporting the 53rd Infantry Bde and were thus still in the vicinity. C Battery was south and south-west of the village of Benay, where their forward guns were potentially in great danger. The enemy infantry attack began at 4.40 a.m. on a misty morning and, supported by a ferocious artillery barrage, it quickly made progress against the thinly spread Allied line. The enemy was slightly held up by machine-gun fire and sniper fire, but not for long as, at around 12.45 p.m., telephone links between the British batteries were damaged as a result of enemy shelling and the enemy broke through the frontal positions.

One artillery gunner, a member of C Battery, was Gunner (Gnr) C.E. Stone MM, who had begun the day working his gun under gas and shellfire for six hours. When Haybittel gave orders to retire to a sunken road between the villages of Hinacourt and Benay, Stone took up a position with a rifle about 100 yards distant from the nearest Germans, in order to give the battery some sort of protective cover from the enemy. Although he was under continuous machine-gun fire, he calmly picked off any Germans who attempted to rush his position. After the artillery moved their guns again, Stone accompanied them and took up a new position on their right flank. He continued to have more success as the enemy attempted to outflank Haybittel's unit. Those few Germans who did get through were summarily dealt with by Stone, who was still operating under heavy machine-gun fire.

At 8.00 p.m. the guns, which were the only field guns left from 83rd Bde, were beginning to seize up and Haybittel was compelled to give the order to withdraw. However, before they did so, the gun that might still have been of use to the enemy when they overran the ground was disabled. This was a process which included 'removing the wheel dust-caps and retaining pins so that if the Germans tried to move the guns the wheels would fall off!

The withdrawal party of six men was led by Lt M.N.S. Jackson, and included Charlie Stone, and re-established itself 300 yards to the rear where new barbed wire had been set up.

Stone was one in a party of six men detailed to provide protective cover. However, the gunners achieved more than that and managed to capture a German machine-gun, together with its team of four men who had managed to get themselves behind Haybittel's position. Stone chased one German for about 100 yards before catching up with him and killing him. By 9 p.m. the men had returned to their wagon lines.

The very depleted 83rd Artillery Bde was rested for a short time, but after three days it replaced the 82nd Artillery Bde, using the former's two remaining guns, and then began to carry out work alongside the French Army until 30 March.

Not surprisingly, Capt. Haybittel recommended Gnr Stone for the VC for all his assistance and courage in helping to keep the two guns working virtually the whole day. In addition, Haybittel received the DSO, as did Lt Ellis, because during the day their two 18-pounders had fired over 1,900 rounds of ammunition in all.

Even the enemy was impressed, for a newspaper published in Kiel printed the following report:

Our men tell me of a heavy English battery which continued coolly to fire behind our German line when our men were already a hundred yards from the guns. Finally the gun crews jumped to some machine guns which were in position for defence at close quarters, and blazed away for all they were worth until overcome by the storming columns.

The 18th Div's line had been withdrawn for 2,000 yards by the end of the day and the attacks against the two farms had been successfully repulsed.

The citation announcing Gnr Stone's VC in the *London Gazette* of 22 May 1918 was very detailed and the geographical position for Stone's action was given as Caponne Farm, which is due east of Hinacourt.

After working hard at his gun for six hours under heavy gas and shell fire, Gunner Stone was sent back to the rear section with an order. He delivered the order and voluntarily, under a very heavy barrage, returned with a rifle to the forward position to assist in holding up the enemy on a sunken road. Lying in the open, about a 100 yards from the enemy, under very heavy machine-gun fire, he calmly and effectively shot the enemy until ordered to retire. He then took up a position on the right flank of the two rear guns, and held the enemy at bay, though they again and again attempted to outflank the guns. During this period one of the enemy managed to break through, and, regardless of fierce machine-gun fire raging at the time, Gunner Stone rushed after him and killed him, thereby saving the flank of the guns. Later he was one of the party which captured the machine-gun and four prisoners who, in the dusk, had got round to the rear of the gun position. This most gallant act undoubtedly saved the detachment serving the guns. Gunner Stone's behaviour throughout the whole day was beyond all praise, and his magnificent example and fine work through these critical periods undoubtedly kept the guns in action, thereby holding up the enemy on the battle zone at the most critical moment.

Charles Edwin Stone was born at Street Lane, Ripley, near Belper in Derbyshire, on 4 February 1889. His parents were George Edward and Mary Ellen Stone and he was the tenth of thirteen children. By the time he had reached the age of 5 or 6 the family moved to a farm cottage on Sandbed Lane, Openwoodgate, Belper, where he attended the local school, Belper Pottery School. In 1901 Stone's mother died, which meant that the younger children were subsequently brought up by their older brothers and sisters. Later, following his father's trade, Stone became a miner, first at New Denby Hall Pit and then at Salterwood near Ripley. After leaving home he shared a house with his brother Joseph in Nottingham Road, Belper.

On 12 September 1914, Charles enlisted as a gunner in the Royal Field Artillery at Sutton-in-Ashfield. He was attached to C Battery, 83rd Bde, which was part of the 18th (Eastern) Div. Their guns combined 18-pound field guns and 4½in Howitzers, and, initially, Stone was stationed in Colchester for artillery training. Stone's brigade left for France at the end of July 1915 and, at first, was part of X Corps of the Third Army, taking part in many of the major campaigns including the Somme. For part of this time Stone served as an officer's servant. His brother Ernest, who was a platoon sergeant, was killed in action in 1917. It was on 28 October during the Battle of Passchendaele in the same year that Stone was to win the MM (*London Gazette*, 4 February 1918), probably for helping to assist in manning the guns when his usual job was working in the wagon lines. The battery subsequently suffered from several direct hits, but Stone, heedless of his own safety, helped to tend the wounded. On returning home in June 1918, Bombardier (Bdr) Stone was presented with his VC by the King at Buckingham Palace on the 28th. He then travelled to Belper, where he was presented with a gold watch and chain, and £100 in War Bonds by the people of Belper and District in the Belper River Gardens. In his speech of thanks he said:

> ... he felt that he could not adequately express his gratitude to them for the beautiful presents they had made him. What he did on March 21st he would gladly repeat if he had the chance because having lost a brother in the war, he had a big score to wipe off with the Huns. He was stimulated with that one thought as he was helping his comrades on the memorable day of March 21st, and performed the deed which brought him the VC. However, he confessed that he had been very lucky in having escaped any serious wounds after 3 years of war ...

The chairman of the meeting read out congratulatory messages from the members of the Belper branch of the Comrades of the Great War and the Federation of Discharged and Wounded Soldiers.

Seemingly not to be outdone, the residents of Ripley also gave Stone a civic reception, which took place in the market place when he was presented with another £100 in War Bonds. He subsequently returned to France where he saw further action and was promoted to lance bombardier (L. Bdr). He was demobilised in January 1919 and returned to the mines at Salterwood Colliery, where he worked for a few more years until 1923. In 1920 he had attended the Royal Garden party on 26 June for holders of the Victoria Cross. During this same time he took a keen interest in the local athletics club at Heage, a nearby village, and in the same year moved to Ashbourne where he worked for Mr Clifford Etches at Heywood Farm. It was during this time that he saved a fellow worker on the farm, Miss Elizabeth Lees (later Mrs Harrison), from severe burns when her clothes caught fire and he smothered the flames with his jacket.

For about twelve years after the war, Stone lodged with the parents of an ex-fellow soldier and he never married, seemingly always being a lodger. From September 1924, when he moved to Derby, he worked for Rolls-Royce for twenty years, and from the early 1930's he lived at 32 Becket Well Lane, Derby. At Rolls-Royce he initially worked in one of the foundries which was nicknamed 'Dante's Inferno'! On 3 June 1926 Stone was invited to attend the opening of the British Legion Club at Allenton and, three years later on 9 November, he was one of the guests at the House of Lords Dinner, which was given for winners of the VC and hosted by the Prince of Wales. Later in the same week he visited the Royal Artillery at Woolwich, where they made a great fuss of him and he was invited to take the salute at a special parade held at Shrapnel Barracks, which was later demolished after the Second World War and is now part of the site of the Queen Elizabeth Hospital. The sergeants' mess has a Stone Room named in his honour, where he carved his name on a wooden chair to commemorate his visit. Also during his visit he was greeted by Brigadier (Brig.) W. Evans, the former commander of the 18th Div. Artillery in France, and the two men talked about 'old times'. When Stone returned to Derby he took with him a cross of poppies, a table decoration from the November Dinner, as well as a copy of the menu which was probably autographed.

During 1940 Stone was introduced to King George VI when he was visiting the Rolls-Royce works in Derby. In June 1949 he was presented to the Duke of Edinburgh on the occasion of another royal visit to the Rolls-Royce plant.

After the war Stone's health began to fail and he died in the City Hospital in Derby of cardiac failure, diabetes and arteriosclerosis on 29 August 1952. He was buried on 3 September in his mother's grave at Belper Cemetery, with full military honours, after a service at the branch of the local British Legion in Strutt Street. His funeral was attended by members of his family, as well as Capt. V. H. Bellringer and representatives of the Heavy Anti-Aircraft Regt, Derby. The Last Post and Reveille were played at the graveside.

Stone's family bequeathed Charlie's VC, MM, 1914–15 Star, BWM, VM and King George VI Coronation Medal to the Royal Artillery Institution in Woolwich, where his name is also included on the VC Memorial in the chapel.

J.S. COLLINGS-WELLS
Marcoing to Albert, France, 22/27 March

On 22 March 1918, the 4th (Extra Reserve) Bn The Bedfordshire Regt, 190th Bde, 63rd Royal Naval Div. was in position south of Bapaume. At the start of what turned out to be a fighting retirement they passed through Ytres, Guedecourt and Martinpuich, and then, on 25 March, they reached High Wood. At this point, the battalion helped to reinforce the 189th Bde, which was being hard pressed in front of the nearby village of Martinpuich. The battalion managed to hang on until it ran out of ammunition and its gallant conduct helped to save the flank of the Naval Div. The battalion then made its way westwards to the Thiepval Ridge and took up positions behind the River Ancre, but only after destroying the bridges.

On the following day the enemy tried to capture Bouzincourt Ridge, which is about 2 miles to the north-west of the town of Albert, directly opposite the village of Aveluy. The Germans managed to capture the eastern edge of it, which they were to lose a few months later. The man mainly responsible for the defence of the ridge was the commanding officer of the 4th Bedfordshire Bn, Lt Col John Collings-Wells. Six days after the Germans began their Spring Offensive on the 21st, the Bedfords were exhausted and severely depleted in men, having fought for nearly a week. Tragically, Wells, who had been wounded twice in the fighting, was killed outright on 27 March in a position quite close to a railway line to the west of Albert. He was killed by a trench mortar shell which also killed two other officers, including his second-in-command, and he was later buried in Bouzincourt Ridge Cemetery (III E 12). The cemetery stands alongside a track that runs from Bouzincourt to Albert and is not frequently visited. When he died, Wells was 37 years old and was awarded a posthumous VC 'For most conspicuous bravery, skilful leader and handling of his battalion in very critical situations during a withdrawal between 22 March and his death on the 27th.'

Wells' VC citation, published in the *London Gazette* less than four weeks later on 27 April, describes what happened:

> When the rearguard was almost surrounded and in great danger of being captured, Lieut.-Colonel Collings-Wells, realising the situation, called for volunteers to remain behind and hold up the enemy whilst the remainder of the rearguard withdrew, and with his small body of volunteers held them up for one and a half hours until they had expended every round of ammunition. During this time he moved freely amongst his men guiding and encouraging them, and by his great courage undoubtedly saved the situation.On a subsequent occasion, when his battalion was ordered to carry out s counter-attack, he showed the greatest bravery. Knowing that his men were extremely tired and after six days' fighting, he placed himself in front and led the attack, and even when twice wounded refused to leave them, but continued to lead and encourage his men until he was killed at the moment of gaining their objective. The successful results of the operation were, without doubt, due to the undaunted courage exhibited by this officer.

Capt. J.H. Blackwell, a witness of the colonel's death when he was at his side, wrote to Collings-Wells's mother twelve days later:

> In the early hours of what turned out to be the saddest day I have ever experienced, we were ordered to attack. The attack started, the Colonel, seeing that the men were very tired said to me that he should lead them himself, as he would be able to cheer them on, and generally control the attack much better. So he took a rifle and went forward with the first wave. When a few hundred yards from the enemy he was slightly wounded in the arm, but continued to lead the Battalion on. A few minutes later he was wounded a second time in the other arm, but still continued to lead them, until he reached a trench, where Major Nunneley and I dressed his wounds. He was killed in the trench just outside Albert a moment afterwards and thank God suffered no pain. We were unable to

recover the bodies as the enemy counter attacked a few hours afterwards. I am so fearfully sorry about this as he always did his best to recover our dead at all times, so I sincerely hope that he has been reverently buried by the enemy. He was the finest and the bravest soldier and the most perfect commanding officer I have ever known. I am proud to have served under him, and I hope, helped him a little. His loss is felt by every unit in the Division . . . I think that you will realise what he did when I tell you he has been recommended for the highest honour a soldier can receive.

John Stanhope Collings-Wells, the son of Arthur and Caroline Mary, was born at Caddington Hall, Markyate, Hertfordshire on 19 July 1880. 'The Hall' was the family home for about twenty years. John was educated at Uppingham and Christ Church College, Oxford (1903–6). After leaving university he worked with his uncle, running the family business in Manchester from 1906–14.

He joined the Army in 1903 and was with the Hertfordshire Militia, which, by 1906, evolved into the 4th (Militia) Bn, Bedfordshire. Collings-Wells had been commissioned into the Bedfordshire Regt in September 1904 and was already a captain by 1907. He arrived in France on 22 August, in the first month of the war, and was appointed company commander. On 6 November he joined the 2nd Bedfordshires, who had been stationed in South Africa on the outbreak of war, and took part in the fighting in Ypres Salient. On 12 January 1915 he was badly wounded at Fleurbaix, south-west of Armentières, suffering from gunshot wounds to his right thigh, and two days later was sent to No. 4 General Hospital, Versailles. He was then invalided home to recuperate and was declared fit for General Service on 5 March after his wounds had healed. Back in France he joined the 4th Bedfordshires and served in the Ancre Battle of 1916. On 4 September he was promoted to major, becoming second-in-command, and from 24 December he became commander and took part in the Third Battle of Ypres.

In March 1917 at Gavrelle during the Battle of Arras, he won the DSO and his citation was published in the *London Gazette* of 18 July 1917:

For conspicuous gallantry in command of a battalion in holding its objectives against heavy counter-attacks, and later for his leadership and bravery in forming and commanding a composite battalion, which achieved its objective under very adverse circumstances.

The circumstances were described by Maj. Gen. Sir Frederick Maurice in his history of the 16th Foot in the following way:

> Simultaneously the 63rd Division attacked a little further north the German trench system about Oppy. For this attack a composite battalion was formed from the 4th Bn and the 7th Royal Fusiliers under Lt Col J.S. Collings-Wells. The battalion attacked at dawn and quickly reached its objective but was driven out by a counter-attack. It was re-formed and attacked again and again and won its objective largely owing to the leadership and personal gallantry of Lt Col J.S. Collings-Wells who was awarded the D.S.O.

In the *Times* of 16 April 1918, a correspondent wrote of Collings-Wells who had been Mentioned in Despatches as well:

> He was one of the best type of the citizen soldier. In pre-war days he devoted much time to the Hertfordshire Militia and subsequently to the Special Reserve. He spent the winter of 1914–15 in France, where in January 1915, he was wounded and invalided home. He returned to France in July, 1916 in command of a company, with the rank of Major. Shortly afterwards he became second in command, and a few days before the Battle of Beaucourt-Beaumont Hamel assumed the position of Lieut. Colonel of his battalion – a post which he held till his death on March 27th. . . . Possessing a wonderful grasp of detail and great organising ability, Lieut. Colonel Collings-Wells raised his battalion to a pitch of high efficiency. . . . He was wedded to his battalion and spared no efforts to promote the welfare and comfort of his men.

Collings-Wells somehow managed to secure the drums used in France by his old regiment and sent them back to Caddington Hall, presumably for safe-keeping. His parents were presented with their son's decorations at Buckingham Palace on 1 June 1918 by the King. Mrs Collings-Wells wrote an account of the presentation to her daughter Betha:

We were to be there at 10.00 a.m. We started from home in the little Motor at 7.45 a.m. to catch the 8.15 train from Luton. But as fate would have it, the car broke down at Woodside and refused to go another yard. So there was nothing for it but to walk. We set off steadily, Father in London clothes and high hat and I, in my best frock and hat etc. We caught the next train at 8.55 a.m. at Luton and were up at St Pancras by 10.00 and with a taxi soon arrived at Buckingham Palace. This was an outdoor Investiture, so we were ushered into the quadrangle, where about 100 people were seated — nothing had commenced.

We sat down where we were told and very soon the King came and took his place on the dais, together with the Duke of Connaught and Sir Derek Keppel. Then began the stream of heroes of various ages, ranks and regiments. There were several Victoria Crosses presented to the living men themselves and they were clapped and cheered tremendously. Then came naval men, airmen and some nurses. Well, we thought we were forgotten but then someone came and ushered us behind the dais and I found myself face to face with King George. I made my curtsey and he began to speak, congratulating us on having such a gallant son. . . .

He then expressed some words of sympathy and presented the medal; John's mother curtsied again and the couple left Buckingham Palace. They then went out into Green Park where they were mobbed by crowds of people who wanted to take their photographs and catch a glimpse of their son's VC.

In 1935 a village hall was set up and dedicated to the memory of Wells. Named The Collings-Wells VC Memorial Hall, it was opened by his surviving brother, Lt Col R.P. Collings-Wells, on 26 January. Mrs Pemberton, one of his sisters, was also present. John's name is written across the front of the building. Together the two brothers had attended a church service at Caddington just prior to the war when the congregation had prayed for peace. Both men were later to earn the DSO during the war. The hall was built in Chaul End behind the church and close to the local schools and could accommodate 250 people. The vicar who had taken a major role in the setting up of the hall was presented with a silver-mounted walking stick as a memento of the occasion.

The Collings-Wells family home, Caddington Hall, was originally built in 1830 becoming the local Manor House. After the family vacated it the house became a nursing home for the elderly and in 1948 was purchased by Bedfordshire County Council for £11,400. It was demolished in the 1970s and a residential care unit for the elderly was built in its place by the County Council. Parts of the original walled gardens can still be traced.

Collings-Wells is remembered in many ways and his name is also included in the family memorial at Hughenden Manor Church, Buckinghamshire. There is also a tablet to his memory at St Ethelreda's Church in Hatfield, Herts. At All Saint's Church, Caddington, a marble plaque near the altar was erected by his parents and an east window to his memory is in the parish church of St John the Baptist at Markyate. Caddington and Markyate are part of the same group of Ecclesiastical Parishes. There is also a plaque in Bedford School and in Caddington a road named after him called Collings-Wells Close. In addition his name is listed on the following memorials: Christ Church, Oxford; Caddington War Memorial, All Saint's Churchyard, Luton Road, Caddington; and at Uppingham School.

In his will he left £7406 Gross and his VC; DSO, 1914–15 Star & Clasp and service medals are kept at the Bedfordshire and Hertfordshire Reginental Museum in Luton. The two battalions had amalgamated in 1919.

H.G. COLUMBINE
Hervilly Wood, France, 22 March

No fewer than nine Victoria Crosses had been won on the first day of the German Spring Offensive of 21 March 1918, an operation which was also known as Kaiserschlacht or 'the Kaiser's Battle', the intention of which was for Germany to knock the British Army out of the war.

With the added advantage of it being a very misty morning great inroads were made by the enemy into the lines of the British Third and Fifth Armies but with hindsight it was clear that the German Army, in making one last desperate bid to end the stalemate of a staticWestern Front had over stretched itself. By evening the writing was already on the wall for the Kaiser's Army and it would only be a matter of time before the Allies; soon to be supported by the involvement of American troops, were to win the last battle of the war eight months later.

Even so there was still a long way to go and as the British Army tried to re-establish itself in new and hastily prepared defensive positions no fewer than five more men were to gain the nation's highest military honour the following day including an extremely courageous machine gunner, Private Herbert Columbine.

Columbine's heroic deed took place in the Fifth Army sector at the village of Hervilly, which had been occupied by British troops since 31 March 1917. The village together with its wood, was 8 miles due east of Péronne and 1½ miles behind the front line of the previous day. The British 1st Cavalry Div. was already in action together with the 66th and 24th Infantry divisions. The divisional front was described by the Official Historian as ' a series of re-entrants and salients down the middle of the Battle Zone'. The 9th Dismounted Bde of the 1st Cavalry Div. was in reserve to the rear of the 66th Div. at Hervilly and

Roisel to the north-west. By about 11 a.m. the enemy, with one tank assisting them, entered Hervilly Wood and captured two posts of the 8th Hussars which were close by. From this position they enfiladed a company of the 9th Royal Sussex who were based in the village and lying flat on their trenches which were too shallow to give them adequate protection. However a temporary respite was provided about an hour later when the Cavalry re-captured a part of the wood.

Pte Columbine of the 9th Squadron, Machine Gun Corps had taken over one of the guns in an advance position in the wood, east of the village and kept it going for four hours until 1.00 p.m. with not even wire to give him even slight protection. During this time waves of German troops tried to overcome his position and he was only checked when a low flying enemy aircraft began to assist the enemy ground troops. The Germans were then able to gain a footing on either side of his position and Columbine could see that he would be soon completely surrounded and cut off. He then gave orders to his two remaining colleagues to get back to safety and although he was now alone and being bombed as well as being fired upon by the enemy, he still managed to inflict heavy losses. Still it was only a matter of time before the uneven struggle came to an end and the cause was a direct hit on both Columbine and his gun by a bomb which was dropped from an aircraft which blew the position sky high. Not surprisingly Columbine's body was not recovered from the battlefield.

About an hour later the enemy entered Hervilly village which was to remain in their hands until the Final Advance. Earlier in the war between 1915–16 the village had been a favourite bombing target for the RFC as a German airfield was in the vicinity.

Fortunately we have an eye-witness statement by Dr. P.G.C. Atkinson which supports the official account of what happened to Columbine when he won his VC and the Doctor wrote as follows:

The enemy attacked in great force. They made considerable headway, and from vantage ground on either side they started to enfilade our trenches, causing very severe casualties among the men. Part of our defence system included a machine-gun post somewhat in advance of the main trench. The men working this were all knocked out. Running the gauntlet of very heavy fire, Private Columbine rushed forward and took charge of this gun. He was followed by some comrades, and in spite of the fact that the whole of the enemy machine guns in the immediate neighbourhood concentrated their heaviest fire against this post, which was almost unprotected by any of the devices commonly used, Columbine kept the machine going for over four hours. All the time the enemy had been working round the position with strong forces, and actually had the post cut off save for one narrow gap, by which it was still possible to communicate with the main position. For the whole of the time, save when he went across the fire-swept ground to bring ammunition, the brave chap remained at his post, and despite repeated rushes, he kept the enemy at bay. In the course of the fight a German officer appeared and repeatedly urged his men to the attack on the isolated post, but every rush of the Germans was stopped in a few yards by the deadly fire from this brave gunner, who was actually wounded, but continued to work his gun in spite of that. Early in the afternoon it became obvious that the position was hopeless, and Columbine told the only two unwounded comrades left that it as folly for them to remain there...

They were reluctant to go, but he insisted, and in the end they came to see the force of his contention that there was no point in sacrificing three lives where one was enough. He shouted a few words of farewell, and that was the last his comrades heard from him ... In the course of the hour, from noon to one, the enemy made eight attempts to rush the post. Each one was brought to a standstill ... At the same time a number of hostile aeroplanes appeared overhead. They were promptly engaged by our machines, but one detached itself from the fighting group and came down to about a hundred feet or so above the machine-gun position. We saw Columbine elevate his gun to attack the new enemy. The fight could only have one ending. A bomb was launched from the aeroplane, and there was a sharp report, gun and gunner blown up. The heroic fight of Columbine was not without its value, for the way in which he delayed the enemy attack gave us time to consolidate our position in the immediate neighbourhood, and when the enemy attacked they found that the four hours' stand made by this man alone had put the German plans hopelessly out of gear as far as the capture of that series of positions was concerned. The comrades of the dead hero speak highly of him.

Lt Eade was the officer in charge of Columbine's sub-section and he described Columbine as 'one of my best gunners' and Capt. MacAndrews, the commander of 9th Machine Gun Squadron, wrote to Columbine's mother with the following information:

I had a full parade of the Squadron this morning to read out the account of his action and also the letter of congratulations which we received from the General ... We all sincerely trust that your great sorrow may be to some extent lessened by your pride of his noble death, so noble that the King has honoured him with the very highest award.

The citation for Columbine' s posthumous VC was published on 3 May 1918 as follows:

... Private Columbine took over command of a gun and kept it firing from 9 a.m. till 1 p.m. In an isolated position with no wire in front. During this time wave after wave of the enemy failed to get up to him. Owing to his being attacked by a low-flying aeroplane, the enemy at last gained a footing in the trench on either side. The position being untenable, he ordered the two remaining men to getaway, and, though being bombed from either side, he kept his gun firing and inflicted tremendous losses. He was eventually killed by a bomb which blew him up and his gun. He showed throughout the highest valour, determination and self-sacrifice. '

Emma, Columbine's widowed mother, was presented with her son's VC by the King three months later on 22 June 1918. For some reason she declined to accept an Army Pension which she was entitled to and the people of Walton set up a street collection on her behalf and collected £312 9 s 2d which was exchanged for War Bonds.

Herbert George Columbine, son of Herbert and Emma Columbine, was born in Chelsea on 28 November 1893 and educated at Melvin Road Council School, Penge. His father, also Herbert, was killed during the Boer War on 11 July 1900 when young Herbert was only six years old. The widowed Emma and Herbert junior lived at 44 Annesley Road, Penge.

Emma came from Suffolk, having been born in Brandon in 1860 and had lived at Methwold. In 1871 her family moved to Whittlesey, near Peterborough and by the time she was 20 she had moved to Kensington where she was in service in Redcliffe Street. At the time she was living with her mother in Lambeth and at some stage met Herbert Columbine and the couple married in 1893.

It is difficult to sort out the links with Walton but prior to 1900 the family used to visit the Essex resort for holidays and at some point Herbert worked with Mr J.W.Hipkins, a carrier who delivered parcels collected from the local railway station. In 1911 Emma's address was 33, Crescent Road, Cottages, Walton (later destroyed in the Second World War) and for an income she had small private means and money from needlework.

Also in 1911 and after leaving school, Columbine enlisted in the 19th (Queen Alexandra's Own Royal) Hussars when he was stationed in Aldershot. He was allocated the service number 5780. The Hussars were then divided into three Squadrons and arrived in France on 22 August 1914. In April 1915 the Hussars were made into one unit becoming part of 9th Cavalry Bde of the 1st Cavalry Div. and they took part in some of the Ypres battles. In October the Machine Gun Corps was established and at the end of June 1916 Columbine was one of the men transferred to the MGC Cavalry. He was then allocated the new number of 50720 and now served with the 9th Squadron MGC who were the Machine Gun element of the 15th and 19th Hussars together with the 1/1 Bedfordshire Yeomanry. They took part in the September 1916 Somme battles and also in the battle of Arras in April 1917.

After the war in 1921 Emma gave her son's posthumous VC to the Walton on the Naze Urban District Council, for display in the Town Hall but when the council was amalgamated in 1934, the VC was given to the local branch of the British Legion who still own it. For security reasons it was transferred to a bank vault. Later, as she had no real links with the town Emma moved back to London to live with her sister in Fulham, dying in 1945.

Columbine's name is commemorated on the Pozieres Memorial, Panels 93 and 94 and a bronze bust of his head was erected on the Marine Parade on the seafront at Walton which was unveiled in 1920 by Lord Byng, former commander of the Third Army. The white stone pedestal supporting the head had a plaque attached to it which quoted a short section of his VC Citation and lower down was a second plaque which contained the following inscription:

Erected by his Friends and Countrymen in ever grateful memory in the year 1920.

The 21cm bust was the work of Newton Abbot Trent (1885–1953) Marine Parade was also the site for the town's war memorial, which was 50 yards distant from the bust and listed the name of the fifty-eight Walton men who fell in the Great War. This memorial was later moved and re-erected in the Cemetery of the local Parish Church. At some point a captured German Howitzer was also on display on the Parade but was probably later removed for scrap. In 1957 a third plaque to Columbine's memory was added to the plinth, by his former regiment.

Two years before Miss Louie Columbine's, one of Columbine's aunts, was taken to a London Hospital where she remained for several months. While there she used to talk about her nephew's award and her doctors considered that it might help with her recovery if she were to set eyes on this decoration again. As a result, Frinton and Walton Council was contacted and agreed to ask the local branch of the British Legion if they would kindly send it in the post for her to see one more time. The request was granted and the Legion posted it, together with a collection of various newspaper cuttings that were kept with it. Miss Columbine had sent a two shilling postal order to cover carriage costs and promised to return the award very quickly. The Legion, however, returned the postal order. Also in the same year this VC allowed out of the bank vault again when displayed at an exhibition arranged by the 15th/ 19th Hussars.

Sadly, in May 1970, both the bust of Columbine as well as the plinth were vandalised and dumped in scrub. There were also other occasions when the memorial became a target for vandals, indeed the head was regularly tossed into the sea. It then dawned on the town that the bust might be less of a temptation if it was moved to a safer position and it was taken to the Parish cemetery. However even the cemetery wasn't a safe haven and a local shopkeeper took it upon himself to commission a series of duplicate heads in order to safeguard against further loss or destruction. In 1996 this same man whose shop was close to the cemetery, informed the writer that the Columbine memorial hadn't been vandalised in the previous three years and at the same meeting he showed the author one of the duplicate heads which he had commissioned and paid for.

Safety of the bust and plinth were not the only problem for also in 1970 a dispute broke out between the 15th/ 19th Hussars, based in Newcastle upon Tyne and the Walton branch of the British Legion, who were responsible for the VC's care. A trustee of the Old Comrades Association was quoted in the *Daily Telegraph* of 13 October saying: 'What is the use of the VC being in a vault in the bank? Surely it is better to put it in a regimental museum where people can come and see it?'

Having set down this complicated story it almost comes as a relief to mention that Columbine's name has also been remembered in more conventional ways. For example when one enters the seaside town from the Colchester direction, one sees a notice pointing to the Columbine

Centre, a large building erected in 1992 and formerly opened in Bath House Meadow the following March. The Centre serves as a base for various activities carried out by members of the local community, and provides a suitable venue for all kinds of local entertainments such as concerts, plays, dances, public meetings etc. In the foyer can be found the original bronze head of Columbine, which has been repaired, and a copy of his VC citation is placed above the head and replicas of his VC and Mons Star are also displayed. His other awards were the BWM and VM service medals. Further commemorative links with the local hero can be found with names of Columbine Gardens and a road called Hervilly Way, in a new housing estate.

In 1992 a bust of Columbine was listed in *Spinks*' sale catalogue of 15 September but the lot was later withdrawn, presumably because the firm founds they might be handling stolen property. The happy ending to this part of the story is that this very bust is the one now on display, in relative security, of the Columbine Centre.

At the time of writing there are active plans to commemorate the memory of Herbert Columbine with a statue on the Walton seafront. John Doubleday is the commissioned sculptor and the project's fund raisers are offering for sale scaled down bronze models of the statue to contribute to funding for the project. They can be purchased for £1200 plus VAT. One can only hope that once it has been erected on the seafront that it doesn't suffer from the same fate as its predecessor.

H. JACKSON
Hermies, France, 22 March

Sgt Harold Jackson of the 7th (S) Bn East Yorkshire Regt won his VC at Hermies on 22 March 1918. The battalion was part of the 50th Bde of the 17th (Northern) Div., which in turn was part of V Corps of the Third Army. Other brigades in the division were the 51st and 52nd. To the right was the 63rd (Royal Naval) Div.. On 21 March, the first day of the German Offensive, the 7th East Yorks had taken up defensive positions awaiting the expected German advance.

The brigade dispositions on the 22nd were as follows: 50th Bde held the line from the Canal du Nord to Hermies, with the 7th East Yorks in exposed positions or outposts called Gong Trench facing a north-easterly direction on the left of the canal; 52nd Bde was to the right and held the defences as far west as the canal and the village of Havrincourt, and the 51st Bde was in the Hermies defences. These lines were called the Hermies–Havrincourt Ridge. Defensive preparations were made in the British lines and when the sun rose on the 22nd it began to disperse the early morning mist. The enemy made slow progress and tried to capture Gong Trench, but the East Yorks held their ground despite the enemy using *Flammenwerfer* (flamethrower). The Germans then made a half-hearted attempt to take the outpost of Jermyn Street across the Canal at around 10.15 a.m. There was a more serious attempt when the enemy attacked the British positions to the west of the Canal du Nord. It was during this period that Jackson won his VC for remarkable gallantry and the details are given in the privately printed *History of the 50th Infantry Brigade 1914–1919*:

> On the morning of 22 March this N.C.O. volunteered for a daylight patrol during a heavy enemy barrage preparatory to their

first assault and was successful in getting in touch with the enemy and brought back valuable intelligence re their concentration. On the same morning, after the enemy had succeeded in entering parts of our front line, he held an important bombing-stop and by his vigorous offensive forced them to withdraw. He later stalked an enemy machine gun which was enfilading our line, and single-handed he bombed the crew and put the gun definitely out of action, killing or wounding the entire crew. He fought with magnificent gallantry for the following seven days during rearguard actions. . . .

At about 2.00 p.m. the East Yorks fell back to positions between Hermies and the Canal, where they remained that night. The Germans were concentrating their attacks on the left of the Salient, in other words on Hermies, from the direction of Doignies and Denicourt. They threw in at least 4,000 men in the attempt to capture the ruined village and as the 51st Div. to the right of the 17th Div. were having to give ground, the 17th was shortly to be in a very dangerous situation itself. In order to assist, divisional reserves were sent up but it was not long before the 17th Div. fell back to the so-called 'Green Line'.

However, late in the evening the line to the south of the Third Army was retiring and plans were already in hand for the 17th Div. to stage a fighting retreat even further to the rear, to the former Somme battlefield in positions to the west of the River Ancre.

On the 23rd the initial enemy attacks were beaten off by the 17th Div. and then the retirement began. The Germans brought up their field artillery and very soon reached Vélu Wood; at about midday the division began to move back. The 50th Bde suffered from hostile shell-fire and attacks from the rear but 'steady fighting' brought them through and the East Yorkshiremen retired through the lines of the 2nd Div. to the Vélu Wood line, and back to Rocquigny.

Eight days later, on 31 March, Jackson was again in the action at Bouzincourt just outside Albert. The account in the 50th Bde history continues:

He took command of his company after all his officers had become casualties, led them to the attack with splendid bravery and initiative, and withdrew when ordered to do so under heavy fire and took up a good new defensive position. He afterwards repeatedly went out into the open and brought back badly wounded men, under a murderous enemy fire.

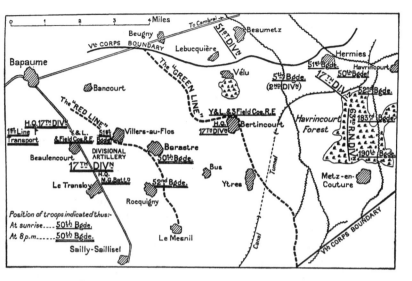

Retreat to the Red Line, 23 March 1918

His wonderful coolness and devotion to duty under the most trying circumstances has set the highest example to everyone.

The attack that Jackson was involved in on the 31st was made with the assistance of four tanks and began at 5.30 a.m. It failed because of severe enemy machine-gun fire from buildings on the outskirts of Albert, and because the tanks were not much use. However despite this failure the German advance was actually stopped and the battle that had begun ten days previously now ended.

The 50th Bde was relieved by the 51st and then went into divisional reserve at Henencourt. The East Yorks in the last ten days of March had lost twenty-one officers and 431 men. Jackson's luck ran out on 24 August when he was killed taking part in the fighting to capture Stuff Redoubt and Mouquet Farm at Thiepval. He was initially buried in the area, but in 1927, when the graves were being concentrated, his remains were transferred to the AIF burial ground at Glass Lane, Flers and his family informed. The village of Flers came into prominence in mid-September 1916 when it was captured by British and New Zealanders who had the use of tanks for the first time. The village was lost in March 1918 and retaken by the British in August.

The AIF cemetery is a mile to the west of Guedecourt and the grave reference is Plot XV. Row A. Grave 21/30.

Harold ('Chummy') Jackson was the son of Thomas and Ann Jackson and born in Allandales, Kirton, near Boston, Lincolnshire on 31 May 1892. Not much is known of his early life, though he was a noted amateur boxer and was initially employed as a drayman before he left his home town at the age of 20 to work on the railways at Nottingham. Later he became a bricklayer with the builders Messrs McAlpine.

In April 1915 he joined the 18th Hussars as a trooper and left for France. A few months later he was transferred to the East Yorkshire Regt. He took part in the attack on Fricourt at the beginning of July 1916 and was wounded two weeks later at Bazentin. He returned to England and served with a reserve battalion before rejoining his regiment in 1917.

His VC was gazetted on 8 May 1918 and he was presented with the VC ribbon by his corps commander on 18 May 1918. The citation was as follows:

> Sergt. Jackson volunteered and went out through the hostile barrage and brought back valuable information regarding the enemy's movements. Later, when the enemy had established themselves in our line, this N. C. O. rushed at them, single handed, bombed then out into the open. Shortly afterwards, again single-handed, he stalked an enemy machine gun, threw Mills bombs at the detachment, and put the gun out of action. On a subsequent occasion, when all his officers had became casualties, this very gallant N. C. O. led his company in the attack, and when ordered to retire, he withdrew the company successfully under heavy fire. He then went out repeatedly heavy fire and carried in wounded.

Jackson was lodging with one of his sisters at 5 Cheshire Road, Bowes Park, Wood Green when his VC was announced. A photograph of him was displayed in Wood Green at the time. On 26 June he went to Buckingham Palace to receive his decoration from the hands of the King and shortly afterwards returned home to Kirton, to a hero's welcome and Kirton Brass Band took part in the ceremonies along with most of the town's inhabitants. In response Sgt Jackson thanked the people of the town for their 'grand and hearty reception'. A photographic portrait of him was on display at the Parish Hall until it later disappeared.

Wounded twice in the war Jackson's medals included the 1914–15 Star, the BWM and the VM, and were sold with various original documents, including a letter from the War Office informing his next of kin of his death, and three letters from the IWGC of spring 1927 giving details of his headstone and its erection. Jackson's bible was also included with an inscription from the Vicar of Kirton dated 1918 along with one from Kirton Church dated January 1902, with an inscription from Kirton Church Sunday School. There were photographs of Jackson's return after his investiture and a large quantity of newspaper cuttings relating to him and his VC. Mrs Mary Searby, one of Jackson's sisters, came into possession of her brother's VC, and she lent the medal to her father, who wished to wear it to a Buckingham Palace garden party. Unfortunately he did not return it and it was only on his death that it was found and returned to her. It then passed to Jackson's niece, Mrs Mabel Scuffham of 154 Sleaford Road, Boston, probably in 1956/57. Jackson's medals, including his VC in the original case provided by Hancocks, were sold at Sothebys on 11 May 1989 and were purchased by Mr George Gambol for £10,450. Harold Jackson's name is commemorated on the war memorials in Kirton; Boston and Wood Green in London.

C.L. KNOX

Tugny, France, 22 March

When the German Spring Offensive began on 21 March 1918 the 36th (Ulster) Div. was part of XVIII Corps, Fifth Army and its Field Coy was 150th Field Coy (Royal Engineers), in which T/2nd Lt Cecil Knox was serving. Before the war he had been a civil engineer and was now given the task of destroying pontoons and bridges on the divisional front, which was 6 or 7 miles south-east of the German-held town of St Quentin, along the Somme Canal. When the German offensive began in thick fog on 21 March at 4.45 a.m. the Sappers had quickly realised that the demolition plan would have to be put into effect and Battle Stations were manned and Knox set off for his bridges (the Artemps Group) which were made ready to blow by mid morning. The enemy bombardment continued for the rest of the day and the predicted enemy advance was expected at any time. During the small hours of the 22nd six bridges and two footbridges were destroyed in the Hamel-Seraucourt area and later and further to the south-east, as we have seen, the 150th Field Coy was allotted the Artemps group of four bridges to destroy and in addition the Tugny and St.Simon group of two footbridges and ten road bridges were the responsibility of another company. A section of the company under the command of Lt W.M.W. Brunyate destroyed the Artemps bridges in the early morning mists between 4.00 and 4.30 a.m and Knox and his section of the company completed the destruction of the Tugny group by 9.30 a.m. At Tugny the enemy was advancing towards one of the bridges – of a steel girder type – when the time-fuse for the detonator failed due to damp caused by the dew or mist. Knox immediately raced forward as the first German soldiers set foot on the other end of the long bridge, and ripped out the time-fuse. He then climbed under the framework of the bridge and lit a replacement fuse of the instantaneous type. Thus the bridge was immediately destroyed, with some German casualties though miraculously Knox was uninjured.

At St Simon, Lt Stapylton-Smith of the same company had successfully destroyed more of the enemy when blowing one of the three main bridges there and as a consequence the enemy advance was considerably delayed in this sector.

Despite the chaotic conditions and the inevitability of an Allied retreat the Sappers had planned the operation very efficiently and all told they were to destroy no fewer than seventy-eight bridges in the six-day period 22–28 March. However, a few were not destroyed, including those allocated to the French engineers, who were understandably reluctant to carry out the demolition. The British had laid up a good supply of gun cotton for the destruction of steel lattice and girder bridges and of ammonal tubes for the destruction of pile bridges The charges were stored in special boxes and placed close to the bridges, in anticipation of the German offensive.

Sec. Lt Knox had earned a VC for his part in the destruction of the Canal bridges and the citation was published in the *London Gazette* of 4 June 1918 as follows:

> Twelve bridges [probably thirteen] were entrusted to this officer for demolition, and all of them were successfully destroyed. In the case of one steel girder bridge, the destruction of which he personally supervised, the time fuse failed to act. Without hesitation, Second. Lieut. Knox ran to the bridge, under heavy fire and machine-gun fire, and when the enemy were actually on the bridge he tore away the time fuse and lit the instantaneous fuse, to do which he had to get under the bridge. This was an act of the highest devotion to duty, entailing the gravest risks, which, as a practical civil engineer, he fully realised.

Cecil Leonard Knox was born in Nuneaton, Warwickshire on 9 May 1889, and was the second of nine brothers of whom six served in the war and of whom two were killed in action. Andrew in December 1915 and James died of wounds in September 1918. They were the children of Mr and Mrs James Knox of The Chase, Higham Lane, Nuneaton. Cecil attended King Edward VI Grammar school in the town, where the Revd S. Waters, later vicar of Meriden, was headmaster. Knox finished his schooling at Oundle Public School, where he developed a passion for fives, a sport played with a gloved hand in a walled court.

Two of Cecil's brothers were working as civil engineers in Alberta at the beginning of the war in Canada and didn't hear news of it for some time and when they did they immediately enlisted. Cecil, already a qualified engineer himself, was commissioned as a temporary 2nd lieutenant into the Royal Engineers and joined the 150th Field Coy, RE, who were then serving with the 36th (Ulster) Div. of IX Corps, Second Army. He was present at the Battle of Messines in June 1917 and two months later the division was transferred to the XIX Corps of the Fifth Army and his field company was used for road work in preparation for the Battle of Langemarck. Knox later served at Cambrai with IV Corps of the Third Army and in November the 36th Div. rejoined VI Corps.

In June 1918 Nuneaton Council moved a resolution of congratulations to Mr and Mrs Knox and to their son Cecil for winning the VC, which had been announced in the *London Gazette* on 4 June. He received the decoration from the King at Second Army Headquarters at Blendecques, 3 miles south of St Omer on 6 August 1918. The HQ was normally based at Cassel but between April and September 1918 it was wisely moved to safety. John Crowe of the Worcestershire and Charles Train of the London Regt were also presented with their VCs at the same ceremony. Knox had already been given the Freedom of the Borough of Nuneaton at a ceremony which took place in Riversley Park on 17 July. He was accompanied by Cpl Beesley VC, who was also presented with the Freedom of the Borough. After the Armistice Knox was promoted to lieutenant on 2 December 1918, although he had already been given the temporary rank of captain in the previous October. In 1919 he was demobilised and returned to civilian life as a civil engineer. He and his brother Kenneth became directors of the family business of Haunchwood Brick and Tile Company and of G.W. Lewis Tileries Ltd. In addition his family also owned the Arley Colliery.

Between the wars Knox attended a couple of VC events and he took up flying and was based at Castle Bromwich aerodrome, serving with 605 (Bombing) Squadron (County of Warwick), Royal Auxiliary Air Force between 1926 and 1932. He was promoted to Flying Officer on 23 May 1928 and later to flight lieutenant on 1 January 1930. In August 1927, when still a Pilot Officer, Knox took part in a volunteer parachute jump which resulted in a spell in hospital with internal injuries after he landed heavily. The jump took place in Manston, Kent, where 605 (Bombing) Squadron was carrying out training. The injuries put an end to Knox's active career in the Air Force – although in June 1928 he did take part in an aerial display in Birmingham – he relinquished his commission in 1931.

In 1931/32 Knox decided to build himself a new house and the site that he chose was in the small hamlet of Caldecote to the north-west of Nuneaton. The site was on a flat hilltop and it was very much a house of its era, with no expense spared. The internal panelling and doors were made largely from cherry wood and what was particularly unusual was that Knox decided to incorporate a fives court on the south side of the house with a gallery for spectators. The house was named Fyves Court, which gives a glimpse of Knox's sense of humour.

When visiting Fyves Court (1996) the writer was shown the site of the court, which was in the process of being changed into a snooker room. The former spectator gallery now has a wooden floor above the table. The outside alterations have been carried out to blend in with the original house and no doubt bricks from the family brickyards were originally used. Knox was also a very keen all-year-round swimmer and built a pool in the garden, also in the process of being altered. Knox was obviously attached to this house and it shows a side of his nature that could be called quirky, as there cannot have been many houses built between the wars which incorporated a fives court. He was also very keen on woodwork and built a modern workshop attached to the house.

Knox's father died in 1931 aged eighty-two, and his mother Florence Elizabeth in 1935. In October 1941 Cecil Knox's wife Eileen Baylor gave birth to a daughter, Katrina Victoria, the couple's only child, in Nuneaton Nursing Home, Watling Street. Under her married name of Barling, Katrina was known to be living in Devon in 1994.

In the Second World War Knox served as a Major and Second-in-Command of the local Home Guard unit. On 4 February 1943 when travelling down Buck's Hill, Nuneaton on his motor bike Knox inexplicably skidded and was thrown on his head and died of his injuries. He was only fifty-three. The accident occurred at about 10.30 a.m. and Knox was taken unconscious to Nuneaton General Hospital, where he died about three hours later. His wife was at his bedside. A witness who was driving a Haunchwood Colliery lorry up Buck's Hill towards Chapel End stated at the inquest:

Just after I saw a motor cyclist coming down the hill towards me, on his proper side. The speed of the motor cyclist was very moderate, about 10 to 15 miles an hour . . . The deceased had plenty of room, and went past all right, still skidding, his wheels towards the kerb. The deceased kept hold of his handle-bars as long as he could, and he fell with his head towards the middle of the road, the motor cycle being still between his legs.

An ambulance was called and the road was said to be slippery in patches. Knox had just taken a right-hand bend, when he went into a skid. This accident was difficult to explain and despite the inquest coming to the conclusion that no other vehicle was involved, it was rumoured that a van was involved and by turning either into or out of Buck's Hill indirectly caused Knox's fatal skid. The private funeral took place at St Peter's Church, Witherley, and the coffin – on which spring flowers from the garden at Fyves Court had been placed – was borne by workers from the three brickyards owned by the Knox family. Knox's body was cremated at Gilroes Crematorium, Leicester, (Refernce 339) and his ashes were scattered in the grounds of his much-loved home.

After Knox's death his widow Eileen moved to Brodwell near Stow-on-the-Wold and presented the casket which had contained the Freeman's Scroll to the Mayor of Nuneaton in April 1972 for safe keeping. In September 1994 Katrina visited the town to meet the Mayor and some old friends and to seek out her family roots. With her she brought her father's VC which she showed to the Mayor; she also met Tim Newcombe, who as a young fireman had been at the scene of her father's fatal accident.

The family memorial is at Oaston Road Cemetery, Nuneaton, and includes the names of Cecil's parents and his brothers killed in the war, Lt Col James and 2nd Lt A. Ronald Knox, though not Cecil's. Knox Crescent on the St Nicholas Park Estate perpetuates the family name and a picture of Knox receiving his VC from the King used to hang in the Nuneaton Art Gallery. His name is also included on the War Memorial in Nuneaton Park and on the VC Memorial at Thiepval close to the Ulster Tower

Riversley Park, where Knox and Beesley were greeted by the citizens of Nuneaton in July 1918, still exists and is the site of the Museum and Art Gallery and the local Registry Office. Also in the park is the town's war memorial and Lt Col James Knox's name heads the list of members of the Royal Warwickshire Regt who lost their lives during the conflict.

The three brick and tile yards owned by the Knox family were still going at the end of the Second World War but between the 1950s and 1970s they were closed down. The clay used for the bricks was frequently found in the same area as coal and the two industries often went hand in hand. The Knox family were major employers in Nuneaton and its environs and were greatly respected; even today the locals still talk of them.

The Chase, the former Knox family home, still exists and is now a public house and hotel. It used to be called The Gatehouse and one can still see the initials of James Knox on two escutcheons on the outside walls of what is now a saloon bar.

Knox's life was one of those commemorated at a special service held in Lichfield Cathedral on 10 June 2007 to the memory of local VC holders who had links with either Warwickshire or Coventry. It was 150 years since Queen Victoria invested the very first VC winner.

Knox's decorations include the VC, 1914–15 Star, BWM VM and the 1937 King George VIth Coronation Medal, are owned by his family.

F.C. ROBERTS

*West of Somme and at Pargny, 22
March to 2 April*

On 22 March the 8th Div., then in GHQ
reserve, was moved by rail from its
concentration area near St Omer down to
the Fifth Army on the Somme, where it was
placed under command of XIX Corps. The
men proceeded to detrain at various stations
from Amiens to Ham and after going up the
line they took up their allotted positions on
23 March, holding the right section of the
Péronne bridgehead. Advance parties of the
24th Bde began to arrive between 8.00 and
9.00 p.m., and to their great surprise they found the enemy occupying
the billets which had been set aside for them. Later on that evening the
divisional orders were changed and their new positions were now to
be an 8 mile section on the west bank of the Somme from Ingon in the
north to Eterpigny. The 24th Bde was sent up to the front line in lorries
and was in position at around 7.00 a.m. on the 23rd, the only part of
the division to be so.

However, the enemy quickly worked round the exposed right flank
and managed to reach the area to the south of the village of Pargny
by noon. Several attempts were made by them to cut the divisional
positions and an enemy party managed to take the ruined canal
bridge at Pargny and subsequently occupy the village. It was at this
point that A/Lt Col Frank Roberts, Commanding Officer of the 1st Bn
The Worcestershire Regt, performed a deed which contributed to his
winning the VC over a period of twelve days between 22 March and
2 April. The 1st Worcesters counter-attacked at Pargny and brought
considerable assistance to the 25th Bde. The *London Gazette* recorded
on 8 May:

During continuous operations which covered over twelve days Lieut.-Colonel Roberts showed most conspicuous bravery, exceptional military skill in dealing with the very difficult situations of the retirement, and amazing endurance and energy in encouraging and inspiring all ranks under his command. On one occasion the enemy attacked a village and had practically cleared it of our troops, when this officer got together an improvised party and led a counter-attack which temporarily drove the enemy out of the village thus covering the retirement of troops on their flanks, who would otherwise have been cut off. The success of this action was entirely due to his personal valour and skill.

This counter-attack by about seventy men of the 1st Worcestershires and 2nd Rifle Bde drove the Germans back, with the loss of many dead, twenty prisoners and four machine guns.

In 1925, seven years after these events, Roberts wrote to H. Fitzmaurice Stacke, the regimental historian of the Worcestershire Regt, that:

... after two companies had returned from Falvy village (a village to the north-east of Pargny on the right bank of the Somme canal) about 5.00 p.m. on the 23rd March, where they had been covering the retreat of the 50th Division, I reinforced the battalion front on the W. of the Canal which we held from N. of Epenancourt to Pargny Bridge inclusive. About 6.00 p.m. I found a few men of another battalion in the southern part of the village and was told the whole battalion was at that time getting into position along the canal to my right. After having fixed up the defence of the bridge (partially blown up) I walked along the canal bank looking at my posts until I reached my battalion HQ in a sunken road just south of Epenacourt; here I had tea, and at dusk started off to go round the battalion again, from N. to S. At about 8 00 p.m. I reached a point 'E' (on map) and found the post there was excited as they were being shot at from houses in the N. portion of Pargny, and had also seen Boche in the village before dark. I was also told that all posts between them and the bridge had ceased to function (afterwards I found a number of men in them had been shot in the back and that the local defence South of the bridge had been broken through about dusk).

I at once realised that the battalion supposed to have been on my right (2nd Rifle Brigade) could not have arrived, and that unless the village was taken back, we should be mopped up during the night, if the enemy continued to advance N.W. of the canal. After about quarter of an hour I managed to collect about 45 ORs from posts N. of 'E' and at once moved across country to 'A' (on map) along 'F' (a sunken road) which prevented the party from being seen by the Boche. Here I organised my three parties behind a few broken-down cottages, telling the R. and Left parties to work along the routes given them, paying attention to any noise that might start in the main street (i.e. 'D' party's route) and to keep up level with me, so as to deal with any enemy who might clear out of the houses in the outskirts of the village and try to get away.

As far as I can recollect we actually started off at about 9 p.m. 'D' party started off with fixed bayonets and magazines loaded. For the first 100 yards or so we went into two parties in single file on each side of the main road, at the walk and as quietly as possible. The first intimation that I had of the Boche, was some shouting from houses we were passing, and both mg and rifle fire (very wild) from windows and doors, with small parties of the enemy dashing into the streets and clearing off in the direction of the bridge. Once this started we all went hell-for-leather up the street, firing at anything we saw and using the bayonet in many cases. From the beginning every man screamed and cheered as hard as he bloody well could, and by the time we reached the Church the village was in an uproar and Boche was legging it hard to the bridge or else chucking his hands up (we only took very few prisoners as I'd told the men to KILL so as to prevent the brutes again coming up in our rear). In the Churchyard itself the hardest fighting took place tombstones being used as if in a game of hide and seek. Here after clearing it we had a few minutes rest and then went smack through to the bridge where a mass of Boche were trying to scramble across, some did and some didn't! That more or less ended it, and we at once brought up some of the Reserve coy. to take over this part of the front. The two flank parties did extremely well as regards turning the Boche into us and helped to make a success of the general muddle which as a matter of fact went far to helping get the village back. We actually captured 6 light machine guns, and about 15–20 prisoners and I think killed approx. 80–100. Our own losses were heavy but I can't quite remember the exact figures …

Roberts also mentioned that the village and church had already been ruined in the earlier part of the war and signed himself with his nickname, 'Cully', in his letter to Stacke.

By the evening of 24 March the 24th Bde's position was left of the line of the canal bank about a mile to the south of the village of St Christ which then ran in a south-westerly direction and joined up with the indented lines of the 25th Bde about a mile south-south-east of the village of Licourt.

By now at least eight German divisions had been identified on the front of the British 8th Div. and the divisional HQ were no longer in control of events and had no knowledge of what was happening at Pargny.

On 27 March Roberts was wounded but in June he returned to his post as CO of the 1st Worcesters. After the Battle of the Aisne in May, every commanding officer of the 8th Div. became a casualty. On 1 August, in the Vimy Ridge sector twenty trench mortar shells containing mustard gas were fired on the positions of the 1st Worcesters, causing about thirty casualties, including Lt Col Roberts; his Second in Command and his Adjutant. Fortunately they were not seriously affected.

On 17 October Colonel Roberts made a personal reconnaissance of the canal near Douai and ascertained that the enemy was still holding it at 9.15 a.m. on the front of the 1st Worcesters. Later in the morning the sounds of heavy traffic moving in Douai were heard and it was assumed, quite correctly, that the Germans were pulling out of the town. Patrols from the 2nd Middlesex entered the town at 2.00 p.m., when they took possession of it and raised the Union Jack and regimental flag. Troops had to be careful as the town had been booby-trapped with mines but they were soon made harmless.

Frank Crowther Roberts was born in Highbury, Middlesex on 2 June 1891 and was the son of the Revd Frank Roberts, Vicar of St John's, Southall and of Mrs Frank Roberts. He was educated at St Lawrence College, Ramsgate and joined the Army in 1911, training at the Royal Military Academy, Sandhurst and on 4 March was commissioned into the 1st Bn The Worcester Regt as a 2nd Lieut. He left with the battalion to Egypt where he won a boxing trophy in 1913. By the outbreak of war he had been promoted to lieutenant and his battalion left Egypt reaching France via England on 6 November 1914. A few months later he was awarded the DSO *London Gazette* of 3 January for work carried out in Neuve Chapelle when he led a party of twenty-five men in a raid on an enemy trench, which was one of the earliest genuine raids to be carried out on the Western Front. The party took the enemy by surprise, bayoneted thirty of them and returned to the British lines after only four minutes. The battalion casualties were two men missing and one wounded. In 1915 Roberts was promoted to captain and gained the MC in 1917 at the Battle of Ypres. The citation published in the *London Gazette* of 9 January 1918 was as follows:

> During two days' very hard fighting he showed marked skill and resource under adverse circumstances, and throughout kept a firm grip on the situation. It was largely due to his excellent staff work that the brigade was able to hold its objectives against heavy-counter-attacks; and, in addition, the daring personal reconnaissances which he made under heavy fire were of the greatest value to headquarters throughout the whole action.

Roberts was made Officer Commanding the 1st Bn 1917–18 and later promoted to being acting brigade major of 23rd Brigade between March and October while the Commanding Officer was absent in England. After winning the VC (*London Gazette*, 8 May 1918) he was presented with his award by the King on 1 June 1918. After the war he became acting lieutenant colonel attached to the Egyptian Army Sudan 1919–20 and was later awarded the OBE on 27 January 1921. He then served with the Rhine Army and in the Far East. On 6 July 1927 he transferred on accelerated promotion to Major with the 2nd Royal Warwickshire Regt and served with them in India; the Middle East and also with the Iraqi Army. This was followed by service in Northern Ireland and in 1937 he became Commanding Officer of the 1st Royal Warwickshire Regt. In 1938 he then served as a brigade commander in India in charge of the Poona Brigade of the British Indian Army and later as GOC 48th (South Midland) Div. (TA) before finally retiring in 1939 with the rank of major general.

On 23 April 1932 at their wedding party he and his wife (formerly Miss Winifred Wragg) had entertained forty-six survivors of H Coy, 5th Bn The Sherwood Foresters to supper at Swadlincote and after his retirement the couple lived at Four Winds, his wife's home in Bretby, Burton-on-Trent, Derbyshire. The couple were never to have children and Winifred pre-deceased her husband by two years dying in 1980. Frank Roberts was ninety years of age a fortnight after the VC/GC reunion dinner in London on 18 May 1981 and died at Four Winds on 12 January 1982. He was the last of the Spring 1918 winners of the VC to die and was cremated at Bretby six days later and his ashes were buried in the Wragg family plot in Bretby Churchyard. His name is included in the Crematorium Reference Book and on the family gravestone.

In his will Frank Roberts left £285,432 gross (£273,997 net) and bequeathed his decorations to the Worcestershire Regt, together with a handsome bequest. The regiment also owns a painting by Gilbert Holiday of Roberts involved in fierce fighting in a churchyard presumably based on Pargny. The decorations are on display in the City Art Gallery and Museum in Worcester and apart from his VC, DSO OBE and MC he was also awarded the 1914 Star with clasp, BWM, VM, Gold Medal of the Order of Mohamed Ali, Khedive's Sudan Medal and clasp (Aliab Dinka) and Iraq Medal, Victory Medal (Second World War) and four other medals including the King George V Silver Jubilee; King George VI Coronation and Queen Elizabeth II Coronation. He had been wounded three times and Mentioned in Despatches on four occasions.

C. BUSHELL

West of St Quentin, Crozat Canal and north of Tergnier, France, 23 March

Approximately 12 miles due south of St Quentin close to where the Fifth Army bordered the French Army the 7th (S) Bn The Queen's (Royal West Surrey Regt) were part of the 55th Bde of the 18th Div. and the other two brigades in the division were the 53rd and 54th.

On 21 March 1918 the division was in the centre of III Corps with the 58th Div. to their right and the 14th Div. to the left. The divisional sector was split into a two-brigade sector with the 55th Bde in divisional reserve at a camp called Haute Tombelle. By 9.00 a.m. the enemy had already crossed the River Oise and the 58th Div. position to the right had been penetrated.

The next day the 55th Bde left its reserve positions and crossed the canal; the 7th Queen's was to the north of the village of Vouel in a valley to the rear of Tergnier the rest of the brigade was in the Bois de Frières. The bridges between Mennesis and Jussy to the north-west were still passable for infantry. In the morning the Queen's took up positions close to the canal where they remained for the rest of the day but later the enemy crossed the canal at Tergnier opposite the 58th Div.

In the early hours of 23 March it was known that a French unit, the 125th Regt, was intending to retake the west bank of the Crozat Canal crossing at Tergnier, a position that the 58th Div. had lost earlier. A conference of senior officers of the 55th Bde, including Lt Col C. Bushell, took place in a hut to the east of the Bois de Frières and it was decided that two companies of the Queen's should go into action with the French infantry and that they should try and reach the high ground at Le Sart to the west of Quessy. At around 6.00 a.m. the French arrived looking well turned-out but unfortunately they did not have very much ammunition with them and they had no knowledge of the local terrain. An hour-long artillery bombardment was laid on by their artillery and the counter-attack, led by Colonel Bushell with his C Coy, began when there was still a thick mist. Although enemy machine-gun fire was very fierce and Tergnier was nearly reached, but the Germans soon recovered themselves and their machine-gun fire took a heavy toll of the French, whose commanding officer was hit. In the action Bushell was struck in the head but this did not stop him rallying his troops and encouraging them to fresh effort and his example kept the line steady. When he considered the position was secure for a while, he returned to Rouez to report to General Wood. His head was bandaged, and after making his report he left for his battalion in front of Faillouel south-west of Mennesis. He fainted twice and was encouraged to leave the battlefield, but in the end had to be carried out of action. Owing to the fog some of the Queen's also lost their way. The 18th Div. history noted 'Though the attack failed, the Queen's did not fail, and glorious gallantry and leadership that gained him the Victoria Cross was shown by Colonel Bushell.'

At 10.00 a.m. the Queen's retired in orderly fashion and a defensive position was then adopted on the western side of the road that ran north–south through Frières Wood which was held for the rest of the day until another withdrawal was organised. Indeed 7th Queen's heavy involvement in the March Retreat continued until 27 March when they were finally relieved near Villers-Bretonneux and went back to camp at Blangy Tronville. The citation for T/Lt Col Bushell's VC was published in the *London Gazette* of 3 May 1918 as follows:

For most conspicuous bravery and devotion to duty when in command of his battalion. Lieut.-Colonel Bushell personally led C company of his battalion, who were co-operating with an Allied regiment in a counter-attack, in face of very heavy machine-gun fire. In the course of this attack he was severely wounded in the head, but he continued to carry on, walking about both in front of English and Allied troops, encouraging them and reorganising them. He refused even to have his wound attended to until he had placed the whole line in a sound position, and formed a defensive flank to meet a turning movement by the enemy. He then went to Brigade Headquarters and reported the situation, had is wound dressed, and returned to the firing line, which had come back a short distance. He visited every portion of the line, both English and Allied. In the face of terrific machine-gun fire, exhorting the troops to remain where they were and to kill the enemy. In spite of the wounds, this gallant officer refuse to go to the rear, and had eventually to be removed to the dressing station in a fainting condition. To the magnificent example of energy, devotion and courage shown by their commanding officer is attributed the fine spirit displayed and the keen fight put up by his battalion, not only on the day in question, but on each succeeding day of the withdrawal.

Bushell received both his VC and DSO from the King at Buckingham Palace on 11 May. He returned to the front eleven days later and was temporarily in command of the 7th Queen's in December 1916; he had served with them as company commander, second-in-command, and finally as CO. It was in this role that he was killed on 8 August 1918, the first day of the Battle of Amiens, a date referred to by Ludendorff as the 'black day of the German Army'. He fell south-west of Morlancourt at Cloncurry Trench, which ran northwards from a position on the Corbie–Bray Road. The Queen's had a rough time on 7 August, when they were faced by machine-gun nests close to their start line. These machine guns were placed in Cloncurry Trench, which was part of the line that the 18th Div. had lost two days earlier. By 7.00 a.m. the Queen's were far from their objective and Bushell left battalion HQ to try and sort out the situation. Once again as in March his presence inspired his men and the Queen's managed to take Cloncurry Trench with the use of bayonet and bomb. When the mist lifted some tanks appeared and success looked within their grasp. In directing the second tank Bushell was hit by a sniper's bullet and Pte A.E. Morris, Bushell's runner, rushed across the open field and gathered up the body of his Commanding Officer, but tragically he had been fatally wounded. However, his sacrifice inspired his men to still greater effort and they managed to hold the Corbie–Bray road for the rest of the day. Bushell was buried in Querrieu British Cemetery 6 miles from Amiens on the Albert road and 9 miles south-west of Albert. The Grave is in Row E, number 6.

Christopher Bushell was the younger son of Reginald and Caroline Bushell of St Margaret's Bay, Kent and was born at Hinderton Lodge, Neston, Cheshire on the Wirral on 31 October 1888. His father was a partner in the Liverpool firm of Bushell Bros and Co. in Castle Street, a firm of wine merchants and shippers. He was also a member of the

Mersey Docks and Harbour Board and JP for the County of Cheshire. He died in 1904.

Christopher was educated at Moorland House, Haswell, Cheshire, and later at Rugby School (1901–6). He was a keen Rugby player with the Notting Dale Club, and also their Treasurer. At Corpus Christi College, Oxford he was captain of his college boat and he also took part in the Henley Regatta. He was called to the Bar at the Inner Temple in 1911 and in the following year, on 8 May, was commissioned as a Special Reserve Officer in the 1st Bn The Queen's Royal (West Surrey) Regt. In 1914 he went to France with the 1st Bn as part of the original BEF and took part in the Retreat from Mons and a few weeks later he was severely wounded on 14 September during the Battle of the Aisne.

After recovering he returned to France in November 1915 and until June 1916 he was ADC to the GOC 33rd Div., and then staff captain 100th Bde during the Battle of the Somme. In December 1916 he was temporarily in command of the 7th Queen's and in due course became the company commander; second-in-command and finally temporary lieutenant colonel (commanding officer) when he was killed. He had been Mentioned in Despatches on 4 January and 7 November 1917 and in January 1918 Bushell was also awarded the DSO for 'distinguished service in the field'.

While he was recuperating from wounds he married Rachel Lambert, on 24 August 1915, she was daughter of the Revd. E. Lambert of Wye in Kent and the officiating vicar was the Revd D.W. Holson, Christopher's brother-in-law. The couple were to have one child, a daughter, Elizabeth Hope, born 15 June 1916, who later became Mrs Betsy MacLehose who lived in Lockerley Vicarage, Romsey, Kent. The family had lived together for a short period at Christopher's mother's home at Hillside, Granville Road, St Margaret's Bay, Kent, after her husband died in 1904.

Christopher is commemorated on the parish church war memorial at St Margaret's-at-Cliffe and the present memorial replaces the original, which was destroyed by enemy action in the Second World War. Rachel Bushell also resided at some time in Boughton Aluph, just across the River Stour from Wye. Christopher Bushell's name is also included on the war memorial at Wye parish church, where there is a bronze tablet in the church porch for each of the two world wars. He is also remembered in Neston with a road named after him and his name is listed on a plaque at the parish church of St Mary and St Helen, also in Neston. The plaque is approximately 30 inches by 18 inches and reads:

To the Glorious Memory of
Christopher Bushell, VC DSO,
T/Lt. Colonel Commanding 7th Battn The Queen's R.W.S. Regt
Younger Son of Reginald and Caroline Bushell
Killed in Action in France
August 8th 1918

E'en as he trod that day to God
So walked he from his birth
To gentleness and simpleness
And honour and clean mirth

Bushell's VC and medals were always in the hands of his family until recently and on the death of Elizabeth MacLehose, his daughter, they were bequeathed his regiment. On 27 April 2003 a special ceremony was held at the Queen's Royal Surrey Regiment Museum in West Clandon when members of the Bushell family officially handed over Christopher's decorations including his VC; DSO, 1914 Star-Clasp, BWM and VM into the care of his regiment. Copies of various letters written to his wife from the trenches were also presented.

J.R. GRIBBLE
Beaumetz, Hermies Ridge,
France, 23 March

On the morning of the first day of the German Spring Offensive (21 March) the 10th (S) Bn The Royal Warwickshire Regt (57th Bde, 19th (Western) Div.) who were in reserve in the Third Army was moved forward to a position to the north-east of the village of Vélu, to the south of Beaumetz and the Bapaume–Cambrai road and about 4½ miles from Bapaume to the west. The positions were close to the Second Army Boundary. The enemy had advanced to the north-east of Vélu having captured the villages of Lagnicourt and Doignies. That evening the Warwicks were placed under the command of the 154th Bde of the 51st (Highland) Div., V Corps, Third Army when their orders were to ' hold out to the last'.

However on the following day they could not prevent themselves from being gradually pushed back by owing to the relentless enemy shelling. On the 23rd the enemy did not begin its attack until 9.30 a.m. in this sector and then the fighting began to move in a south-westerly direction. After about an hour the Germans broke through on the left of the village of Beaumetz and after a prolonged fight, managed to get behind the 8th (S) Bn The Gloucestershire Regt which was in a salient. This advance forced the Glosters together with the supporting 10th Warwicks to retire to the railway line Vélu-Lebucquière, which ran southwards towards the village of Bertincourt. Close to the line a defensive left flank facing the northern edge of Vélu Wood was then formed. The wood was south of the village of that name. Troops from battalion HQ had been drafted in to assist in holding this position together with some stragglers from the 51st (Highland) Div.

Soon after 1 pm. attacking troops could be seen entering the wood and a short time later the right of the brigade defensive flank was under threat The enemy could now be seen pouring into Vélu Wood and at about 1.30 p.m. were seen threatening the right of the position from the high ground. The British plan was to keep the Germans bottled up in the wood as long as possible in order to give as much time for their troops to retire from the area for new defensive positions. The 57th Bde was only saved from annihilation by the actions of D Coy of the Gloucestershires, and the 10th Warwickshires who somehow between them managed successfully to stop the enemy on the edge of the wood, and at the same time save a battery of 18-pounders of the 2nd Div. which was firing over open sights from being captured. The two battalions had continued to fight having been unaware that orders had been give to retire.

Capt. J. Gribble, of D Coy of the 10th Warwicks, reported that troops on his right were withdrawing, and soon afterwards all the battalion except for D Coy was pushed back from the east–west Beaumetz–Hermies Ridge. This was at about 1.30 p.m. The gallant stand made by the company under Capt. Gribble was very similar to that made by Capt. Manley James of the Gloucesters (see pp. 23–8). Gribble proceeded to interpret his orders of 'hold on to the last' quite literally, although his right flank was now in the air. He sent a runner back to battalion HQ with a message that they were going to hold on until he received further orders. He inspired his small party with his heroism, and although they could have escaped when the rest of the battalion fell back they hung on and fought to the last before becoming surrounded. Not surprisingly they suffered heavy casualties and Gribble himself, who had been wounded in the head, was taken prisoner. This glorious stand, which lasted for three hours, was not to be in vain as it had prevented the Germans from completely commanding the Ridge for several hours, and not only did the British force in that sector get away but so did three batteries of 104th Artillery Bde, RFA, under RSM Hopcroft, in spite of the enemy reaching within 500 yards of their positions.

The severity of the fighting in this area is made all to clear from the graves in the Commonwealth War Graves Commission Cemetery on the high ground of the ridge named Beaumetz-les-Cambrai which contains the remains of men who were killed in the March and September battles of 1918.

Sadly while Capt. Gribble was in captivity in the officer's prison in Mainz Castle he contracted pneumonia having earlier been brought low by influenza and died in the Royal Fortress Hospital, in Mainz. Initially he had been a patient at Karlsruhe (Seucher) Isolation Hospital which was also in Mainz. He was buried at the Niederzwehren Cemetery, Cassel, Germany, Plot III, Row F, Grave 11. The date of death on his gravestone is 25 November 1918 but some sources have his date of death as 24 November this may be because of different time zones and as he died close to midnight. His brother Philip, in *Off the Cuff*, his autobiography, and also Arthur Mee in his book on Dorset both inexplicably give Julian's date of death as Armistice Day, namely 11 November.

Gribble's very worthy VC had been published in the *London Gazette* on 28 June 1918, five months prior to his death in Germany. He did know of the award and to celebrate his brother officers had taken him around the barrack square on their shoulders.

Capt. Gribble was in command of the right company of the battalion when the enemy attacked, and his orders were to hold on to the last. His company was eventually entirely isolated, though he could easily have withdrawn them at one period, when the rest of the battalion on his left were driven back to a secondary position. His right flank was' in the air' owing to the withdrawal of all troops of a neighbouring division. By means of a runner to the company on his left, he intimated his determination to hold on till other orders were received from Battalion Headquarters and this he inspired his command to accomplish. His company was eventually surrounded by the enemy at close range, and he was see fighting to the last. By his splendid example of grit, Capt. Gribble was materially instrumental in preventing for some hours the enemy obtaining complete mastery of the crest of the ridge, and by his magnificent self-sacrifice he enabled the remainder of his own brigade to be withdrawn, as well as another garrison and three batteries of field artillery.

Julian Royds Gribble together with his elder brother Philip and four daughters sisters were the children of Mr George J. Gribble, a wealthy merchant and Mrs Norah Gribble (nee Royds) of 34 Eaton Square, London and Kingston Russell House in Long Bredy, Dorset. The family was not only wealthy but also privileged. Julian was born at 34 Lennox Gardens in London SW1 on 5 January 1897 and until the age of ten was educated privately until September 1908 when he then attended Hillside School in Godalming until July 1910. This was followed by four years at Eton, from September 1910 until December 1914.

At first he tried for the Royal Navy but was turned down by an Admiralty Board and then he enlisted in the Army giving his occupation in his attestation papers as student and he then spent the next few months training at RMC Sandhurst before beginning his active military service as a 2nd leiutenant. By 15 May 1915 he was attached to the 10th Royal Warwicks and then posted to Albany Barracks in Parkhurst, Isle of Wight. His job was to assist in training new recruits and three months later he injured his foot and remained on the island for about a year. Occasionally his duties included escorting batches of newly drafted troops as far as the French channel ports. In April 1916 it was his turn to be sent to France and over the next few months he took an active part in the Battle of the Somme. In October he was wounded and sent to Corbie CCS on the 2nd and then sent home diagnosed with 'trench fever' becoming a patient at 2nd Western General Hospital in Manchester. He was then given leave of absence from 13 October to 17 November 1916 and declared fit again for general service on 5 December when he joined the 3rd Reserve Bn. He had returned to Parkhurst and from there was posted to the 10th Royal Warwicks with the rank of captain. In the spring of 1917 he was unfit again for three weeks this time with laryngitis. On 10 April he attended a medical board and soon returned to active service and took part in the Battle of Passchendaele later in the year.

After Julian's death his parents were presented with his posthumous VC in September 1919 by Maj. Gen. L.D. Jackson, commander of the Southern Area, at their country home in Long Bredy, Bridport. In 1913 Mr Gribble had purchased Kingston Russell House, which was in a ruinous state, from the Bedford Estate and set about restoring it. His oldest son, Philip purchased 740 acres in the area at around the same time and lived in Piddletrenthide Manor. On news of his son's death in November 1918 his father built a hall extension to the farmhouse situated at the end of the drive to his Kingston Russell House in Julian's memory.

On 26 June 1920 Mrs and Mrs Gribble attended the VC holder's Buckingham Palace Garden Party and three years later Norah died followed by her husband's death in June 1927. Kingston Russell House and estate was then sold by Philip who also inherited Julian's decoration. In 1948 Philip moved from Dorset to Suffolk when he purchased Warmill Hall a house near Mildenhall. It was in this house where his brother's VC and medals were now kept. Sadly the building was badly damaged by fire in February 1958 and the VC and medals destroyed. A duplicate Cross was commissioned by Philip which is the one now on display in the Royal Warwickshire Museum in Warwick.

Julian Gribble's name is commemorated on a pillar on the south side of the chapel in the Chapel Royal Military Academy, Camberley and his name is also listed amongst those on a brass plaque on a column in St Peter's Church, Long Bredy. Finally he is also remembered in St Martin's Church, Preston, Hertfordshire with a stained glass window in the wall of the south chancel where St Martin's face has been replaced by Gribble's. This memorial was designed by his sister Vivienne and there is a plaque to his memory at the base of the window. Another sister, Lesley Grace, married Hugh Exton Seebohm and lived in Poynders End n the village but she died suddenly at the age of 30 and was buried in the graveyard. It is her memorial which is opposite her brother's window which was restored and re-dedicated in 2006 in the presence of Gribble family members.

Norah Gribble, the mother of the two sisters was so stricken by the death of her youngest son Julian, that she gave instructions to the effect that she should be buried close to the window dedicated to him and also near her daughter Lesley's grave. She would then have had a sense of being close to him.

A.C. HERRING

Montagne Bridge, France, 23/24 March

T/2nd Lt Alfred Herring was a member of the Royal Army Service Corps attached to the 6th (S) Bn Northamptonshire (54th Bde, 18th (Eastern) Div.) and won his VC at Montagne Bridge. By 22 March the 6th Northants were in positions to the south-west of the village of Remigny, approximately 8 miles south of the German held town of St Quentin. The St Quentin Canal (although the section between the Rivers Somme and Oise is known as the Crozat Canal) ran quite close to a railway at this point. Soon after 10.00 a.m. on the 22nd the morning fog began to thin and the front of the 54th Bde, which formed the right of the 14th Div., to the left of the 18th Div. and close to Jussy was swept with machine gun and trench mortar fire. The enemy infantry took advantage of the situation creeping up to their side of the canal bank. However although Montagne Railway bridge was undamaged the enemy took no action until 6 p.m., when under the cover of heavy artillery they rushed the bridge and pushed back the defenders and gained a position on the south side of the canal. Herring, having received no orders had decided to take his party up to the canal bank but the actual company responsible for the defence of the bridge was from the 7th (S) Bn The Bedfordshire Regt also of the 54th Bde but under Herring's leadership it fought back with the aid of two companies from Herring's own battalion. In spite of Herring's expert leadership there was nothing he could do to prevent an enemy advance as his post was cut off from supporting troops on either side and he and his party became surrounded. Despite this dire situation he counter-attacked as soon as possible and with such dash that the bridge was re-taken together with the capture of six machine guns and twenty prisoners. Herring and his men then remained and despite all attempts by the enemy to shift them when during the night the post was continuously attacked. This was largely due to the splendid leadership and heroism displayed by T/2nd Lieut. Herring, who continually visited his men and cheered them on, thus managing to hold up the German advance in this sector.

However his party was captured in the end on 23 March when they were made POWs. After his capture, together with other officers, Herring was presented to the Kaiser at St Quentin and the Emperor shook Herring by the hand congratulating him on a very fine fight. Herring was later imprisoned at Graudanz prisoner-of-war camp in West Prussia.

His VC was published in the *London Gazette* of 7 June 1918:

> ... after severe fighting the enemy gained a position on the south bank of the canal. His post was cut off from the troops on both flanks and surrounded. Second Lieut. Herring, however, immediately counter-attacked, and recaptured the position, together with 20 prisoners and six machine guns. During the night the post was continually attacked, but all attacks were beaten off. This was largely due to the splendid heroism displayed by Second Lieut. Herring, who continually visited his men and cheered them up. It was entirely due to the bravery and initiative of this officer that the enemy advantage was held up for 11 hours at an exceedingly critical period. His magnificent heroism, coupled with the skilful handling of this troops, were most important factors leading to success.

Major Herring wrote about the VC action in note form and was dated 12 April 1919. The enemy crossed the Crozat Canal at about 5 p.m. on 22 March 1918: 'We drove him back over canal capturing prisoners and guns.' He was the only officer left. They had positions in front of the Bridge until 10 a.m. on 23 March. He received orders to withdraw to railway embankment about 500 yards back. They first put the captured guns out of action. On reaching embankment they received the embankment had another order telling him to return to his original position. However the enemy had got down to the canal bank with mgs and out of about 50 only two men reached the original position. Subjected to very heavy mg fire the enemy then crossed the canal in boats and surrounded them. Communication by this time had broken down.

Alfred Cecil Herring was born in Tottenham, Middlesex on 26 October 1888, the son of George Edward who worked in a solicitor's office and Cecilia Emily Herring. He was educated at Tottenham County School and was captain of cricket and football. He was a member of the Cadet Corps from 1906. He chose accountancy as a career and served his articles with D.S. Fripp and past his final examinations in December 1912 becoming a Chartered Accountant.

Herring was of medium height and joined the Army on 10 December 1914, as a Paymaster in the Army Service Corps, serving in Chatham from 1914–16 and then as a temporary 2nd lieutenant in France for a year between November 1916 and November 1917. In January 1918 he was attached to the 6th (Service) Bn Northamptonshire Regt and took part in his first action which led to him winning a VC in March 1918. He was promoted to lieutenant on 26 April and after being a POW for nine months was repatriated to England 23 December. On 27 January 1919 he was promoted temporary Major and served as Group Accountant with the Cost Accounting Committee. Herring was presented with his VC by the King on 15 February 1919, and resigned his commission leaving the Army in 1922, when he returned as a partner in the firm of Evans Fripp Deed & Co. In May 1925 he became a member of the Stock Exchange and was a partner in a stockbroking firm from 1925 to 1961.In addition he held various directorships, including one with the Austin Motor Company.

While working in London between the wars, he lived in Fernleigh, 143 Fox Lane, Palmer's Green. In February 1922 he married Miss Winifred Frankland at St Barnabas Church, North Dulwich, and in April 1929 a daughter was born to them. He was an active golfer and having been captain of football and cricket at school he later captained the Old Boys' Football Club. He attended two VC events in 1920, namely the Buckingham Palace Garden Party in June and the burial of the Unknown Warrior in Westminster Abbey in November when he was also a member of the Honour Guard. He also attended the 1956 centenary review in Hyde Park.

Alfred Herring died on 10 August 1966 in the Ascot Nursing Home, Sunninghill at the age of 78. At the time his address was care of the Oatlands Park Hotel, Weybridge. He was cremated at Woking Crematorium, Reference 6521 and his ashes scattered in the Chaucer south area in the Garden if Remembrance.

For some reason his name was not on the list of VCs who were eligible for a pension of £100 per year but this error was rectified on 1 August 1959 when payments were also back dated. In his will he left £82,681 gross, a sum which perhaps made him one of the most prosperous VCs of 1918. The ASC became Royal in January 1918 and Part of the Royal Logistic Corps in 1993. His VC and two service medals together with Coronation Medals for 1937 and 1953 are in the care of the Officers Mess of the Royal Logistic Corps in Camberley, Surrey.

Finally, in 2006 and as he had lived in Palmers Green, North London, J.D. Wetherspoon named a pub after him called The Alfred Herring which can be visited in Green Lanes.

J.T. DAVIES
Near Eppeville, France, 24 March

Cpl John Davies was a member of the 11th (S) Bn (St Helens Pioneers) The Prince of Wales' Volunteers (South Lancashire Regt) and won his VC on 24 March 1918 near Eppeville, about 12 miles south-west of St Quentin close to the Somme Canal. The 11th South Lancs was the Pioneer Battalion of the 30th Div. and had been in France since November 1915 and was part of the Fifth Army of XVIII Corps. The 30th Div. consisted of the 21st, 89th and 90th brigades. About 1½ miles to the south-west of Eppeville a thinly held line of the 90th Bde was in support to the remnants of the 89th Bde, which had been formed into a composite battalion. The weak 21st Bde together with the 11th South Lancs was dug-in on the northern side of the village of Esmery Hallon. After heavy shelling of the line of the river the enemy advanced from the bridgehead at Ham between 7.00 and 8.00 a.m., also by using boats and pontoons he crossed the Somme canal at Canizy and northwards.

Such was the speed of the enemy advance that two forward companies of the South Lancs quickly became almost completely surrounded. They only had one slight chance of escape but that would involve retiring across a stream which had been barricaded with barbed wire. However their lives were protected through the heroic actions of the crews of the battalion Lewis gunners who by serving their guns until they were either killed or wounded inflicted heavy damage on the enemy. Even so there was to be only one outcome and by mid-morning the British withdrawal was forced to continue.

The chief figure amongst the Lewis Gunners was a Cpl John Davies who earned a VC for his involvement in the actions when he mounted the parapet, thus achieving a more effective field of fire, and through his heroic efforts enabled most of his colleagues to escape. When last seen this brave NCO was still firing his gun when the enemy was almost on top of his position.

The two companies then managed to make their escape fighting when fighting a rearguard action while at the same time moving in a westerly direction towards the village of Moyencourt. At 6.30 p.m. they took up positions between the village and Cressy to the west.

The rest of the 30th Div. was also in trouble and by 9 a.m. the left and central sections were falling back southwards to Esmery Hallon. After sending the artillery on ahead the infantry then began to cross the Canal du Nord close to the west of Moyencourt. They then formed up behind the canal together with the 20th Div. where the French 62nd Div. was already in position.

By the night of the 24th the enemy had made great progress and was in position on a line stretching from Mesnil to Chauny to the west of the canal.

On 20 May the announcement of the award of the VC to 20765 Cpl J.T. Davies was included in the 11th South Lancs Bn Routine Orders which was signed by the commanding officer, Maj. J.E.S. Pethick. It had been assumed that Davies had been 'probably killed at his gun' when winning his VC and this was confirmed within the text of the citation for the award which was published in the *London Gazette* on 22 May. However, almost at exactly the same time, information that Davies was in fact alive and a POW in Germany was received. The citation was as follows:

> For most conspicuous bravery and devotion to duty under heavy rifle and machine-gun fire. When his company – outflanked on both sides – received orders to withdrew. Corpl. Davies knew that the only line of withdrawal lay through a deep stream lined wit a belt of barbed wire, and that it was imperative to hold up the enemy as long as possible. He mounted the parapet, fully exposing himself, in order to get a more effective field of fire, and kept his Lewis gun in action to the last, causing the enemy many casualties and checking their advance. By his very great devotion to duty he enabled part of his company to get across the river, which they would otherwise have been unable to do, this undoubtedly saving the lives of many of his comrades. When last see this gallant N.C.O. Was still firing his gun, with the enemy close on top of him, and was in all probability killed at his gun.

John Thomas Davies was born at Rockferry, Cheshire on 29 September 1896 at 19 Railway Road, Tranmere, Birkenhead. He was the eldest son of John Davies of Birkenhead and Margaret Davies of Mostyn, North Wales. His father was a labourer. When John was still very young the family moved to St Helens and Davies senior became an employee at Cannington & Shaw's glass bottle factory. John attended Arthur Street School in St Helens and became a brick worker at the Ravenhead Brick and Tile Works in St Helens. In September 1914 he enlisted joining the South Lancashire Regt and was posted to the 11th Bn becoming one of the St Helens 'Pals'.

After initial training he served in France from 6 November 1915, and in 1916 he was wounded twice on the Somme front. He was taken prisoner at St Quentin on 24 March 1918, the same day that he won his VC. His parents were led to believe that their son had been killed but a request for food from a POW camp at Zagan, Silesia (now Poland) informed them otherwise.

On 1 January 1919 Davies was repatriated to England and in early January received a very special welcome when he returned to his home at Alma Street, Peasley Cross, St Helens. He was presented with £650 worth of bonds by the people of the borough of St Helens and also an illuminated address.

On 5 April Davies was presented with his VC by the King in the Ballroom of Buckingham Palace and later in the same year he was discharged from the Army. In civilian life Davies was employed in a local glass bottle factory and during in the Second World War he served with the 75th Bn of the West Lancashire Home Guard (South Lancashire Regt), becoming a captain by the end of the war.

In later life Davies was a regular visitor to the Regimental Depot and was a friend of another holder of the VC, John Molyneux of the Royal Fusiliers, who won his VC in 1917. The two men used to attend functions together and in the 1930s were presented to the then Prince of Wales. Before that on 19 July 1924 the new cathedral at Liverpool was consecrated and when in the afternoon the King reviewed the 55th West Lancashire (TF) Div. at Wavertree Playgound, Davies was one of the nine VCs present.

John Thomas Davies was married to Beatrice nee Travers and the couple had one daughter and two sons, one of whom, whom Alan, pre-deceased his parents dying at the age of 20 in 1943. John died suddenly on 28 October 1955 at the age of sixty, at 27 Leslie Road, St Helens and was given a funeral with full military honours and buried in the Church of England section of St Helens Borough Cemetery, Area 59. Grave 426. His widow died twenty years later on 27 August 1976.

Davies's name is remembered as part of a collage on display in the heroes' gallery in the Wirral Museum, Birkenhead and his VC, 1914–15 Star, BWM, VM and two Coronation Medals (1937 and 1953) are on display in the Lord Ashcroft Gallery in the Imperial War Museum.

W.H. ANDERSON

Bois Favières, near Maricourt,
France, 25 March

The 35th Div. of VII Corps included 104, 105 and 106 brigades and one of the battalions in the last named was the 12th (S) Highland Light Infantry, under the command of Lt Col William Anderson. VII Corps also included the 9th and 21st Infantry divisions together with the 1st Dismounted Bde.

By the night of 24 March and after three days of very heavy fighting, the enemy had reached a line stretching from the village of Longueval, near Delville Wood to a point on the eastern side of Curlu on the River Somme.

The 35th Div. was more or less fresh but during the night of the 24th/25th, the 51st Bde of the 17th (Northern) Div. to their left was having a hard time finding sufficient numbers of men to fill a 1½ mile gap which had opened up between V Corps and VII Corps. The latter Corps therefore supplied men of the 1st Dismounted Bde to assist in forming a defensive flank but even then the gap was not adequately plugged and Germans could be seen streaming past into Mametz Wood. However, the danger was to come mainly from the front rather than from the flanks and 105th and 106th brigades had between them a front line of 6,000 yards to look after.

The enemy began a heavy barrage at 7.45 a.m. on 25 March and then followed this up with a strong frontal attack, as well as an attack on the weakened Allied left flank. An outpost line, part of Bois Favières was driven in and captured by men of the German 199th Div. The wood was north-east of Maricourt and south of Bernafay and Trônes Woods. Realising the seriousness of the situation Lt Col Anderson of the 12th (S) HLI made his way across open ground towards the positions where his right companies were placed which had become disorganised. Getting them together again he set up and led a brilliant counter-attack which resulted in the lost ground being recovered together with twelve machine guns and 70 enemy captured prisoners. The left flank was reinforced by the 19th (S) Bn (2nd Tyneside Pioneers) Northumberland Fusiliers (35th Div.) as it had been slightly driven in. The fighting continued until 10 a.m. when on the right, the 105th began to have serious losses as a results of artillery fire. He defending battalions then fell back to a second line. At one point the 12th HLI were in real danger of becoming surrounded and in their retreat they moved into a timber yard about 300 yards outside Maricourt.

Further attacks were made by 106 Bde as the fighting swung back and forth. At about 5.00 p.m., when the 19th (S) Bn (2nd County) The Durham Light Infantry (104th Bde) 35th Div. had made progress during a counter-attack Anderson took the opportunity to try to drive the enemy out of Maricourt Wood as well as from the timber yard which they had taken and then packed with machine guns. At this time there were no front line troops to assist the 12th HLI and a whole group of men who were not usually used as front line soldiers were summoned from 104th Bde and were detailed to form up on the right of the HLI. The Germans were then so surprised by the ferocity of the counter-attack that they fell back down a slope for a distance of a 1,000 yards. Unfortunately Anderson himself was killed during this counter-attack and the details of events leading up to his death can be described in the following way.

The attack began on the Albert–Péronne road and moved through the timber yard. The attackers then came to a railway line where they took cover in order to avoid German machine-gun fire, and then, in a north-westerly direction, the attack moved towards a small road close to an old trench which was the objective. It was at this point that Anderson was killed when leading his men.

Later in the evening orders were received that VII Corps was to withdraw to a line Bray-Albert and by the evening of the next day the enemy had reached Albert, about 6 miles to the west of Maricourt.

Lt Col Anderson is buried in Péronne Road Cemetery, Maricourt in Plot II, Row G, Grave 36 and the cemetery is on the north side of the road from Albert to Péronne and although it was taken in March by the Germans it was recaptured five months later. Maricourt was close to the junction point of the British and French Armies.

Anderson's body was found where he had fallen, together with some of his effects, which were sent home to his wife. In addition, Capt. A. Campbell and Capt. R.H.J. Stewart, who was the padre, also claimed to have found Anderson's original grave. However, Mrs Anderson was not convinced that they had indeed found her husband's correct grave and corresponded with the man who first discovered her husband's remains. On 5 April the War Office informed Mrs Anderson, staying in Baloch at the time, that her husband had been killed on 26 March but later changed the date to the 25th.

As was the normal practice the enemy had removed Anderson's identity disc and sent it to the HQ of the Red Cross in Geneva. It was returned to the War Office after the War via diplomatic channels.

The citation for Lt Col Anderson's posthumous VC was published in the *London Gazette* on 3 May 1918 as follows:

> For most conspicuous bravery, determination and gallant leading of his command. The enemy attacked on the right of the battalion frontage, and succeeded in penetrating the wood held by our men. Owing to successive lines of the enemy following on closely, there was the gravest danger that the flank of the whole position would be turned. Grasping the seriousness of the situation, Colonel Anderson made his way across the open in full view of the enemy, now holding the wood on the right, and after much effort succeeded in gathering the remainder of the two right companies. He personally led the counter-attack, and drove the enemy from the wood, capturing twelve machine guns and seventy prisoners, and restoring the original line. His conduct in leading the charge was quite fearless, and his most splendid example was the means of rallying and inspiring the men during a most critical hour. Later on the same day, in another position, the enemy had penetrated to within three hundred yards of the village and were holding a timber yard in force. Colonel Anderson reorganised his men after they had been driven in, and brought them forward to a position of readiness for a counter-attack. He led the attack in person, and throughout showed the utmost disregard for his own safety. The counter-attack drove the enemy from his position, but resulted in this very gallant officer losing his life. He died fighting within the enemy's lines, setting a magnificent example to all who were privileged to serve under him.

William Herbert Anderson was born in Glasgow on 29 December 1881. His father, William J. Anderson who was a prosperous chartered accountant with Messrs Kerr, Anderson and Macleod and his mother was Eleanor Kay, daughter of Alexander Kay of Cornhill,

Biggar, Lanarkshire. The Anderson family had two houses, one in the country at Upper Largo, Fife and the other one Lansdowne Crescent in a prosperous district in the west of Glasgow. William Junior, known in the family as Bertie, was educated at Glasgow Academy and then at Fettes College, Edinburgh where he studied French language and literature at Tours.

Following in the steps of his father William became a Chartered Accountant and in 1900 joined the 1st Lanark Rifle Volunteers ('Gallant Greys'), which later became the 5th Scottish Rifles (Cameronians). In 1905 he took up horse riding and three years later, when the Territorial Army replaced the Volunteers, he retired with the rank of lieutenant becoming a partner in his father's accountancy firm. In addition he also took a keen interest in politics.

On 4 July 1909 William married Miss Gertrude Campbell Gilmour of Woodback, Baloch, Dunbartonshire and the couple were to have two sons, William Alan Campbell born in 1911 and Charles Patrick in 1913. In 1914 the Anderson home address was 149 West George Street, Glasgow and a month after the war began in August William joined the 17th (S) Bn (3rd Glasgow) The Highland Light Infantry with the rank of captain, when he was to become deeply involved with the unit's training in Scotland and England. Before his battalion left Codford, however, Anderson was instructed to carry out a similar training job from November 1915 while serving as second-in-command to Colonel William Auld of the 19th (Reserve) Bn The Highland Light Infantry. On reaching France in September 1916 William was attached to the 9th (S) Bn The East Surrey Regt as their second-in-command in October a month when he was wounded on the 31st. In the following year he was hospitalised on 3 March 1917 and two days later was sent home to England, returning to France in June of that year when he became second-in-command of the 12th HLI. By the time of his death in March 1918 he was the battalion's CO, having been promoted in February. Two of his brothers also served with the HLI and were also killed in the war; nor did his third brother survive. After the war a brass plaque was put up to the memory of the four brothers close to the south-west door of Glasgow Cathedral.

William's VC was presented to his widow by the King at the Orthopaedic Hospital, Becketts Park, Leeds on 31 May 1918, and at the time of writing is on loan to the Lord Ashcroft Gallery in the Imperial War Museum together with the 1914–15 Star, BWM and VM.

The youngest of Anderson's two sons, Charles Patrick, served as a lieutenant with the Argyle and Sutherland Highlanders in the Second World War.

A.H. CROSS
Ervillers, France, 25 March

On 24 March 1918 A/L. Cpl Arthur Cross was serving with 121 Coy, 40th Bn Machine Gun Corps, 40th Div., in the region of the village of Ervillers, about 4 ½ miles north-west of the important town of Bapaume. On the 40th Div's left was the 31st Div. and the Guards were with the 3rd Div. further north. IV Corps was having to withdraw and it was planned that the 40th Div. should bring back its right to the area of Favreuil, about 3 miles to the south of Ervillers, in order to keep in line with its neighbour. It was also planned that the 42nd Div. would take over from the 40th Div. that evening, but this order was countermanded because of the rapid progress of the German attack. They had reached a line running southwards from St Léger, keeping to the west of Mory and to Avesnes, just outside Bapaume, which had recently fallen. Cross was with a machine-gun section near a line of infantry which had been hastily assembled near Ervillers, when the enemy was making an attack resulting in two of Cross's machine-gun teams becoming surrounded and he was compelled to fall back with the other two. Although the battlefield conditions were chaotic Cross felt that he was going to have to try and recapture the two guns. So early the following morning he sought his Sergeant's agreement for him to go over the top in search of the two guns. Arming himself with a service revolver and moving carefully up to his former positions he saw his two guns in the hands of a group of enemy soldiers. Some men might then have called it a day but Cross considered that a surprise attack on the men could possibly be successful. Leaping up with his revolver pointed directly at the startled enemy Cross and not only compelled the group to surrender but also persuaded them to carry the guns, together with their tripods and ammunition, back to his own section.

He then handed over his prisoners and collected teams for his guns and within a short time the guns that he had recovered came into action again when they were used to destroy further German attacks. At 9.30 p.m., after the remaining troops of the IV Corps had retired, the village of Ervillers was evacuated by the 1/10th Bn (TF) The Manchester Regt, (East Lancs. Bde) 42nd Div. who had held been holding it for some hours. The new positions were 1,000 yards back.

Through his heroic deeds L. Cpl Cross had won the VC and the citation was published in the *London Gazette* of 4 June 1918 as follows:

> … Cross volunteered to make a reconnaissance of the position of two machine guns which had been captured by the enemy. He advanced single-handed to the enemy trench, and with his revolver forced seven of the enemy to surrender and carry the machine guns with their tripods and ammunition to our lines. He then handed over his prisoners, collected teams for his guns, which he brought into action with exceptional dash and skill, annihilating a very heavy attack by the enemy. It is impossible to speak too highly of the extreme gallantry, initiative and dash displayed by this N.C.O., who showed throughout four days of operations supreme devotion to duty.

A few weeks later Cross won a further award for gallantry, this time the Military Medal, (*LG* 29 August 1918) when he had held a bridge against a German attack.

Arthur Henry Cross was born in a cottage opposite a chapel in Shipdham, Thetford, Norfolk on 13 December 1884. Although he was named Arthur Henry he was always to be known as either Henry or 'Crossy'. He was the son of William Cross, a wheelwright and carpenter of Shipdham, and at the age of seventeen left home and went to work in Camberwell, being employed on the Great Eastern Railway. He later worked at Woolwich Dockyard.

After the Great War had been raging for two years Arthur Cross took part in the Derby Scheme as a Private and enlisted in the 21st London Regt (1st Surrey Rifles) on 30 May 1916 with the number 62990.

His battalion was part of the 142 Bde of the 47th (London) Div. but in 1917 he joined 121 Coy, 40th Bn MGC, 40th Div. He was decorated with his VC at Buckingham Palace on 4 September 1918.

On 16 September 1918 on the village green in Shipdham, Cross was presented with a gold watch by the local vicar, inscribed 'Presented by the people of Shipdham to Lance Corporal A.H. Cross VC, September 1918'.

Soon afterwards and not one for army discipline Cross was charged with being absent without leave from the Army and at Dereham, Norfolk. He stated that he had been granted extra leave, to continue after his presentation, in order to visit his mother in Shipdham. Cross was then handed over to the Army authorities. On 31 March 1919 he was discharged from the Army with the rank of Corporal but as was the case with thousands of other former servicemen he was to find it very difficult to get employment in this post-war period and after his gratuity ran out he fell on bad times.

In April 1920 he lived at Trinity Buildings, Mermaid Court, Southwark and was unemployed for some time as he was suffering from gastritis. Unable to keep his family on his disability pension, he accepted the job of council scavenger at £3 17s per week. In 1923 he was again up before the courts when he was charged with loitering for the purposes of street betting. On another occasion he was bound over for stealing a postal order when in the employment of the Post Office before he became a city messenger.

He was first married to Frances Harrison, who subsequently died and is buried in an unmarked grave in Streatham Vale Cemetery. During the Second World War his second wife, Minnie Rosina together with two of their children were killed in an air raid in May 1941, when they had gone down into the air raid shelter while Cross remained in his flat. Tragically the shelter received a direct hit.

Subsequently Cross continued his job as a city messenger and was now living alone. In the 1950s he answered an appeal by the makers of the film *Carrington VC*, who wanted the star, David Niven, to wear a genuine Victoria Cross during the courtroom scenes. Cross lent them his and had his photograph taken with the actor. Cross was a tall man while Niven was much shorter and the picture of the two men doesn't show that Niven is actually standing on a wooden crate and appears to be taller than Cross! During his life Cross attended several VC events including the centenary in Hyde Park in June 1956.

Cross lived for thirty years in the same flat on top of a tenement block in Marshalsea Road, Lambeth and when one of his daughters visited him on 26 November 1965 she found him dead. He was then buried in the family grave in Streatham Vale Cemetery, Plot E, Square 27, Grave 885 where he joined his second wife Minnie Rosina Cross and their two children. His funeral was a low key affair organised by the OCA of the Machine Gun Corps of whom thirteen members attended and of whom Cross had been an active member. Originally his name was not included on the headstone above the grave.

In 1969 one of the roads in a new housing estate in the village where he was born eighty-five years before was named 'Henry Cross Close'. This seems to be the only commemoration in Shipdham, apart from a portrait of him in the small village hall. Obviously, his name is not on the parish war memorial, although another Cross is listed there from the Great War, possibly a relative. There is a plaque in Shipdham church which is connected with the Victoria Cross but it is to the memory of Mark Haggard, September 1914, whose rescuer gained a VC during the Battle of the Aisne in September 1914.

As the result of efforts made by Victor Cross, a son of Arthur by his first wife, Frances, funds were found to pay for a proper stone to the hero's memory in Streatham Vale Cemetery. This new headstone made of rich green granite with silver lettering was dedicated on 27 September 2001 with about twenty-five people attending. After forty-six years justice had at last been done to Arthur Cross's memory. Sadly Victor died prior to the dedication

During his long and troubled life Henry Cross fathered ten children and was known to be quite fond of alcohol. His decorations apart from the VC and MM include the BWM, VM and two Coronation medals and were sold by Spink on 19 April 2012 for £185,000 to an unnamed buyer.

A.M. TOYE

Eterpigny Bridge, France, 25 March

On the night of 24/25 March the 2nd Bn The Duke of Cambridge's Own (Middlesex Regt) (23rd Bde, 8th Div.) was allocated the Somme bridges to cover to the south of Péronne at Happlincourt, Brie and Eterpigny. Before 8.00 a.m. on 25 March the enemy had managed to cross the Somme Canal to the north of Eterpigny and they chose the joining point of the 50th Div. and the 23rd Bde. The men of the 8th Div. already knew that in attempting to hold the enemy back from crossing the Canal they were facing an impossible task and Sappers had prepared for the bridges to be blown.

C Coy of the 2nd Middlesex under A/Capt. Alfred Toye was holding the bridge at Eterpigny and had been given orders to hold on until the last. In all they lost and regained it three times. However, the enemy had worked itself around the back of C Coy and Toye decided to fight himself out of the trap, which he succeeded in doing with only a handful of men to assist him. Out of the four company platoons only ten men managed to escape: the rest either became casualties or were taken prisoner. Not content with this action, Toye decided to turn the tables on the enemy and gathering up about seventy men of the 1/7th Durham LI (Pioneers) from the 50th Div. on his left flank who were leaderless, he led them in a daring counter-attack and subsequently held on to the Eterpigny–Villers Carbonnel road.

Assistance too came from the 2nd Bn The Prince of Wales's Own (West Yorkshire Regt) also of the 23rd Bde who were in support and who made a counter-attack and filled the gap between the Middlesex and the battalion to the north of them. The enemy still managed to keep to the British side of the river and a new defensive position was therefore set up on the Eterpigny Ridge which allowed further assaults during the day to be repelled. Despite the Middlesex battling on throughout the enemy continued to pour over Eterpigny bridge and at points further to the north as well.

To the south of Eterpigny, Brie Bridge was also under tremendous pressure, not only from enemy troops coming across it but also from attacking infantry coming in from the north on the West (i.e. British) side. At around 6.45 p.m. orders came at last for the withdrawal of the 23rd Bde but it was far too late for the Middlesex men except for the greater part of one company. Nearly three-quarters of the battalion had fallen at their posts and the remainder escaped under the leadership of Lt Col C.A.S. Page. In coming from the east side of the Somme as well as from the north, the enemy was just too much for the brigade to cope with.

Eterpigny Bridge was destroyed during the fightingin 1918 but the outline of its position along with the road leading towards Villers Carbonnel can still be traced (July 1996). The River Somme over which the bridge was built was 'canalised' in the late 1920s.

For his considerable courage and leadership Toye was awarded the VC for his work on this day and also for similar acts at Rosieres on 26/27 March, Caix on the 28th, Moreuil on the 31st and Villers-Bretonneux on 24 April.

The citation was published in the *London Gazette* of 8 May 1918 as follows:

For most conspicuous bravery and fine leadership displayed in extremely critical circumstances. When the enemy captured a trench at a bridge-head, he three times re-established the post, which was eventually re-captured by fresh enemy attacks. After ascertaining that his three other posts were cut off, he fought his way through the enemy with one officer and six men of his company. Finding 70 men of the battalion on his left retiring, he collected them, counter-attacked and took up a line which he maintained until reinforcements arrived. Without this action the defence of the bridge must have been turned. In two subsequent operations, when in command of a complete company, he covered the retirement of his battalion with skill and courage. Later, with a party of battalion headquarters, he pressed through the enemy in the village, firing at them in the streets, thus covering the left flank of the battalion retirement. Finally, on a still later occasion, when in command of a mixed force of the brigade, he re-established after hard fighting, a line that had been abandoned before his arrival. He was twice wounded within ten days, but remained on duty. His valour and skilful leading throughout this prolonged period of intense operations were most conspicuous.

The Brigadier in command of the 23rd Bde was George Grogan who later won a VC on 27 May in the third Battle of the Aisne, and with whom Toye was going to go to Russia at the end of the war. At Eterpigny Communal Cemetery Extension lie the remains of some of Toye's colleagues from the 2nd Middlesex.

Alfred Maurice Toye (known as Maurice) was the eldest son of Dgt. Maj. James R. Toye, Chief Clerk, General Registry, Aldershot Command, and was born in Aldershot on 15 April 1897. He was born at 'D' Terrace, Stanhope Lines, Aldershot and was educated at Garrison School, Aldershot.

Toye's father was a practising Christian Scientist and also ran a troop of Boy Scouts, the 2nd Aldershot, which had its HQ in a hut in Wellington Lines, Aldershot. Alfred was a First Patrol Leader and also a King's Scout. Henry, his younger brother, was also in the troop. At the age of fourteen Toye enlisted as a trumpeter in the Royal Engineers on boy's service and went to train at The Curragh, County Kildare. On 4 August 1915 when he was still only eighteen Toye went to France and became an Acting Corporal. At the end of 1916 he applied to become an officer and went to the Cadet School at Blendecques, near St Omer.

Canon Lummis recalls meeting him at this period and wrote:

In January 1917 I was in charge of a couple of Army lorries sent from Pernois to Watten to pick up stores belonging to my Regiment, 2nd Battalion Suffolk Regiment. These had been left there before we went to the Somme. On my way I called at Somerset House, Cadet School, Blendecques and there I met Alfred Toye. He appeared to be a very smart soldier. Later he was given a regular commission into the 2nd Battalion The Middlesex Regiment.

Toye was posted to them on 15 February 1917 from the Royal Engineers and in October he won the MC in the Passchendaele Offensive 'when in charge of communications he went to a most forward position and carried out his duties under heavy and continuous fire of every kind with great ability and fearlessness...'

He was then made acting captain and given the command of a company on 15 August 1917. He served in France and Belgium until 24 April 1918 and again from 23 August to 11 November 1918. He was promoted to lieutenant on 15 August 1918 and was acting major from 29 September 1918 to 21 July 1919. He was wounded three times in all during the war and decorated by the King on Queen's Parade, Aldershot on 8 June 1918 when he was not fully fit, having only recently been a patient at a military hospital in Winchester. His parents had been invited to the Queen's Parade ceremony as well. When Toye's turn came to be presented to the King he gave the salute and the VC citation was read out and after the King had had spoken to him for a few moments he pinned the decoration on the hero's chest.. Toye then left the dais for a seat on the far side of the ground to the sound of renewed cheering.

On another occasion Toye was also presented with the Freedom of Aldershot by Aldershot Town Council, who placed the document in a silver casket which was accompanied by a large portrait. At the same time his wife, whom he had married on 15 June 1918, received a diamond pendant. She was formerly Miss Flora Robertson, an Army School teacher and daughter of Mr G.P. Robertson, a bandmaster of the RAMC. The couple were to have two daughters.

Toye was the only soldier brought up in Aldershot, home of the British Army, to win the VC, and he ended the war as second-in-command of the 2nd Middlesex Regt.

After the Armistice which brought to an end the fighting on the Western Front in November 1918 Toye was one of six holders of the VC who were specially selected for service in the North Russian campaign under T/Brig. Gen. G.W.St G. Grogan VC. He served on the General Staff and arrived there in April 1919 as a lieutenant. He had been surprised by his selection for this job and he had been expecting to be sent to India.

He was present at the Garden Party given by the King and Queen to recipients of the VC at Buckingham Palace on 26 June 1920 and between 1922 and 1924 he worked in a special appointment with the Rhine Army, during which time he was based in Cologne.

On 26 April 1924 Toye was transferred to the Oxfordshire & Bucks Light Infantry and with this transfer came promotion. From November 1925 he was appointed Chief Instructor, Royal Egyptian Military College in Cairo for seven years and was awarded the Order of the Nile (Commander). In 1937 he was back in England and living with his wife in married quarters at Ypres Road, Reed Hall, Colchester. In March 1938 he was promoted Major and again promoted on 1 July 1939 to brevet lieutenant colonel. He was in charge of Tregantle Fort,

Cornwall. He was temporary lieutenant colonel from 18 January 1940 to 9 September 1940, when he was acting colonel. Between 1940 and 1942 he was commander of the War Office School of Chemical Warfare and in 1943 became an instructor at the Staff College at Camberley. In 1943/44 he was brigade commander with the 6th Airborne Div., and later served in GHQ, Cairo between 1945 and 1948. He was promoted to brigadier on 1 July 1948 and retired from the Army on 19 January 1949.

In what turned out to be his last years he was appointed Commandant at the Home Office Defence School at Falfield, Gloucestershire. His address at the time was Eastwood Park, Falfield where he was taken ill with cancer and for the last seven months of his life was almost totally paralysed. He died at the Madame Curie Memorial Foundation, Tidcombe Hall, Tiverton, Devon on 6 September 1955. The building still exists and is now a hospice called the Marie Curie Centre. Toye was buried in Section XF in Grave 36 of Tiverton Cemetery.

Toye's club was the Army and Navy and his VC and other decorations are at present in the hands of the National Army Museum, they had been offered for sale at Sothebys on 17 September 1992 and were expected to fetch between £17,000 and £19, 000, but in fact reached £25, 000. Apart from the VC, MC and Order of Nile he also earned a 1914–15 Star, British War Medal, Victory Medal and two Coronation Medals. For his role in the Second World War he was awarded a Defence Medal; Victory Medal, War Medal and General Service Medal. During the Great War Toye had also been Mentioned in Despatches for his services as an Intelligence Officer. A final tribute was to have an Aldershot Scout Troop named after him – Toye's Own.

Toye's wife Flora died in January 1979.

T. YOUNG

Bucquoy, France, 25/31 March

On 24 March the 42nd Div. was transferred from VI Corps to IV Corps and late that night the 62nd Div. moved from the Arras front to Ayette, 4 miles NNW of Ervillers, where it too came under the orders of IV Corps. In the small hours of the 25th the 185th and 186th Bdes. continued moving on south-westerly towards Bucquoy having to cope with extremely chaotic and congested roads when traffic was moving in both directions.

Of the 62nd Div's three infantry brigades; the 185th was not concentrated on Bucquoy until noon, and the 186th not until 2.00 p.m. They were followed by their Pioneer Battalion, the 9th Durham Light Infantry, who remained in the village in order to dig trenches, while the 185th and 186th Bdes. advanced in the direction of the village of Achiet le Petit arriving there at 5 p.m. The third brigade, the 187th, arrived in Bucquoy late in the afternoon.

With at least fifteen German divisions against them the two divisions knew that it would be only a short time before they would be forced back in retreat and by the end of the 25th a 3 miles gap had been opened up between the Corps and its nearest neighbour. After this very wearing day the 62nd Div. had hardly had time to settle in that on the following morning when at 8.45 a.m. when it was still misty, the enemy made an attack against Bucquoy. They were slightly delayed by fire a quarter of a mile from the British line but the enemy advance was so rapid that the 186th Bde forming a defensive position on the right flank was almost overwhelmed. Fortunately the 1/9th Durhams Pioneer Battalion moved up to support the brigade and together with the 2/5th Duke of Wellington's Regt (186th Bde), helped to extend the flank and their positions then became the front line for the next five days until relief on the night of the 31st. It was during this fighting at Bucquoy that Private

Thomas Young, a member of the 9th Durhams was to win a VC for work in the six day period (25th–31st) when he managed to save the lives of no fewer than nine men when acting as stretcher-bearer.

The story of how he achieved the award cannot be better told than in the words of the official citation published in the *London Gazette* of 4 June 1918.

> For most conspicuous bravery in face of the enemy while acting as a stretcher-bearer. He showed throughout the whole course of the operations a most magnificent example of courage and devotion to duty. On nine different occasions he went out in front of our line in broad daylight under heavy rifle, machine-gun and shell fire, which was directed on him, and brought back wounded to safety, those too badly wounded to be moved before he dressing he dressed under this harassing fire, and carried them unaided to our lines and safety; he rescued and saved nine live in this manner. His untiring energy, coupled with an absolute disregard of personal danger, and the great skill he showed in dealing with casualties, is beyond all praise. For five days Private Young worked unceasingly, evacuating wounded from seemingly impossible places...

Thomas Young was born in Boldon, County Durham on 28 January 1895 and after he left school became a miner working in High Spen near Blaydon as a hewer. He joined up with the Gateshead Territorials in 1914 at the age of nineteen and was given the service number 203590. His real name was Morrell but in the Army he used the name of Young, which was his stepmother's surname. After training, Young arrived in France with his battalion on 20 April 1915, just in time to take part in the Second Battle of Ypres. His battalion was part of 151st Bde of the 50th Div. at this period and during 1915 he was gassed and on 16 September 1916, as a result of wounds received in High Wood, he was in hospital for ten weeks. He didn't return to France until May 1917 and took part in the Battle of Third Ypres in the second half of the year

Young was presented with his VC by the King on 29 June 1918 and on the following day returned to Gateshead for a spell of leave. However, much to his surprise he was met at the Central Station by five coal mine officials who were waiting to take him to his home in a pony and trap. The pony took the small party along Scotswood Road to Blaydon, where it was rested, and then on to High Spen. Tommy

Young lived in a house in East Street, a long curved street which still exists and the place was dressed with flags and bunting.

In the evening Young was fêted in front of a crowd of 15,000 people at Saltwell Park, Gateshead. The mayor presided and there was a good attendance of local organisations such as the Boy Scouts. The Earl of Durham presented Young with a watch; some War Bonds and a silver cigarette case and further presentations were made by Blaydon council and the local pit owners also gave Young a gold watch and chain. Col F.J. Cheverton, a former curate, conducted a drumhead service and in his speech of thanks Young said, amidst a storm of cheers, that 'any of the Durhams would have done the same thing'.

After the war Young went back to work in the mines but he was unable to keep his job as a hewer because of ill-health and took on a new job as a £9-a-week baths attendant where he worked. In 1920 he joined the 9th Durhams, when the territorial battalion was reformed but it didn't work out.

In 1923 Young appeared in court along with a companion, Samuel Cutter, on a charge of having stolen some chickens. He was put on probation and his solicitor stated that: 'Young was so drunk that he did not know what he was doing. Young slept on the kitchen floor that night and next morning woke to find the hens beside him.'

In 1936 his VC was spotted by a former officer in the 9th Durhams in a pawnbroker's shop along with a gold watch that was inscribed to him. The prices were £50 and £60 respectively, at a time when the going rate for a VC was about £40. The regiment organised their purchase and the VC is on display at the Regimental Museum in the City of Durham. In 1939 Young rejoined the Durhams for a short period but Rachel his wife died at this point (21 April 1940) and he was discharged in order that he could look after the family.

In Durham there are two stories about Young which have often been told and which may or may not be true. The first is that he used to march on to the stage at the Empire Theatre in Newcastle (later demolished) and the audience used to throw money at him. The second story concerns the time when he was in the Home Guard during the Second World War, and used to be on guard duty at the end of one of the Tyne bridges with a tin box placed at his feet. Here he asked for contributions to an old VC.

Unfortunately Young, who was never fully fit, his health having been permanently damaged by gas in May 1915 and by the wounds that he sustained in 1916, and after the war his health continued to decline and he had also taken to drink and found it very difficult to keep a job and as a consequence was constantly in dire financial straits.

After moving from his East Street home in July 1966 he ended up at a council-run men's hostel, The Hermitage, Front Street, Whickham, Co. Durham where he died three months later on 15 October. The Hermitage later became a hostel for people with learning difficulties. At the beginning of the 20th century the building had been the home of a local surgeon, James Osterley McCreery, and had also been a library.

Young was buried at St Patrick's Cemetery, High Spen and at his funeral the military was represented. His VC and medals were displayed and the Last Post sounded. Young's son was one of the mourners.

During his life Young had attended several of the special VC commemorations but the gaining of the nation's highest military honour through his wonderful bravery and selflessness never brought him much luck. In recent years though, Young together with Frank Dobson VC, both of who had lived in High Spen and both of whom died in County Durham, have been remembered with a memorial stone made from sandstone and erected in the grounds of High Spen Primary School, Huger Road, Gateshead. It was unveiled on 8 July 2008.

Young's VC but not his medals which would have included the 1914–15 Star; BWM, VM and two Coronation medals, is on display in the Durham Light Infantry Museum & Durham Art Gallery in Durham City.

A. MOUNTAIN
Hamelincourt, France, 26 March

On the night of 25 March the 15th/17th Bn The Prince of Wales's Own (West Yorkshire Regt) of 93rd Bde (31st Div.) (the two battalions, the 1st and 2nd Leeds battalions had been amalgamated in December 1917) was withdrawn from its position close to Judas Farm (near St Léger) to the Boyelles–Ervillers road, the battalion having been heavily engaged with the enemy. The next day it withdrew westwards, to a position close to the cemetery at Hamelincourt. During the day the brigade fought off an enemy attack, but suffered many casualties from artillery and machine-gun fire. Sgt Albert Mountain a member of the 15/17th West Yorks won an extremely well deserved VC for his courage and leadership throughout two days' fighting. His company had dug themselves in on a sunken road close to the Hamelincourt village cemetery but the position proved to be very exposed and they were forced to leave it. At the time the enemy was advancing in large numbers preceded by a patrol of an estimated two hundred men. A call for volunteers was then made to the West Yorks Bn in order to stage a counter-attack, and Sgt Albert Mountain volunteered, as did his party of ten men. They moved forward on the flank and, with the use of a Lewis gun and rifle fire, enfiladed a German patrol and killed about a hundred men.

In the meantime the rest of the company made a counter-attack and the remainder of the German patrol was cut up and thirty prisoners were taken. Soon the main body of the enemy appeared and bore down on the West Yorkshiremen, and at the sight of such numbers Mountain's group began to waver. However, he quickly rallied them and, after securing a defensive position, was able to cover the retreat of the rest of his company, together with the prisoners. After holding up six hundred

Germans for half an hour Mountain and his colleagues decided to retire and rejoin their company. The fighting had been so intense that wounded men could not possibly be attended to, let alone be moved.

Sgt Mountain then took charge of an isolated flank post and held on to it for just over a day until his group was surrounded by the enemy. An order to withdraw had been sent but had never reached them. This chaotic state resulted in only a small number of men escaping to rejoin their brigade, Sgt Mountain being one of them. The remaining men of the 31st Div. had been saved by the deeds of the West Yorkshiremen and in particular by the very great contribution made by Sgt Mountain. His 'fearlessness and initiative undoubtedly saved the whole situation'.

The divisional withdrawal continued to a position south-east of Moyenneville and finally, on the 30th, they were relieved and went into billets in the village of Bienvillers further westwards.

Sgt Mountain's VC citation was published in the *London Gazette* of 7 June 1918 as follows:

> For most conspicuous bravery and devotion to duty during an enemy attack, when his company was in an exposed position on a sunken road, having hastily dug themselves in. Owing to the intense artillery fire, they were obliged to vacate the road and fall back. The enemy in the meantime was advancing in mass preceded by an advanced patrol about 200 strong. The situation was critical, and volunteers for a counter-attack were called for. Sergt. Mountain immediately stepped forward and his party of ten men followed him. He then advanced on the flank with a Lewis gun, and brought enfilade fire to bear on the enemy patrol., killing about 100. In the meantime the remainder of the company made a frontal attack, and the entire enemy patrol was cut up and thirty prisoners taken. At this time the enemy main body appeared, and the men, who were numerically many times weaker than the enemy, began to waver. Sergt. Mountain rallied and organised his party and formed a defensive position from which to recover the retirement of the rest of the company and the prisoners. With this party of one Non-commissioned Officer and four me he successfully held at bay 600 of the enemy for half an hour, eventually retiring and rejoining his company. He then took command of the flank post of the battalion which was ' in the air,' and held on there for 27 ours until finally surrounded by the enemy. Sergt. Mountain was one of the few who managed to fight their way back. His supreme fearlessness and initiative undoubtedly saved the whole situation.

When the author visited the cemetery at Hamelincourt in March 1995 the only sign of what might have been war damage was the then relatively new brick-work in part of the cemetery wall.

Albert Mountain was born in Leeds on 19 April 1895. When the war began Mountain joined the Leeds Bantams before transferring to the Leeds Pals. The 15th and 17th battalions amalgamated on 7 December 1917 at Acq and Mountain's unit thus became the 15/17 The West Yorkshire Regt. He was presented with the ribbon of the VC by Maj. T.G. Gibson commanding the 15/17 The West Yorkshire Regt at a battalion parade held in the field in France on 10 June 1918, three days after the citation had been published and he sewed the ribbon on his uniform. Nearly three weeks later he was presented with the award itself by the King in the Quadrangle of Buckingham Palace on 29 June 1918. During the following year he was discharged and after the war he was chauffeur to the Lord Mayor of Leeds for a time and also worked as a timekeeper in Burton's clothing factory, Leeds. The restructured firm of Burtons used to operate from Leeds with branches in many British towns and cities.

From 1942 until his death Mountain was the licensee for the Miners Arms public house in Garforth, owned by the Tetley Brewery, where there is now a blue plaque to commemorate him. In the 1920s he attended a couple of VC functions and was present on 21 March 1930 at a dinner in honour of the West Riding VCs. In November 1929 he attended the funeral of Sgt John Crawshaw Raynes VC and in 1950 he attended the funeral of another Leeds VC, Cpl (later Capt.) George Sanders. He was also a friend of Tommy Young. In 1956 he took part in the Hyde Park VC centenary and after a long illness he died at his home in Aberford Road, Garforth, Leeds on 7 January 1967. He left a widow, a son and three daughters. His funeral was at Garforth parish church, where his regiment was represented and a bugler from the 1st Bn sounded the Last Post. Capt. W. Edwards, another Leeds VC, attended the funeral. Mountain's body was cremated at Lawns Wood Crematorium. Reference 82479 and his ashes placed in New Adel Lane Avenue, Plot K2-380 in the Garden of Remembrance and after his death his VC was presented by his son to the curator of the West Yorkshire Regiment Museum in 1967 and at the present time is in the Yorkshire Regiments Museum in York. Mountain's other decorations included the Croix de Guerre (France) and the Médaille Militaire (France), the BWM, VM, and two Coronation Medals.

Mountain is one of a dozen VC holders from the First World War to have strong local connections having either been born or buried in Leeds and he has name listed on a VC Memorial in the Victoria Gardens in the centre of the city on the Headrow side of Cookridge Street outside the Henry Moore Institute. The memorial was unveiled in November 1992 and the list of local VCs includes a chum of Albert Mountain, Pte William Boynton Butler of the 17th a fellow VC of the Leeds Pals. His final home in Aberford Road where he had lived for fourteen years boasts a plaque to his memory which was set up by the Garforth Historical Society.

B.A. HORSFALL

*Between Moyenneville and
Ablainzeville, France, 27 March*

At about 4.00 p.m. on 26 March news reached the 11th (S) Bn Accrington) The East Lancashire Regt (92nd Bde, 31st Div.) in their positions that the enemy had occupied the village of Moyenneville due west of Hamelincourt and St Léger where the Germans had been forty-eight hours before. The East Lancs were between Moyenneville and Ablainzeville to the south-west, both flanks were under pressure and the battalion was suffering from artillery fire from both the British and the German artillery. British shells were falling on their own support trenches as well as on the rear of battalion HQ. Urgent messages were sent to brigade to ask for their artillery range to be lengthened but to no avail. However, the enemy didn't seize the opportunity that the open flanks offered.

Next morning the German 16th Bavarian Div. made a frontal attack at 11.20 a.m. against the whole of the 92nd Bde and during what became very fierce fighting the village of Ablainzeville fell and at midday a further attack was launched and the East Lancs had to hang on grimly in their hastily dug trenches.

Twenty minutes later the Germans launched a stronger attack, this time with the assistance of low flying aircraft. Although they were held, it was at considerable loss to the 92nd Bde. According to captured German prisoners, the enemy's destination was the village of Ayette to the north.

It was during this fighting that 2nd Lt Basil Horsfall of the 3rd (Reserve) Bn The East Lancashire Regt attached to the 11th East Lancs won his VC when his company was astride the Courcelle-le-Comte–Ayette road and the Ablainzeville–Moyenneville Ridge, along which the road ran.

At 1.30 p.m. the enemy was seen to be advancing in large numbers from the direction of Ablainzeville and a company of the 10th (S) Bn (1st Hull) The East Yorkshire Regt (92nd Bde, 31st Div.) was ordered to reinforce the 11th East Lancs reserves. A platoon was sent forward to assist the right-hand company but heavy machine-gun fire coming from the village prevented them from reaching the front line. At 2.00 p.m. the ridge was still being held, but with very few men. Reinforcements from the 10th East Yorks had so far been unable to reach the beleaguered company.

Soon the whole defence began to break down as the sheer number of attackers took its toll on the Allied positions. Battalion communication with 92nd Bde HQ was made impossible owing to ground mist, and other forms of communication had been severed. At 4.25 p.m. Col Rickman assumed command of the brigade, ordered the 11th East Lancs, less one company, to retire to high ground to the south-east of Ayette, and instructed the 10th East Yorks to move to the high ground to the north-east of the same village.

The 11th East Lancs then moved again from the south-east of Ayette to the south-west and reformed under the cover of the banks of the River Cojeul. It was at the commencement of this withdrawal to the river that the gallant Horsfall was killed.

The battalion soon withdrew to new positions at Adinfer Wood, about 2 miles to the west of Moyenneville and by this time, owing to the stubborn brigade resistance put up on the 27th, the main enemy thrust was over and the west of Ayette was as far as the Germans reached. On the same day the East Lancs were relieved by the 1st Dorsets of the 32nd Div.

According to Horsfall's VC citation published on 22 May 1918 in the *London Gazette* he carried out the following deeds:

Foe most conspicuous bravery and devotion to duty. Second Lieut. Horsfall was in command of the centre platoon during an attack on our positions When the enemy first attacked his three forward sections were driven back and he was wounded in the head. Nevertheless, he immediately organised the remainder of his men and made a counter-attack, which recovered his original positions. On hearing that out of the three remaining officers of his company two were killed and one was wounded, he refused to go to the dressing station, although his wound was severe. Later his platoon had to be withdrawn to escape very heavy shell fire, but immediately the shelling lifted he made a second counter-attack and again recovered his positions. When the order to withdraw was given he was the last to leave his position, and, although exhausted, said he could have held on if it had been necessary. His conduct was a splendid example to his men, and he showed throughout the utmost disregards of danger. This very gallant officer was killed when retiring to the positions in rear.

Basil Athur Horsfall was born in Colombo, Ceylon on 4 October 1887. He was the youngest of the four sons of Mr and Mrs Charles W.F. Horsfall, who had a total of eight children. Charles Horsfall had gone to Ceylon in the 1860s and became one of the pioneers of the island's tea and coffee industry. By the time of his retirement he had become a very rich man.

Horsfall's first school was in Ceylon itself where he was a pupil at St Thomas's College, Mount Lavinia. On arriving in England he joined the St William Borase's Grammar School in Marlow, Buckinghamshire. He was a sports all-rounder and excelled at cricket. His first job was with a branch of Barclays Bank before he returned to Ceylon where he began working with the Public Works Department as an accountant. When war broke out he was acting as financial assistant. He had already joined the Ceylon Engineer Volunteers, a unit which was mobilised at the outbreak of war. He requested leave in order to travel to England and was released from his civil appointment but not allowed to leave the Ceylon Engineers, who were carrying out important work. In 1916, however, he did get clearance and joined the East Lancashire Regt on 19 December of that year. He went to France in the spring of 1917 and was subsequently wounded. Two of his three brothers were also wounded on the same day. He returned to front line duties in the winter.

Horsfall's VC, in its leather case, was presented to his parents at a very grand military parade on the Galle Face in Colombo on 16 August 1918. The Governor of Ceylon also presented a letter from the King to his parents. In March 1982 Horsfall's VC; 1914–15 Star, BWM, and VM medals, accompanied by a wealth of documentation, were offered for sale in Spinks' catalogue with the suggested selling price of £9,750. Horsfall's name is commemorated on the Arras Memorial to the Missing and his decorations are with The Queens' Lancashire Regiment Museum, Fulwood, Barracks, Preston.

B.M. CASSIDY

Arras, France, 28 March

In early 1918 the 2nd Lancashire Fusiliers (12th Bde) 4th Div. were positioned in the Arras area, with which they had become very familiar, as they had taken part in the Battle of Arras the previous spring. After several weeks of training and rest they moved to billets in Arras itself on 11 March. Eight days later the battalion moved into brigade reserve at St Laurent Blangy, a village about a mile to the north-east of Arras. While here on the 26th they learned that if the German Army was to continue with the successful advance further south, that the battalion was to withdraw to a position covering the village of Fampoux, 2 miles eastwards. This move would prevent the forming of a dangerous salient. By this time the battalion had moved into the support positions which it was destined to hold on to in the 28/29 March period.

On the 28th the enemy launched a massive attack to the north of Arras on the day that was designated as the first day of the Second Battle of Arras. The attack was designed to recapture Vimy Ridge, which had fallen to the Canadians nearly a year before. At 3.00 a.m. the enemy began a heavy bombardment and at 5.50 a.m. when the 169th Bde (56th Div.), which was on the immediate left of the 2nd LF, sent up a distress signal as their frontal wire was being destroyed by enemy artillery. It was the 2nd Essex, also of the 12th Bde, who bore the brunt of the shelling as, with the help of the early morning mist, the enemy got around behind the infantrymen, thus cutting them off. The defenders were then 'submerged by sheer weight of numbers' and by 10.30 a.m. they had been overwhelmed but despite this the enemy made little actual progress between 10.00 a.m. and 1.00 p.m. against the 4th and 56th divisions as they were finding that attacking over open ground was proving too costly for them and they decided to change tactics and began to work up communication trenches instead; supported by a strong artillery response. It was at this period that the 2nd LF suffered the same fate as the 2nd Essex had as when the enemy bombed their way down a communication trench they found themselves cut off and only six unwounded men managed to escape. A Coy under Cassidy had held positions called Civil Avenue and Humid Trench. Making one of the 'arms' that formed a cross which ran northeast to south-west. Cassidy was one of the casualties. In effect the enemy had driven a wedge between A & D companies and although the defenders fought heroically A Coy was short of ammunition and had almost no bombs left. It was during this desperate fighting and his attempts to hold his men together that 2nd Lt Bernard Cassidy won his VC in a position about 150 yards to the north of Fampoux. In the words used in the Regimental History:

> ... they held up the whole of the German attack at this point and saved the left flank of the 4th Division.

On the 30th the battalion counter-attacked but ran out of steam and on the night of 30/31 March they were relieved by the King's Own and went into support in Missourie, Mississippi and Effie Trenches, about a 1,000 yards to the rear of their previous positions.

For his bravery and ultimate self-sacrifice Cassidy was to be awarded a posthumous VC which was published in the *London Gazette* of 3 May 1918 as follows:

> At a time when the flank of the division was in danger, Lieut. Cassidy was in command of the left company of his battalion, which was in close support. He was given orders prior to the attack that he must hold onto his position to the last. He most nobly carried this out to the letter. The enemy came on in overwhelming numbers and endeavoured to turn the flank. He, however, continually rallied his men under a terrific bombardment. The enemy were several times cleared out of the trench by his personal leadership. His company was eventually surrounded, but Lieut. Cassidy still fought on, encouraging and exhorting his men until eventually killed. By his most gallant conduct the whole line was held up at this point, and the left flank was undoubtedly saved from what might have been a disaster.

Bernard Matthew Cassidy was born in Canning Town, London on 17 August 1892, although some accounts say Manchester, and he came from a family of Irish extraction. His parents were Bernard and Julia who had five other children and Bernard and his brother John both enlisted in 1915 and were both commissioned on the same day.

His posthumous VC was presented to his mother at Buckingham Palace by the King on 26 June 1918 and at the present time is on loan to the Ashcroft Gallery in the Imperial War Museum. Apart from the VC; Cassidy's medals included the 1914–15 Star, the BWM and VM.

As Bernard has no known grave his name is listed in Bay Five of the Arras Memorial to the Missing and in Canning Town there is Bernard Cassidy Street after him but that seems to be all in the way of commemoration of his life.

S.R. MCDOUGALL
Dernancourt, France, 28 March

Sgt Stanley Mcdougall was a member of the 47th Bn (Queensland), 12th Australian Infantry Bde, 4th Australian Div. AIF. The scene of his VC action, the first Australian one of the spring of 1918, was a railway cutting at Dernancourt, south of Albert. The forward posts of the division were responsible for holding the rail line between Dernancourt and Albert, and the 48th Bn was on the left. Despite having only arrived the previous night and so having had little rest, the Australians were keeping a close watch as they were expecting an attempted German breakthough at any moment. The rail embankment was strongly guarded and it was felt that it would not be possible for it to be captured in a frontal assault.

On the right flank of the 47th Bn was one of their platoons, guarding a cutting close to the embankment. A second platoon held a low bank to the north of a former French practice trench. Two machine gunners were set in position at a level-crossing, with their closest supports in the cutting to the south, and as an extra precaution Sergeant McDougall, acting as a scout together with two men, watched the crossing from a position behind the embankment.

Patrols during the night had already identified the enemy close by on the Albert–Dernancourt road, which was nearly 300 yards away and which ran parallel to the front line.

At dawn on 28 March McDougall who was about to win a Victoria cross was on guard and a short time later when an officer came on his rounds inspecting the advance posts. At about 4.30 a.m. through the early morning mist McDougall suddenly heard the sound of bayonet scabbards slapping against thighs at the cutting near the railway. He immediately woke his two sleeping colleagues and the officer alerted the rest of the advance posts. McDougall's citation published in the *London Gazette* of 3 May 1918 tells the story of what happened in the following way:

> For most conspicuous bravery and devotion to duty when the enemy attacked our line and his first wave succeeded in gaining an entry. Sergt. McDougall, who was at a post in a flank company, realised the situation and at once charged the enemy's second wave single-handed with rifle and bayonet, killing seven and capturing a machine gun which they had. This he turned on to them, firing from the hip, causing many casualties and routing that wave. He then turned his attention to those who had entered, until his ammunition ran out, all the time firing at close quarters, when he seized a bayonet and charged again, killing three men and an enemy officer, who was just about to kill one of our officers. He used a Lewis gun on the enemy, killing many and enabling us to capture 33 prisoners. The prompt action of this non-commissioned officer saved the line and enabled the enemy's advance to be stopped.

Eight days later on 5 April when McDougall was still in the same area he won a Military Medal, when the enemy was attacking again and he enfiladed them at close quarters. His gun was knocked out and he then crawled about 300 yards in order to find a replacement and to take charge of the by then leaderless platoon for the rest of the action. On 28 May he was posted to the 48th Bn.

Stanley Robert McDougall was born in Recherche, Hobart, Tasmania on 23 July 1889, the son of John Henry McDougall, a sawmiller, and his wife Susannah nee Cate.. After leaving school McDougall worked as a blacksmith and became an excellent rider and shot. He was also an amateur boxer of some repute. Illness had prevented him from joining the Army earlier but on 31 August 1915 he enlisted in Hobart with the service number 4061 and was posted to 12th Reinforcements to the 15th Bn. Despite his usefulness with horses he remained with the infantry and in March 1916, when training in Egypt, he joined the 47th Bn. In June he landed in France with his unit and afterwards they fought at Pozières in August 1916 and at Messines and Broodseinde in 1917. McDougall was promoted Lance Corporal on 5 May 1917 and Corporal in September. In November he became temporary Sergeant and was substantive Sergeant on 23 January 1918. On 28 May he was posted to the 48th Bn and he was decorated by the King on 19 August 1918 at Windsor Castle and soon afterwards he returned to Australia with nine other VC holders on HMAT *Medic*. He then travelled to Tasmania where he was demobilised in Hobart on 15 December 1918.

After the war he was employed by the Tasmanian Forestry Department and by the early 1930s had become an inspector responsible for all the forests in the north-western part of the state. In 1956 he travelled with the Australian VC contingent for the centenary celebrations of the award and took part in the ceremonies in Hyde Park as a member of the Australian contingent. On 28 March 1968, fifty years after he won the VC, he celebrated the event in Launceston Hospital, in Tasmania, where he was then a patient but three months later he died on 7 July in Hobart at the North East Soldiers' Hospital, Scottsdale. He was cremated in Norwood Crematorium, Mitchell, Canberra, ACT where a plaque commemorates his memory and his ashes are buried there. He was survived by his wife, Martha Florence McDougall, whom he married in 1926; they had no children. At the time of his death their home was at 10 Christopher Street, Scottsdale.

McDougall's uniform and the Lewis gun that he used at Dernancourt are on display at the Hall of Valour in the Australian War Memorial, Canberra together with his VC and MM and his other medals; the BWM, VM and two Coronation Medals. The Memorial also owns a portrait of him by Frank Crozier. He is also remembered with a McDougall Street in the city and in the Victoria Cross Memorial in Victoria Cross Park and lastly in Sydney as part of the Victoria Cross Memorial in the Queen Victoria building.

O.C.S. WATSON
Rossignol Wood, France, 28 March

A/Lt Col Oliver Watson was on attachment from the 1st County of London Yeomanry as commander of the 5th King's Own Yorkshire Light Infantry (KOYLI) when he won his VC in the battle for Rossignol Wood on 28 March 1918. This wood (in English, Nightingale Wood), which is close to the villages of Gommecourt and Hébuterne, was also known as Copse 125 and the German writer and soldier Ernst Jünger wrote a book called *Copse 125* in addition to his more famous *The Storm of Steel*. The wood was also connected with two other men who were to win the VC, Theodore Hardy and Dick Travis.

When the writer last visited the wood in March 1995 it was still very full of reminders of the war. There were fallen trees, gas shells, trench lines and hundreds of shell holes. Cowslips were growing in profusion and the only signs of animal life were three deer who shied away at the presence of visitors. As Watson has no known grave it is even possible that his body is still buried there.

The 5th KOYLI were part of 187th Bde of the 62nd Div. and on 23 March the division marched southwards on its way to the village of Bucquoy, about 2 miles east of Gommecourt. The battalion, along with the 2/4th, detached to become part of the reserve to the XVII Corps and was billeted in Arras at the Communal Colleges. The considerable aerial activity suggested that the town was about to be attacked and the following day the 187th Bde moved again and took up positions quite close to the village of Ronville.

On the 25th the brigade was ordered to rejoin the division at Bucquoy, which it marched to through the heavy traffic of a retreating army at night, arriving there in the small hours of the 26th. It was about to take its part in the stemming of the German advance which had been going on for five days. To the south Albert was about to fall.

The 62nd Div. was on the extreme right flank of the IV Corps on the Bucquoy–Puisieux line. Defensive lines were taken up facing the south-east and Rossignol Wood itself was reported to be controlled by enemy machine-gun posts along its near edge. That night contact was made with the 4th Australian Bde to the right.

At 9.00 a.m. large numbers of the enemy were seen getting ready to attack; bombs were requested but none were available. The position that the brigade occupied was a system of former trench lines which could easily be used by bombing parties in an attack. Defence with no bombs was to prove difficult. The two KOYLI battalions were both under the command of Lt Col Watson.

The companies fought an uneven struggle all day against their attackers and at about 10.00 p.m. four tanks were brought up to help the defenders. Together with two companies they moved out towards Rossignol Wood and found that it was clear of the enemy. During the night (27/28th) all the companies of the 5th Bn were moved into the right of the line to be ready for a counter-attack, planned to recover the ground that had been lost. It was hoped to push on from the right and then to take up a line running from the uninhabited Rossignol Wood in a south-westerly direction and then to link up with the Australians.

The first part of the counter-attack went well and three trenches were recaptured in the darkness. But the companies on their way to Rossignol Wood found that they were up against a very strongly held German outpost. At daybreak the attackers were in a south-east-facing position with a road and a light railway between them and Rossignol Wood.

The supply of bombs had been resumed and at daylight another supply was called for. Two tanks which had been left in the south-east corner of Rossignol Wood were now being used by the enemy as strong points.

The British had the sun in their eyes, which made it difficult to spot targets below the skyline, but they could make out the enemy in numbers on the left, advancing down the hill. Their advance was well protected by their own machine guns which harassed the KOYLIs greatly. The position was becoming completely untenable as the enemy was using communication trenches to advance on the KOYLIs from the rear. At about 5.30 a.m. Lt Col Watson was left with only D Coy to reinforce his line as his other companies had become surrounded and he lingered a while before bowing to the inevitable and retreating down a communication trench, emptying his revolver at the approaching Germans as he went and he was killed at this time while covering his company's withdrawal.

The remaining men in the two KOYLI battalions held their defensive flank against further attacks for the rest of the day, before linking up with the Australians, who had fought their way to them from the south. The brigade was relieved three days later and after a short break it continued to repel the German advance. By 5 April the first stage of the German Spring Offensive had petered out as for ten days they had been trying to break through in the Gommecourt sector and for ten days their attacks had been beaten off.

Watson's posthumous VC was published in the *London Gazette* of 18 May 1918 as follows:

> For most conspicuous bravery, self-sacrifice devotion to duty, and exceptionally gallant leading during a critical period of operation. His command was at a point where continual attacks were made by the enemy in order to pierce the line, and an intricate system of old trenches in front, coupled with the fact that his position was under constant rifle and machine-gun fire, rendered the situation still more dangerous. A counter-attack had been made against the enemy position, which at first achieved its object, but as they were holding out in two improvised strong points, Lieut.-Colonel Watson saw that immediate action was necessary, and he led his remaining small reserve to the attack, organising bombing parties and leading attacks under intense rife and machine-gun fire. Outnumbered, he finally ordered his men to retire, remaining himself in a communication trench to cover his retirement, though he faced almost certain death by so doing. The assault he led was at a critical moment, and without doubt saved the line. Both in the assault and in the covering his men's retirement he held his life as nothing, and his splendid bravery inspired all troops in the vicinity to rise to the occasion and save a breach being made in a hardly tried and attenuated line. Lieut.-Colonel Watson was killed while covering the withdrawal.

After he a posthumous VC the decoration was presented to his sister by General Officer Commanding Home Forces.

Oliver Cyril Spencer Watson was born in Cavendish Square, London on 7 September 1876. He was the youngest son of Mr William Spencer Watson MB, FRCS, of London and his wife Georgina Mary Jane Watson. Oliver was educated at St Paul's School and then left for the Royal Military College Sandhurst. On 20 February 1897 he was gazetted to the 2nd Bn Yorkshire Regt. He served on the North West Frontier as part of the Tirah Expedition of 1897–8, in which he was badly wounded in the chest. On 17 August 1898 he was made a full lieutenant and two years later served in the Boxer Rebellion in the China Expedition of 1900. However in 1903 he was severely ill and in the following year on 16 January retired from the Army when his name was placed on the Reserve of Officers at the age of twenty-eight. He then became estate agent to Sir Charles Henry Bart MP at Parkwood and Crazies Hill.

Five years later, on 8 September 1909, and having been a keen huntsman he was commissioned into the Middlesex Yeomanry, a unit which many of his hunting chums were members of, becoming a lieutenant on 24 November 1911 and later captain in November 1913.

In 1914 he was recalled with other officer reservists and left for Egypt and later served in Gallipoli from April 1915, when he became Temporary Major on 28 July 1915. Returning to England he was then attached to the 2nd/5th KOYLI as their second-in-command in 1916 and left for France with them early the following year. A few months later he was awarded the DSO for work at Bullecourt on 20 May 1917. When his commanding officer was killed in an initial attack Watson was sent up to take over the line and on arrival at a railway cutting found the men from units of the brigade who had survived the first attack. Watson promptly reorganised the men and led them forward in a second attack. They were held up by an enemy machine gun which prevented any progress and Watson decided to carry on alone in an attempt to reach men who were holding on in front until he was badly wounded.

In the following January 1918, although not completely fit, he returned to the front as acting lieutenant colonel and was killed a few weeks later.

The Green Howards, who have their museum at Richmond, North Yorkshire, had Watson's medals on loan from 1956; they were donated by the family, Mrs CatherineWhittuck as an outright gift in 1992. The group consisted of the VC, DSO, India Medal 1895–1902 with clasps, Tirah 1897–8, Punjab Frontier 1897–8, China War Medal 1900, BWM and Victory Medal with oak leaf as Watson had been Mentioned in Despatches.

Watson's name is listed on the Arras Memorial under 'Middlesex Yeomanry' and he is commemorated at St Mary's Church, Wargrave, Berkshire as well as included on the Regimental Memorial in St Paul's Cathedral, London.

G.M. FLOWERDEW

North-east of Bois de Moreuil,
France, 30 March

Half of the men in this book who won the VC gained the award in a period of only weeks beginning on 21 March, an indication of the heroism shown when tackling the might of the German Army in what was to be their final attempt to break the stalemate of the Western Front. On 23 March a few miles to the south-east of Amiens a mounted detachment numbering about 500 men was formed from what was left of the 3rd Cavalry Div. Brig. Gen. J.E.B.Seely (Canadian Cavalry Bde) provided 200 cavalrymen, and his brigade staff and the British provided two brigades of 150 men each. For the next few days they helped to re-establish infantry lines which had been destroyed, and on occasions carried out small counter-attacks on enemy positions.

On the 27th, the Canadian Bde was put under the control of the 2nd Cavalry Div. and on the 28th the Anglo-Canadian Cavalry passed under the control of the French First Army. The French then linked up with the right flank of the British Army.

On the 29th, the 2nd Cavalry Div. was once more put under British command, where it joined up with the left of the French Army. Units of the German 243rd Div. began to occupy Moreuil Ridge, a very commanding position, and were beginning to move into the Bois de Moreuil on the Amiens side of the ridge. The position commanded the right embankment of the River Avre.

Brig. -Gen. Seely had learnt the bad news of the German progress from the GOC 2nd Cavalry Div., Brig. Gen. T.T. Pitman. In his book *Adventure*, Seely recalls galloping forward to the village of Castel, leaving his brigade 2 miles behind. He found the village to be very close to the enemy: and when he rode down the main street, it was being spattered with bullets. Seely was accompanied by Major Connolly, commander of Lord Strathcona's Horse, and his aide-de-camp. At a crossroads he saw the Allied line spread out in front of him at a distance of about 600 yards, just beyond the River Luce. The enemy fire was coming from the lower part of the Bois de Moreuil, some 1,400 yards away. However, as Seely turned a corner he found himself shielded from the enemy fire and was able to converse with a French General (unnamed in Seely's book). It appeared to the Frenchman that to take the ridge was just not possible with Seely's small force against perhaps a whole German division. Seely, however, was keen to make the attempt and wrote later that this was a 'big moment' in the war for him. It was agreed between the two men that the French should take the town of Moreuil to the south of the wood and that Seely's force should capture the wood itself. The two Allied armies would then link up and the German advance on Amiens would be halted. Seely gave his orders to Major Connolly for the capture of the ridge.

The plan was for three mounted squadrons of the Royal Canadian Dragoons to attack initially, to be followed up by attacks from mounted and unmounted men from Lord Strathcona's Horse. The Canadian Bde was to attack in three separate but converging thrusts. Seely had a few words with Lt Flowerdew and told him he was confident that he would succeed in taking the wood. 'With his gentle smile he turned to me and said: "I know, sir, I know, it is a splendid moment. I will try not to fail you." 'With orders to take the wood, Lt Gordon Flowerdew (who had been made C Squadron commander in January) began his gallant charge, with men from Lord Strathcona's Horse and they rode for about a mile, over the River Luce and around the north-eastern part of the Bois de Moreuil.

In coping with the cavalry, the German infantry put up a strong resistance and there was a lot of hand-to-hand fighting, but by 11.00 a.m. the northern section of the wood had been captured by the Canadians. It was at this point that Flowerdew, with sword raised, led his men to almost certain death in a suicidal attack on two lines of the enemy, each with about sixty men and three machine guns. Flowerdew had ordered one troop, under Lt Frederick Harvey VC, to dismount while he led the remaining three troops in the charge. Harvey had won his VC at Guyencourt on 27 March 1917.

By midday the wood was clear of the enemy but they soon counter-attacked and after continuous fighting three improvised battalions from the 8th Div. relieved the cavalry during the night and by a coincidence this group was under the command of Brig. Gen. G.W. St G. Grogan, who himself was to win a VC a couple of months later in the third

Battle of the Aisne. However by the 31st, most of the wood, together with Rifle Wood to the north, had been retaken by the enemy but the following day Rifle Wood was back in Allied hands, as was most of the Bois de Moreuil.

During the fierce fighting Flowerdew himself had been cut down by bullets that hit his chest and legs and was he was mortally wounded and taken to a field hospital near Moreuil where he was operated on and one of his legs amputated. His life could not be saved however and he succumbed the next day and was buried in Namps-au-Val British Cemetery, Plot 1, Row H, Grave 1. His age on the headstone installed after the war was given as thirty-two instead of thirty-three. The cemetery is 11 miles south-west of Amiens and was made at the end of March 1918, when the German advance was beginning to fade. The casualties were mostly brought from the 41st, 50th and 55th Casualty Clearing Stations. Also in the cemetery are the remains of twenty-four members of the Canadian Forces, most of whom were cavalrymen, almost certainly Flowerdew's colleagues in the famous charge.

Moreuil Wood is on the top of a high ridge and close to the road is a French war memorial which, according to the inscription, was destroyed by 'Hitler's Soldiers' in the Second World War. The area again came into the limelight on 8 August 1918, the beginning of the end of the German Army, and in Moreuil there is a street commemorating this date.

The citation for Flowerdew's posthumous VC was published in the *London Gazette* of 24 April 1918 as follows:

> For most conspicuous bravery and dash when in command of a squadron detailed for special service of a very important nature. On reaching the first objective, Lieut. Flowerdew saw two lines of the enemy, each about sixty strong, with machine guns in the centre and flanks, one line being about two hundred yards behind the other. Realising the critical nature of the operation, and how much depended upon it, Lieut. Flowerdew ordered a troop under Lieut. Harvey, V.C., to dismount and carry out a special movement while he led the remaining three troops to the charge. The squadron (less one troop) passed over the lines, killing many of the enemy with the sword, and, wheeling about, galloped at them again. Although the squadron had then lost about seventy per cent of its numbers, killed and wounded, from rifle and machine-gun fire directed on it from the front and both flanks, the enemy broke and retired. The survivors of the squadron then established themselves in a position where they were joined, after

much hand-to-hand fighting, by Lieut. Harvey's party. Lieut. Flowerdew was dangerously wounded through both thighs during the operations, but continued to cheer on his men. There can be no doubt that this officer's great valour was the prime factor in the capture of the position.

Two months later Gordon's mother, accompanied by her daughters Eleanor and Florence, was presented with her son's VC by the King in the Quadrangle at Buckingham Palace on 29 June.

Gordon Muriel Flowerdew was born at Billingford Hall, a farm in Billingford, near Scole in Norfolk, on 2 January 1885 and baptised in St Leonard's, the village church. He was the eighth son of ten boys and four girls who were the children of Arthur John Blomfield Flowerdew and Hannah Flowerdew (nee Symonds).

The main part of the village of Billingford, including a fine windmill, is adjacent to the main road running from Scole to Great Yarmouth. The Hall, though, is off the road and has to be approached up a track that rises through fields to the summit of a ridge. There are three main buildings in the area: the Hall, whose origins are several hundred years old, and from where the farming in the area has been organised for generations; the small church of St Leonard's, which lost its tower in the early part of the nineteenth century; and beyond the church, the former rectory. These three buildings dominate the ridge and appear almost to 'keep an eye' on what is happening below in the rest of the village, situated in the Waveney Valley which also separates Suffolk from Norfolk.

Flowerdew attended Framlingham College between 1894 and 1899 and at the age of seventeen emigrated to Canada where he took up work as a cowboy and later worked in various occupations including that of a farmer. In 1911 he became a member of the Regiment of Cavalry (31st Regt, British Columbia Horse) and three years later when war broke out he joined Lord Strathcona's Horse (Royal Canadians) and after training in England they embarked for France in May 1915 as part of the Canadian Cavalry Bde. Flowerdew who had been made a sergeant, was commissioned in 1916 and became very popular with his men.

After the action at Moreuil Wood, Alfred Munnings, a fellow pupil at Framingham College for a short time, painted the famous charge of the Canadian horsemen, the original of which hangs in the Canadian War

Memorial in Ottawa. A copy of the picture, *The Flowerdew Charge*, was presented to the College in 1991 at a special ceremony when guests included officials from the Canadian High Commission and also Lord Strathcona, the great-grandson of the founder of the regiment.

Flowerdew's decorations were owned by Framlingham College and originally presented by one of his brothers and sisters, who each kept a miniature cross. Apart from the VC the decorations included the 1914–15 Star, BWM and VM. The VC itself was later collected from the college by a Canadian official for display in Canada, where Flowerdew had become quite a folk hero, and was then displayed at the Lord Strathcona's Horse Museum (1990–2003) .

In the college chapel is displayed the wooden cross from Flowerdew's original grave in France and citations of the three men from Framlingham who won the VC in the Great War are also on display. Apart from Flowerdew the names of the two men are William Hewitt (1894–1900) and Augustine Agar. The citations are displayed on the chapel wall together with replicas of the medals. Arthur Flowerdew was also a student at the college and is also commemorated. At the entrance to the college is an ante-room with displays of various aspects of the history of the college, which was founded as a memorial to Prince Albert. In addition to a copy of Munnings' painting of the Charge is a second painting of the Canadian Cavalry during the war and copies of newspaper articles, etc.

The man who had recommended Flowerdew for the VC was Brig. -Gen. J.E.B. Seely, later a friend of Alfred Munnings, who went to France in 1918 to carry out commissions for the Canadian government. In St Leonard's Church, Billingford there is a memorial to the men from the village who died in the Great War, and Flowerdew's name is the first one listed. There is also a second memorial that lists the names of the men who served in the war but who survived, and on this list there are no fewer that four Flowerdews. There is also a brass plaque to Arthur Blomfield Flowerdew, one of Flowerdew's brothers, who died in the Boer War; and lastly there is a brass plaque, erected by her then surviving children, to Hannah Flowerdew (1850–1930), who lived at the Hall for fifty years. By 1970, of the original fourteen Flowerdew children only three were still living.

Flowerdew's VC, returned to the college during a special presentation on 3 February 2003, and his deeds have always attracted a lot of interest and he was even written up as 'the man who won the war' on one occasion, surely something of an exaggeration? Certainly, what he and his colleagues achieved thoroughly surprised the German attackers, who were only 11 miles from the outskirts of Amiens. The

Bois de Moreuil was in a very commanding position and perhaps the enemy didn't really appreciate just how important it was to hold onto this last real objective and of the advantage to gain by driving a wedge between the French and the British Armies before moving on to reach the vitally important city of Amiens. On the other hand, the enemy which had been on the offensive for nine continuous days was surely beginning to run out of steam and the possibility of the German Army losing the war was already apparent to the Allies by the beginning of April as clearly by then the enemy had simply overstretched itself while the Allied armies had absorbed whatever had been thrown at them. A final reason for the attraction of the Flowerdew story may be that it was because his VC action was a cavalry charge, which in 1918 surely belonged to another age? Even so, the charge will forever have a romantic appeal.

In April 2004 Framingham College presented Flowerdew's VC together with Lance. Cpl William Hewitt's to the Imperial War Museum where they joined that of Lt Augustine Agar RN.

P. V. STORKEY

Bois de Hangard, France, 7 April

Lt Percy Storkey of the 19th Bn (NSW) 5th Bde 2nd Australian Div. won his VC in Hangard Wood, close to near Villers Brettoneux, on 7 April 1918, a week after Gordon Flowerdew earned his and a day after the enemy had advanced from Chauny to the Oise-Aisne.

The 19th Bn was ordered to clear the ground to the north of Hangard Wood which was 'lightly held' by the enemy. The attacking company was already exhausted and at dawn lay down at the start line; Storkey, who was second in command, actually dozed off. His company advanced without him and they had gone 80 yards before he woke up and realised what had happened. His men were reduced by 25 per cent by heavy machine-gun fire before the leading companies reached the edge of the wood. The company commander, Capt. Wallach, was wounded in both legs and Storkey took over from the stricken officer and led six men through high saplings in the wood in order to try and cut off and get behind the enemy machine-gun team. Another group, made up of four men and one officer broke into some trenches where the enemy was firing on the rest of Storkey's company. One of the Australian troops yelled out and a German suddenly looked around and saw what was about to befall him. It became a fight to the death, and Storkey who was counting on surprise, trying to give the impression that the enemy were up against a much larger force than the small group that the attackers actually were. Thirty of the enemy were killed and fifty taken prisoner. However, when night fell the survivors of the two Australian companies were forced to return. After winning his VC Storkey was wounded again.

The official citation for Storkey's heroism was published in the *London Gazette*, of 7 June and tells the story in the following way:

On emerging from the wood the enemy trench line was encountered, and Lieut. Storkey found himself with six men. While continuing his move forward a large enemy party – about 80 to 100 strong – armed with several machine guns, was noticed to be holding up the advance of the troops on the right. Lieut. Storkey immediately decided to attack this party from the flank and rear, and while moving forward in the attack was joined by Lieut. Lipscomb and four men. Under the leadership of Lieut. Storkey, this small party of two officers, and 10 other ranks charged the enemy position with fixed bayonets, driving the enemy out, killing and wounding about 30, and capturing three officers and 50 men, also one machine gun. The splendid courage shown by this officer in quickly deciding his course of action, and his skilful method of attacking against such great odds, removed a dangerous obstacle to the advance of the troops on the right, and inspired the remainder of our small party with the utmost confidence when advancing to the objective line.

After winning his VC Storkey was presented with the decoration by the King in the Quadrangle of Buckingham Palace on 25 July 1918.

Percy Valentine Storkey was born in Napier, Hawkes Bay, New Zealand, on 9 September 1893, the son of Samual James Storkey who had been born in England and his wife Sarah Edith (nee Dean) born in New Zealand. Percy was educated at Napier High School and Victoria College, Wellington. In 1911 he moved to Sydney and then joined a steamship company as a clerk before enrolling at the Law School of Sydney University in 1912. However his legal studies were interrupted by the war and he enlisted on 10 May 1915. He had military experience having served for five years with the Wellington Infantry. He left for England in December and together with other reinforcements destined for the 19th Bn, he joined his unit in In France on 14 November 1916. Soon involved in the fighting he was wounded five days later north of Flers when attacking the Gird system of trenches He was promoted to lieutenant the following January and again wounded in the Third Battle of Ypres on 10 October 1917. He was appointed temporary company commander the following month.

After winning his VC at Hangard Wood he was again wounded in action and in June his temporary rank of company commander was confirmed. He returned to Australia six months later and left the AIF in January 1919.

In the same year Storkey returned to his interrupted legal studies and graduated from Sydney University and he was called to the bar in New South Wales in June 1921. Practicing common law he became Crown Prosecutor in 1922 and served on the South-Western district for eighteen years. Also in 1922 on 15 April, he married an Englishwoman, Minnie Molly Mary Gordon (née Burnett), at St Stephen's Presbyterian Church, Sydney, and the couple set up home in Vaucluse.

In May 1939 Storkey became a Judge of the District Court and Chairman of Quarter Sessions in the Northern District of New South Wales, a position which he held for sixteen years until retiring in 1955. He then moved to England with his wife where they lived at 20 Trowlock Avenue, Teddington close to the River Thames and from there he attended several of the VC functions, including the 1956 centenary. He had already been active in the RSL when in Austrlia.

Living on to the age of 76 Storkey died at his home on 3 October 1969 and was cremated at the South West Middlesex Crematorium, Hansworth and his ashes scattered on Lawn 3-B3. He bequeathed his VC and medals which include the BWM, VM, and two Coronation Medals to his school, the Napier Boy's School, New Zealand, where his VC was to be displayed as the governors saw fit. In 1983 the School's Parents' League decided to sell Storkey's VC which was then estimated to be worth at least £30,000 and to establish a scholarship fund in his memory with some of the proceeds. However, they underestimated the strength of public feeling and subsequently changed their minds about the scheme. At the present time a replica VC is on display in the school's memorial library and his decorations are on permanent loan to the National Army Museum, Waioura. The machine gun he captured in Hangard Wood is on display in the Australian War Memorial in Canberra. Other commemorations of his memory include a street, Storkey Place, named after him in Canberra ACT; his name listed in the Crematorium Remembrance Book; on the Victoria Cross Memorial in Sydney; the Victoria Cross Memorial Park in Canberra; and his portrait by Max Meldrum is displayed in the Archives Building, Wellington;

J.H. COLLIN
Givenchy, France, 9 April

The 1/4 Bn T.F. King's Own (Royal Lancaster Regt) was part of the 164th Bde of the 55th Div. and in the period from February to early April 1918 the division was in position in the area of the village of Givenchy. Givenchy was a particular important position to the west of Béthune as it stood on a slight rise which gave observation in all directions and in particular towards the west or Allied side of the Western Front. As a consequence the British were very keen to hang on to the village and had made a strong defence, along with a well-dug front trench-line. This line was lightly held and was supported by a series of support and reserve lines, along with switches. These defences or 'keeps' were to be defended at all costs and companies or platoons were in position behind them in case they were overrun. A counter-attack would then be quickly made if such a position was in danger of being surrounded.

On the morning of 9 April, the first day of the German (Lys) Offensive in Flanders and the battle of Estaires, there was a heavy fog and it was cold and raw. At about 4.15 a.m. the enemy began a bombardment on the 55th Div. front and on roads, crossings, tracks and the La Bassée canal bridges using 4.2s and 5.9s together with gas shells which decreased as the other shells increased. The British front line was virtually destroyed by only a few shells and the enemy bombardment eased at around 6.30 a.m. The attackers then attacked two Portuguese brigades to the north of the King's Own, which had been in the line for several days and were now exhausted. At about 8.45 a.m. with the bombardment continuing, the Portuguese were forced to retreat and the flank was therefore 'in the air'. The attack against the rest of the 55th Div. began about an hour later and the thick mist allowed the enemy to get close to the divisional positions before being seen and exposed to fire. The 164th Bde front was penetrated and the enemy made considerable progress during the rest of the morning.

The position held by Lt J.H. Collin (1/4th King's Own) north of the canal was called Orchard Keep and he held it with the assistance of sixteen men, who were gradually reduced to five. Then Collin began to slowly withdraw from the position, while fighting every inch of the way. The enemy pressed the group hard with ever more men, using bombs and machine-gun fire at very close range.

Collin took on the German machine-gun team single-handed and after firing his revolver he threw a Mills bomb which killed four of the team; wounded two others and put the gun out of action. Spying a second machine gun Collin placed a Lewis gun at a high point of advantage on the parapet and kept the enemy at bay until he was mortally wounded.

The Keep was completely in enemy hands by 12.55 p.m. but by 3.35 p.m. it was back in British hands, having been reclaimed by C Coy.

At first the rest of Collin's group had been reported killed; however a L. Cpl J. Pollitt had been wounded and taken prisoner but he killed his escort and fought his way back to his own lines, though he did not receive the credit he deserved. Gradually the other advance posts fell but some were retaken. The Germans were able to reach a group of houses known as Windy Corner. By midday the British had made a counter-attack and had regained some of the positions that they had lost in the morning. The 1/4 King's Own had done well and had the advantage of having good trenches which they had occupied for some time prior to the battle. The battle had been fought to defend the village of Givenchy and it was part of what has become known as the Battle of Estaires.

The position of the 55th Div. at dawn the next day was that with the assistance of the 154th Bde of the 51st Div. it held a line of about 11,000 yards from the La Bassée to the Lawe Canal. The gap left by the Portuguese had been closed.

Collin is buried in Vieille-Chapelle New Military Cemetery, Lacouture, which is 5 miles north-north-east of Béthune. The grave is in Plot III. Row A, Grave 11. The cemetery was used by Field Ambulances and fighting units until the end of March 1918 and in April the village and the cemetery fell into the hands of the Germans until they retired five months later in September. At one point 506 Portuguese troops were buried there but in 1925 they were reburied at their national cemetery at Richebourg-l'Avoué. A few feet away in Row C. Grave 8 is the grave of an officer who won the VC on the same day, T/2nd Lt John Schofield of the 2/5th Lancashire Fusiliers.

Collin's posthumous VC was published in the *London Gazette* of 28 June as follows:

> After offering a long and gallant resistance against heavy odds in the Keep held by his platoon, this officer, with only five of his men remaining, slowly withdrew in the face of superior numbers, contesting every inch of the ground. The enemy were pressing him hard with bombs and machine-gun fire from close range. Single-handed, Second Lieut. Collin attacked the machine gun and team. After firing his revolver in the enemy, he seized a Mills grenade and three it into the hostile team and wounding two others. Observing a second hostile machine gun firing, he took a Lewis gun, and selecting a high point of vantage on the parapet whence he could engage the gun, he, unaided, kept the enemy at bay until he fell mortally wounded. The heroic self-sacrifice of Second Lieut. Collin was a magnificent example to us all.

Joseph Henry Collin was born in Jarrow, Co. Durham on 11 April 1893, the second son of a railworker, also named Joseph, of 8 Petterie Terrace, Carlisle and his wife Mary. Joseph junior was educated at St Patrick's School in Carlisle and during his youth won prizes for sprinting and was an enthusiastic footballer. After leaving school he went to work for the clothiers Messrs Joseph Hepworth & Son of Leeds. In 1915 he joined the Argyll & Sutherland Highlanders as a Private and during his training was promoted to Sergeant. In 1916 he took part in the Battles of the Somme and Ancre and was awarded a commission. After officer training he returned to France in October 1917 and served as a 2nd lieutenant with the 1/4th King's Own.

At Buckingham Palace on 25 July 1918 his parents were presented with their son's VC by the King which nearly forty years later was presented to the King's Own Regimental Museum in 1956. The Museum is in Lancaster and also holds Collin's memorial plaque purchased in in an auction. His other decorations included the 1914–15 Star; the BWM and VM. In the regimental chapel is also a plaque which commemorates his life and each year schools in Carlisle compete for the 'Collin Shield', a trophy for a one mile race originally presented in his memory by his family.

R.G. MASTERS
Near Béthune, France, 9 April

In addition to 2nd Lt Joseph Collin and T/2nd Lt John Schofield, both members of the 164th Bde of the 55th (West Lancs.) Div., Pte Richard Masters of the Royal Army Service Corps, attached to the 141st Field Ambulance, also won the VC on 9 April 1918 at the beginning of the Battle of Estaires.

To quote from his citation (*London Gazette*, 8 May 1918):

Owing to an enemy attack, communications were cut off and wounded could not be evacuated. The road was reported impassable, but Private Masters volunteered to try and get through, and after the greatest difficulty succeeded, although he had to clear the road of all sorts of debris. He made journey after journey throughout the afternoon, over a road constantly shelled and swept by machine-gun fire, and was on one occasion bombed by an aeroplane. The greater part of the wounded cleared from this area were evacuated by Private Masters, as his was the only car that could get through during this particular time.

He carried out these acts of bravery behind Givenchy and the lines of the 55th Div. close to Gorre, a village just to the north of the La Bassée Canal, about 2 miles east of the important town of Béthune. The road, which had become impassable, was between Gorre and the 'Tuning Fork', which was one of the strong defensive positions in the Allied lines.

Richard George Masters was born at 61 Everton Road, Birkdale, Southport, Lancashire on 23 March 1877, son of David Brown and Margaret Alice Masters. His father was a carter by trade. Masters junior was educated at Bury Road School in Southport.

Masters was already thirty-seven when war broke out and was well known in his home town, with a reputation as a man who took great pride in his personal appearance. He worked as a chauffeur in the employ of Mr Pennington of Birkdale. He was also an expert cyclist and together with W. Birtwistle won championships for cycling sprints. In the winter months he kept himself fit by running in cross-country championships, some of which he won. He also used to take regular 5-mile walks with his Cairn terriers.

Masters was married to Alice and the family lived at 102 Norwood Road, Southport, and very soon after the war began, as one of five serving sons, he became a driver with the Army Service Corps which was attached to 141st Field Ambulance. On 7 March 1917, a year before he won his VC, Masters took part in a bombing raid on the Somme when he volunteered to go forward to an advance dressing station which was located in a quarry. From there he made a total of four trips under very heavy fire in order to rescue the wounded who were trapped in a quarry. For this action he was awarded the French Croix de Guerre which was presented by Brig. Gen. Edwards at a ceremony which took place at the Town Hall, Southport. A public subscription was set up in the town and a sum of £500 was invested in War Bonds and his wife and daughter were presented with jewelery. After being demobilised with the rank of Private, Masters became a private chauffeur once more. Also after the war he attended the Garden Party given by the King and Queen at Buckingham Palace on 26 June 1920 for the holders of the VC, and much later the VC centenary review at Hyde Park on 26 June 1956.He was an enthusiastic supporter of the RASC and became Life President of the Southport branch.

After a few months' illness, Richard George Masters died aged eighty-six at 35 Palmerston Road, Southport, on 4 April 1963. His wife Alice had predeceased him by twenty years. His funeral took place at St Cuthbert's, Churchtown, Southport, where he was buried on 8 April. The British Legion supplied bearers and a Junior Lance Corporal played the Last Post at the graveside. Two months later his family presented his VC to the Royal Corps of Transport in June 1963 and it can be seen at the Royal Logistic Corps Museum, Camberley, Surrey together with his other medals. In the early 1970s the RAF Establishment at Farnborough acquired a former inshore minesweeper for research purposes and it was named after Masters at a ceremony at Gun Wharf,

Portsmouth. The naming ceremony was carried out by Masters' sister but the boat, a large towing vessel was later paid off when her hull became suspect after been in use for thirty years. His name is also used for A Troop of 96 Squadrons RLC based at Pirbright and again with the name of the TAVR Centre at 30, Pelham Drive, Bootle, Lancashire. His decorations which also include the 1914–15 Star, BWM, VM and two Coronation Medals can be seen by appointment at the HQ RLC Officers' Mess, (RASC/RCT Institute).

In April 2006 a commemorative service was held in St Cuthbert's and his name is one of five VC holders named on a plaque in the Southport Garden of Remembrance.

J. SCHOFIELD

Givenchy, France, 9 April

At the end of 1917 the 2nd/5th T.F. Lancashire Fusiliers (164th Bde) 55th (West Lancashire) Div. moved to the training area of Coyecque, a village 10 miles west of Aire.. Two months later they took over from the 1st/7th LF in their positions to the south of the La Bassée Canal. On 17 March the battalion carried out its first tour of duty in a section of the Givenchy battlefield, to the immediate north of the canal. It was a a key position on a slight rise and was to become an area the men were to be very well acquainted with over the following few month. On 7 April the 2nd/5th Bn was relieved and went into support and reserve positions in a rear system called the Village Line which was north of the canal and ran along the Cambrin–Festubert road. The headquarters of the battalion was in Gorre.

Two days later on 9 April, the attempts of the German Army's Offensive in Flanders to reach the River Lys and Estaires began at 4.15 am on what was a foggy and raw morning and by the end of the day three British soldiers had won the VC on this the first day of the battle. The German artillery sent over a mixture of shells of different types, including gas shells and with both rear positions and their front line being targeted it was obvious to the battalion that a serious attack was impending.

Lt Col G.S. Brighten, the battalion CO, decided to send the headquarters staff slightly forward in small groups in order that they might be protected from the worst of the bombardment. The German infantry attack began at 8.45 am but the Portuguese division to the left of the 55th Div. gave way very quickly and as a consequence a wide gap on the inner flank of the British division was soon opened up. In addition the left brigade of the 55th Div. was then forced to swing back owing to the failure of their Portuguese allies and a gap appeared between it and the rest of the 164th Bde which was holding Givenchy village. With the mist in their favour and the collapse of the Portuguese division the enemy made rapid progress reaching parts of the Village Line, the main line of resistance in the 55th Div's Battle Zone which ran from Givenchy to Laventie via Lacouture reaching Pont Fixe on the La Bassée Canal and Windy Corner to the north-west.

When Colonel Brighten was informed that Windy Corner was occupied he gave orders that D Coy was to form a defensive flank and that C Coy should support it. Later B Coy, which had been in reserve at Gorre, 2 miles to the rear and close to the canal was ordered to move up to an intermediate line which ran through a wood which was about half a mile to the west of Windy Corner. Here it met up with the enemy and were forced to deploy. Reinforcements were then sent up by Colonel Brighten and the defensive flank at Windy Corner was reinforced at around 12.30 p.m.

Two remaining platoons of B Coy were then ordered to move up Wolfe Road and Orchard Road, which were communication trenches to the left and centre of the 1/5th King's Own's positions. In charge of one of them was 2nd Lt John Schofield, who led a group of nine men against a very heavily defended strong point when he was attacked by a large group of Germans who were heavily armed with bombs. However, Schofield skilfully organised his small group and with clever use of rifles and a Lewis gun pinned down the enemy, forcing them to take cover in dug-outs. In addition he captured a party of twenty Germans, and with assistance managed to clear the position that they were holding. He then gathered the survivors of his party, which now numbered ten men, and sent a message to Col Brighten to inform him that he was going to try and retake the front line. He quickly came across large pockets of the enemy both in communication trenches and in a drain to the right and left. He gave his party orders to give him covering fire and then climbed out on to the top of the trench, coming under point-blank machine-gun fire. However, he forced the Germans to surrender and this time captured about 120 men, including several officers. A short time later when still moving forward to the front line this very gallant officer was killed. He had been ably assisted by Pte C. McGill, who won the DCM and who had also stood up on the parapet.

As the day wore on Brighten continued to send up small parties to the front as they became available. Windy Corner was eventually retaken, and by 2.00 a.m. the following morning the whole brigade sector had been cleared of the invader and the British line was restored to its former position. The German attack had failed with many casualties as well as a large number of men taken prisoner. The total casualties of the 2/5th Bn amounted to 113, including the MO.

2nd Lt John Schofield was buried 5 miles NNE of Béthune in the Vieille-Chapelle New Military Cemetery in Plot III. Row C. Grave 8. Close by is the grave of 2nd Lt Joseph Collin in Grave 11 of Row A. The two men, both members of the 164th Bde of the 55th (West Lancashire) Div. and both killed on the same day defending the village of Givenchy.

The citation for Schofield's posthumous VC was published in the *London Gazette* of 28 June 1918 as follows:

> Second Lieut. Schofield led a party of nine men against a strong point which was reported strongly held by the enemy, and was attacked by about one hundred of the enemy with bombs. He deposed his men so skilfully and made such good use of rifle and Lewis-gun fire that the enemy took cover in dug-outs. This officer himself then held up and captured a party of twenty. With the help of other parties this position was then cleared of the enemy, who were all killed or captured. He then collected the remainder of his men, made his party up to ten, and proceeded towards the front line, previously informing his commanding officer as to the position, and that he was proceeding to retake the front line. He met large numbers of the enemy in a communication trench in front of him and in a drain on his right and left. His party opened rapid rifle fire, and he climbed out onto the parapet under point-blank machine-gun fire, and by his fearless demeanour and bravery forced the enemy to surrender. As a result, 123 of the enemy, including several officers, were captured by Second Lieut. Schofield and his party. This very gallant officer was killed a few minutes later.

John Schofield was born in 16 Wycollar Road, Revidge, Blackburn, Lancashire on 4 March 1892 and educated at Arnold House School. Schofield's name is also remembered at St Michael's Churchyard War Memorial and on the War Memorial in St Thomas's Church also in the town. The church was demolished some years ago when the memorial was then transferred to a nearby garden. John's brother Fred is also remembered on this memorial as he is also on the Blackburn Old Town

Hall Memorial and both men are also listed on the local golf club war memorial board together with name of Percy Thompson Dean a Zeebrugge VC.

In 1989 Schofield's decorations were presented by his niece, Mrs Janet Pratt, to the Lancashire Fusiliers Regimental Museum now called the Fusiliers Museum, where they are on display. Apart from the VC they include the 1914–15 Star, BWM and VM.

'To hell with surrender!' How Second Lieutenant J.C. Buchan won the VC.
(The Sphere, 22 June 1918)

De Wind Drive, Comber. (Keith Haines)

Manchester Redoubt.
(Peter Batchelor)

A.E. Ker in later life.
(Author)

Lt. Col. J.S. Collings-Wells VC, DSO (back row, centre). (Author)

C.L. Knox receiving his VC from King George V. (Author)

Sketch of O.C.S. Watson.
(Author)

Moreuil Wood, as seen from the French memorial. (Peter Batchelor)

Henry Cross VC at Buckingham Palace. (Author)

David Niven and Henry Cross for Carrington VC publicity pictures. (Author)

'How Lt. Col. Forbes-Robertson saved the western line from
breaking.' (The Sphere, 18 June 1918)

Captain Crowe receives his VC from King George V. (Author)

First Day Cover, British Legion Anniversary. (Author)

The Presentation by Terence Cuneo. T.B. Hardy receives his VC from King George V. (Author)

German troops moving to the front. (Martin Kitchen)

Here Lies
L/Cpl. JAMES HEWITSON V.C.
15883

Died March 2nd., 1963
And
His Wife MARY ELIZABETH
Died 2nd., June 1971 Aged 82

Rest in Peace

The grave of L. Cpl James Hewitson VC (Margaret Dickinson)

Private W. Beesley is awarded his VC by King George V. (Author)

German troops in the debris-strewn streets of Bailleul. (Martin Kitchen)

The German high command. Lef to right: Hindenburg, the Kaiser, Ludendorff. (Martin Kitchen)

German frontline troops prepare to advance. (Martin Kitchen)

British soldiers wiring trees felled across a canal to hold up the German advance. (Martin Kitchen)

Canal bridge, south of St Quentin. (Peter Batchelor)

A German soldier emerging from a dugout to surrender to advancing British troops. (Martin Kitchen)

British soldiers clearing out frontline trenches taken over from the French. (Martin Kitchen)

Chemin des Dames. (Martin Kitchen)

Prisoners captured by the Germans in a wood near Reims. (Martin Kitchen)

E.S. DOUGALL

Messines, Belgium, 10 April

A/Capt. Eric Dougall was in command of A Battery, 88th Bde RFA, 19th Div.. The fighting which took place on 10 April 1918, north of the town of Armentières, was called the Battle of Messines. Three divisions of IX Corps were involved and their strength had been severely depleted by the March offensive. These divisions were the 25th, 19th and 9th. We are concerned here with the 19th Div. Artillery and the Official History has this to say:

> Fire at short range through the lifting mist now kept the Germans from making further rapid progress, and this resistance was considerably aided by the artillery of the 19th and 9th Divs, and the three Army brigades with the 25th Division The guns not only remained in action until the infantry were pressed back in line with them, but the artillery officers undertook to keep the guns in action as long as the infantry remained. The batteries were either shooting or moving back, always keeping some guns in action.

Good communication was paramount to this plan.

In his diary Dougall made the following laconic entry on 10 April, the day he gained the VC:

> Hun attacked. Fought guns all day till 7 pm & then got them all out to behind Wytschaete. Moved to Klein Vierstraat.

The citation (*London Gazette* 4 June 1918) for what was to become his posthumous VC tells the story in greater detail:

Capt. Dougall maintained his guns in action from early morning throughout a heavy concentration of gas and high-explosive shell. Finding that he could not clear the crest, owing to the withdrawal of our line, Capt. Dougall ran his guns on to the top of the ridge to fire over open sights. By this time our infantry had been pressed back in line with the guns. Capt. Dougall at once assumed command of the situation, rallied and organised the infantry, supplied them with Lewis guns, and armed as many gunners as he could spare with rifles. With these he formed a line in front of his battery, which during this period was harassing the advancing enemy with a rapid rate of fire. Although exposed to both rifle and machine-gun fire, this officer fearlessly walked about as though on parade, calmly giving orders and encouraging everybody. He inspired the infantry with his assurance that 'so long as you stick to your trenches I will keep my guns here.' This line was maintained throughout the day, thereby delaying the enemy's advance for over 12 hours. In the evening, having expended all ammunition, the battery received orders to withdraw. This was done by man-handling the guns over a distance of about 800 yards of shell-cratered country, an almost impossible feat considering the ground and the intense machine-gun fire. Owing to Capt. Dougall's personality and skilful leadership throughout this trying day, there is no doubt that a serious breach in the line was averted.

This gallant officer was killed four days later while directing the line of fire of his battery near Kemmel and was buried in the village of Westoutre, at the British Cemetery, and he has a special memorial which means that he is buried in the cemetery but it is not known where. The village was in West Flanders, close to the French border, 7 miles south-west of Ypres and remained in Allied hands throughout the war.

Eric Stuart Dougall was born at Brookside, Tunbridge Wells, Kent on 13 April 1886, the only son of Andrew and Emily Dougall of 13 Mount Ephraim. Eric had two sisters, Ellen Mary and Kathleen Jerrett. Andrew Dougall worked as an engineer with the Tunbridge Wells Gas Company.

From 1899 Dougall was educated at Tonbridge School and in 1905 went to Pembroke College, Cambridge, to which he had won an Exhibition. He was a very talented sportsman and achieved a 'blue' in athletics and for his studies read Natural Sciences, graduating in 1908 with a Third in the Mechanical Science Tripos. After leaving Cambridge he worked for four years with the Mersey Docks and Harbour Board as a civil engineer and then from April 1912 worked for the Bombay Port Trust as an assistant engineer for three and a half years. As he was unable to get home at this time he joined the Bombay Light Horse having previously served in the OTC at Pembroke College. In January 1916 he managed to return to England on leave and retired from the company in February. He then attested in the Royal Field Artillery on 21 February and applied for a commission which was granted to the Special Reserve on 7 July. He served in France and Flanders from 24 July, initially in the Battle of the Somme including the capture of Beaumont Hamel in November and won the MC during the Battle of Messines 7 to 14 June 1917 (*London Gazette*, 25 August 1917) . By this time he had been promoted to captain and four weeks later he was made second in command of his battery. He had been serving as a group intelligence officer and took up a succession of observation posts in advanced and exposed positions and during this time was slightly wounded in the face but remained on duty.

On 4 April 1918 Dougall was made Acting Major and took over command of A Battery 88th Bde RFA and was in action during the first part of the German offensive in March/April 1918 including the Battle of Lys on 9 April and Messines 10/11 April when his VC was won on Messines Ridge. Three days later he was struck by a shell on the left hand side of his neck and died instantaneously when directing the fire of his battery on Mount Kemmel. He was buried the next day just outside Westoutre. He died four days after his thirty-second birthday.

Dougall's Adjutant described his colleague in the following terms:

> A finer man never breathed, and his place in the brigade can never be filled. He was in command of his battery at the time of his death, and for the past week had been performing most gallant work.

After her brother's death his posthumous VC was presented by the King to his sister Ellen during a private ceremony at Buckingham Palace on 10 July 1918, as her parents were unable to attend and Andrew died in March the following year. Forty odd years later, Ellen, a former nurse, bequeathed the VC to Pembroke College in 1969, together with some of Eric's diaries which cover the war period as well as other related documents. Dougall's name is also listed on the war memorial in Liverpool Club and in 1986 the Club, established in 1881, opened two refurbished lounges and named them after Chavasse and Dougall, local winners of the VC. A picture and their VC citations were also displayed. Dougall's name is also commemorated on a brass plaque in St Thomas's Cathedral, Bombay.

In 1994 the rest of Dougall's decorations including the MC, BWM and VM together with a replica of his VC were sold at Glendinings for £3,000. Other medals in the lot belonged to his sister Ellen, a former nurse. In 1996 virtually the same lot was offered for sale by Spinks with a reserve price of £2,500 and fetched £2,900. They joined his VC at Pembroke College.

A. POULTER
Lys Erquinghem, France, 10 April

At the end of March 1918 the 34th Div. arrived in the Houplines sector and held 8,000 yards of the line in front of Armentières. The enemy soon began to bombard the town with gas shells and causing heavy casualties.

On 9/10 April the 1/4 West Riding Regt (Duke of Wellington's) Territorial Force 147th Bde 49th (West Riding) Div. (TF) moved to the area north-west of Armentières to join the 34th Div. at Erquinghem, and were to cover a crossing of the River Lys. That evening the 147th Bde was defending Nieppe in support of the 34th Div., which was pulling out of Armentières.

On the 10th, in its attempts to stem the German advance and after crossing the River Lys, the Duke of Wellington's C Coy assembled near the top of the Rue Delpierre while two officers and three NCOs went forward to reconnoitre. The ground was swept by machine-gun fire and the party had to crawl to a point where the road crossed a railway. One of the officers assumed that the original objective could not in fact be reached and decided that the line of the railway should be held instead. He therefore returned to his company in order to inform them of the change of plan. However, already men were being hit while waiting for their officers and when the platoons that made up the company moved up to take positions along the railway. The right of the company was turned back to face south-west. Heavy enfilade fire from a nearby position at the Rue du Moulin was, however, making this a dangerous position. Losses mounted and stretcher-bearers became very hard pressed. One of the platoons was then sent across the railway line to a more advanced position which turned out to be safer. The company stretcher-bearers meanwhile were being hit and soon there were just not enough helpers to cope with the high numbers of casualties. It was during this period that Pte Arthur Poulter of the 1/4th Duke of Wellington's won his VC, the second to be won on the Western Front that day when he tended the wounded for hour after hour and also somehow got them to safety. However the situation grew steadily worse and the enemy brought up a field gun which they used against the company's positions at a range of only a few hundred yards. Soon there were only about twenty men remaining unwounded and the position of the railway became completely untenable. Those men who could crossed the line and took up a position to the south of it.

The battalion to the left was the 11th Suffolks (34th Div.) and in mid-afternoon they received orders to withdraw. Orders had also been issued to the 1/4th Duke of Wellington's but the runners who carried the instructions became casualties, resulting in the battalion hanging on until it was almost too late. As it was, some of the few who remained were captured when the survivors made a dash for temporary safety, taking up any wounded men that they found on their way and making for the village of Erquinghem, which fell to the enemy a short time later.

The citation (*London Gazette*, 28 June 1918) told Poulter's story in the following way:

> On ten occasions Pte Poulter carried badly wounded men on his back to a safer locality through a particularly heavy artillery and machine-gun barrage. Two of these were hit a second time whilst on his back. Again, after a withdrawal over the river [Lys] had been ordered, Pte Poulter returned in full view of the enemy, who were advancing and carried back another man who had been left behind wounded. He bandaged up over 40 men under fire, and his conduct throughout the whole day was a magnificent example to all ranks. This very gallant soldier was subsequently seriously wounded when attempting another rescue in the face of the enemy.

In Poulter's own account he wrote:

> Gradually all the stretcher bearers in my company were killed or wounded and I was left to 'carry on'. How I got through the first day alone I do not know. It is a 'wonder' to me. The enemy artillery and rifle fire was directed at us from a range that could not have been much more than 50 to 100 yards, and each time I went out a hail of shrapnel was falling around, the artillery and machine-gun barrage was terrific. . . . The first day I went out

ten times to bring back some of our wounded and had to carry them a distance of 400 or 500 yards across a bridge over a river to where the R.A.M.C. men were. I carried them on my back, and two of them were hit again before I could get them to the rear.

So from Poulter's own account published in the *Yorkshire Press* it is clear that he was performing very brave deeds for several days until on the 27th near Kemmel he was hit and badly wounded in the neck by a bullet while attending a wounded man. He was able to walk to the field ambulance station, and from there he was sent on to a French hospital, where he had an operation which was followed by two more in Croydon. When he wrote home from hospital Poulter said:

The bullet went in just behind the ear and came out against my eye. So you can tell I have had a near thing of being killed. I am living just like a baby. But my eyesight is not affected so far.

In fact Poulter had been temporarily blinded, had received six stitches to his face and had great difficulty in chewing even bread. A later letter home said:

I had another operation the same day as I received your letter. I am in bed again, I feel very weak still, and my jaws are still fast. It looks to me as if I am never going to get my mouth open again, and that will be rather awkward for me, I can tell you. I am fed up with having this sort of food and I think I should have been better off if I had been in the trenches still.

A few months later he was looking 'exceptionally well' and had only a slight scar on the right cheek and a stiffness of his lower jaw to show for his serious wounds of April.

Arthur Poulter was born in Kilgram Bridge, 4 miles east of the village of East Witton, North Yorkshire, on 16 December 1893. His father was Robert Poulter, a farmer. Arthur was one of twelve children, three daughters and nine sons, all of whom served in the war, and lived on the home farm until 1908, when Arthur left to become a farm servant. At the age of nineteen he arrived in the city of Leeds when he became a drayman with Messrs Timothy Taylor at their maltings in the Gelderd Road depot. He then changed his job and worked for Mr T. Rochford as a cartman and used to deliver firewood in the New Wortley district. In 1916 he married Ada Briggs, daughter of his then boss and the couple were to have ten children, eight boys and two girls. He enlisted in the same year with the West Riding Regt and on winning the VC became the eighth Leeds man to be so honoured. At this time his home address was 5 Thirteenth Avenue, New Wortley.

When Arthur Poulter was recovering from his war wounds at the Stamford Road Military Hospital, Norbury, the Recorder of Hull, Mr H.T. Kemp KC, who was chairman of the Society of Yorkshiremen in London, presented him with a silver watch on behalf of that institution. Poulter was in Croydon War Hospital at the end of the war and was later presented with his VC in the Ballroom at Buckingham Palace on 13 December 1918. He was discharged in 1919 and was declared fit enough to work again.

First Poulter worked in the Leeds Transport Depot and was later employed by Price (Tailors) Ltd.and over time he was to become a popular local figure. In 1953 he was involved in an accident when he was hit by a police car and had to be taken to hospital. He stopped work with Price (which had become a large tailoring concern) in February 1956 and soon after became seriously ill, dying six months later on 29 August. Ada had died two years earlier in March 1954 and their home had been in Florence Road, Wortley.

Arthur's funeral was on 1 September at St Mary's Church and he was buried at New Wortley Cemetery, Tong Road Leeds where his parents and his three infant sons are also buried. Arthur's grave reference is 2500. One of the couple's other sons, Arthur, served in the Second World War with the 8th KRRC and was reported missing in France but had been taken prisoner. He died in 1947, at he age of twenty-seven.

In December 1956 Poulter's VC and his other decorations including the 1914–15 Star, BWM, VM and two Coronation medals passed from his family to the Leeds City Museum on indefinite loan until 1999. On 14 November 1998 a new memorial, a brick plinth was unveiled in France at the place where Poulter carried the wounded to safety close to the railway in the southern end of the Rue Delpierre. It was jointly arranged by a great-grand daughter of Poulter and a daughter of the organiser, Mr Jack Thorpe, the son of a Normandy veteran who had stayed on in France after the Second World War. The memorial was the brainchild of the Erquinghem Historical Society. At the service of unveiling The 1st Bn The Duke of Wellington's Regt supplied buglers, drummers and also a guard of honour and the service was conducted by the padre and the town curé and in addition a tree was planted as part of the proceedings. At the reception after the ceremony beer was provided by Timothy Taylor & Co. the brewer from Leeds who had employed Poulter for many years and where he developed the physique which was to stand him in good stead when coping with rescuing the wounded from the battlefield.

In the Victoria Gardens in Leeds, on The Headrow side of Cookridge Street are various memorials including one to the Victoria Cross holders who were born or buried in Leeds. It is outside the Henry Moore Institute and unveiled in November 1992 and Poulter is one of 17 names inscribed on it. The Leeds War Memorial had been moved to this site in 1937 from a site in the City Square.

Poulter's VC and other medals were presented to the Regimental Museum of the Duke of Wellington's Regt which is part of the Bankfield Museum in Halifax on 11 Sept 1999 by Pat Harrison one of Poulter's daughters who lived in Wortley together with two of her surviving brothers, John and Leslie. Pat recalled the day when the VC no longer belonged to the family when Tommy, a late brother ' was about 11, and you know what kids are line – they'll swop anything. Well, the medal was in a drawer and Tommy knew this lad down the road had a bag of marbles and he thought he would swop them for the medal. ' When his mother heard of the deal she 'frog-marched her son back down the road and got the VC back, and the lad got his marbles back too'.

Poulter used to keep his VC in a drawer in the sideboard and it was taken out on occasions of street festivals and one a year Arthur would wear it next to a poppy on Remembrance Sundays. During the Second World War it was even used to raise funds when it would be wrapped up and people were invited to guess what was inside.

At a service on 31 August 2010 a new headstone on Poulter' s grave in New Wortley Cemetery was dedicated.

J. FORBES-ROBERTSON
Near Vieux Berguin, France, 11/12 April

On 11 April 1918, the third day of the Battle of Estaires, the enemy was still attacking strongly and a gradual retirement was made by the 86th and 87th infantry brigades of the 29th Div. in the direction of the village of Doulieu to the north-east of Estaires. The retirement continued the following day through the village of Bleu to Vieux Berguin north–west of the Nieppe Forest. A lack of artillery support made it even harder to keep the enemy at bay but fortunately for the British Army a stray shell hit a German ammunition dump at Bleu causing considerable havoc. It was against this backdrop that Lt Col Forbes-Robertson (1st Border Regt, 8th Bde, 29th Div.) began what was to become a series of extraordinary exploits that won him a very well earned VC. His official was published in the *London Gazette* of 22 May 1918 and told the story in the following words:

For most conspicuous bravery while commanding his battalion [1st Borders] during the heavy fighting. Through his quick judgement, resource, untiring energy and magnificent example, Lieut.-Colonel Forbes-Robertson on four separate occasions saved the line from breaking, and averted a situation which might have had the most serious and far reaching results. On the first occasion, when troops in front were falling back, he made a rapid reconnaissance on horseback, in full view of the enemy, under heavy machine gun and close-range shell fire. He then organised, and still mounted, led a counter-attack, which was completely successful in re-establishing our line. When his horse was shot under him he continued on foot. Later on the same day, when troops to the left of his line were giving way, he went to that flank and checked and steadied the line, inspiring confidence by his splendid coolness and disregard of personal danger. His horse was wounded three times, and he was thrown five times. The following day when troops on both his flanks were forced to retire, he formed a post at battalion headquarters, and with his battalion still held his ground, thereby covering the retreat of troops on his flanks. Under the heaviest fire this gallant officer fearlessly exposed himself when collecting parties, organising and encouraging. On a subsequent occasion, when troops were retiring on his left, and the condition of things on his right was obscure, he again saved the situation by his magnificent example and cool judgement. Losing a second horse, he continued alone on foot until he had established a line to which his own troops could withdraw and so conform to the general situation.

By now men of the 29th and adjacent 31st divisions were becoming severely depleted in strength and became thinly strung out over a front to the east of the Forest of Nieppe of over 10,000 yards. The line was to be held at all costs until the arrival of the 1st Australian Div., who were to take over the positions.

A Capt. J.C. Ogilvie was quoted in *The Story of the 29th Division* and added to the official Forbes-Robertson citation:

At dawn on the 11th April the regiment found itself grouped in a number of small farms in front of the Meteren Becque, at right angles to the [Vieux-Berguin–Estaires road]. . . The day opened in perfect stillness and dense fog, but out of the fog arrived the Boche with trench mortars and machine guns mounted on lorries . . . Colonel Forbes-Robertson, realising the critical state of affairs, mounted and rode alone from farm to farm, utterly regardless of his personal safety, and organised an effective defence.

The next day Forbes-Robertson continued to ride around to each farm building, which offered little protection, encouraging his men to hold on by his personal example. The distance between Bleu and Vieux Berguin was about 800 yards and was constantly swept by rifle and machine-gun fire. Forbes-Robertson even rode across this open ground and that evening he guided a retirement to a railway cutting in front of Mont de Merris to the north, where he met up with men of the Australian division at dawn the next day. Forbes-Robertson certainly seemed to live a charmed life and was to all intents and purposes omnipresent.

General Jackson, his brigade commander, another witness to Forbes-Robertson's gallantry, wrote that he 'borrowed a horse (not his own, as he considered his old dun mare too good to risk), and said to one or two of his headquarters, "The time has now come for me to take a hand"'.

On 10 August 1918 Forbes-Robertson was made a Temporary Brigadier General when serving as a staff officer.

James Forbes-Robertson was born in Strathpeffer, Ross and Cromarty, Scotland, on 7 July 1884 and was the younger of two sons of Mr and Mrs Farquhar Forbes-Robertson of 2 Keynsham Bank, Cheltenham. Mr Forbes-Robertson died in 1912 soon after the family which also included five girls, had moved from their original Cheltenham home at Langton Lodge, Charlton Kings. His wife lived to the age of 96, dying in 1946.

James attended Cheltenham College between 1897 and 1902 where his elder brother Kenneth, born in 1882 had also been a pupil.

James joined the Border Regt as a 2nd lieutenant on 2 March 1904 and on 31 August 1906 became a full lieutenant. He was made captain on 3 November and was appointed staff captain on 28 November, the same month that his brother had been killed in Belgium. He served in Gallipoli as a Transport Officer, where he was wounded, and on 12 June 1915 rejoined his battalion on the Western Front. In 1916 he won the MC (*London Gazette*, 1 January 1917). He had rejoined the Newfoundland Regt in June 1916 from the 1st Border Regt; both of whom were part of the 29th Div. Forbes-Robertson replaced Major Drew, who had been sent home on health grounds. He supervised the Newfoundlanders' training for the impending Somme offensive. On 1 July Forbes-Robertson remained behind at Louvencourt together with the 10 per cent cadre of the Newfoundlanders, a decision that almost certainly saved his life, as the battalion was virtually destroyed at Beaumont Hamel on that day. Soon after the end of the Somme battle in November 1916 he achieved the rank of temporary lieutenant colonel, and in early March 1917 he was in command of the Newfoundland Bn at the fighting, still on the Somme, in the village of Sailly-Saillisel (1–3 March), when he directed operations from his HQ set up in a position behind a trench called Cheese Trench. The battalion was relieved by the Lancashire Fusiliers on 3 March. Later the Newfoundland Bn was billeted in the village of Méaulte, still on the Somme, where Forbes-Robertson did his best to keep up the morale of the men with 'purposeful occupations'. A few weeks later the Newfoundlanders and the rest of the 29th Div. were involved in the first and second Battles of the Scarpe, part of the Battle of Arras. On 11 April the battalion was heading down the Cambrai road towards the sound of the guns and, as darkness fell, they halted at a group of wrecked buildings called Les Fosses Farm, south of the main road. They were less than a mile from Monchy, where on 14 April 1917 Forbes-Robertson won the DSO for gallantry, which was gazetted on 18 June 1917. The citation was as follows:

For conspicuous gallantry and devotion to duty when in command of his battalion during an enemy attack on Monchy. He collected all the men he could find, and taking up a position on the outskirts of the village, brought the hostile advance to an end by his fire. He undoubtedly saved a very critical situation by his promptness, bravery and example.

By coincidence attacks had been planned by the 29th Div. and the enemy on 14 April and the enemy plan was to overrun the village of Monchy le Preux. Involved in an unexpected attack, the Germans were slowly moving into Monchy instead of overwhelming it. However, the situation was still serious for the 29th Div. as there was a severe shortage of men. At 10.10 a.m. Forbes-Robertson received reports of what was happening in Monchy and sent forward his signal officer to reconnoitre. At the same time he sent his adjutant to report and also request reinforcements.

Meanwhile Forbes-Robertson organised headquarters personnel of about twenty men and the reserve of the 1st Essex Bn to man barricades and prevent the enemy from getting a foothold in the village. To the south-east of the village 2,000 of the enemy were advancing with artillery support and allied reserves were not expected for at least two hours. The small party fired vigorously at the enemy shooting forty at close range. They even put a machine gun out of action before being assisted by the 2nd Hampshires in the afternoon and as a result Monchy was saved.

On 29 August Forbes-Robertson was appointed to command the 16th Middlesex Regt in the 86th Bde and fought with them during the Battle of Cambrai in November 1917, when he was temporarily blinded yet still managed to direct operations. The 86th Bde occupied Masnières or right sector with outposts at Mon Plaisir Farm and a lock. The battalion, whose left rested on the Cambrai road and faced Rumilly, was the 1st Lancashire Fusiliers; to their right were the

16th Middlesex. On 22 March 1918 the citation for a bar to Forbes-Robertson's DSO when serving as a lieutenant colonel was published in the *London Gazette* of 26 March 1918.

> For conspicuous gallantry and devotion to duty. He led his battalion with great dash and determination in a successful attack. Later, during continual enemy attack, though wounded in the eye and unable to see, he was led about by an orderly among his men in the front line, encouraging and inspiring them by his magnificent example of courage and determination.

After the war Forbes-Robertson served with the Army of Occupation as temporary lieutenant colonel and was in turn in command of various battalions and, finally, as 155th Bde commander. He had been Mentioned in Despatches three times. His rank reverted to captain but he was increased to lieutenant colonel in October 1921, and in September 1922 he was made commander of the 2nd Borders.

In 1926 he was lieutenant colonel with the Gordon Highlanders and commanded the 2nd Bn Gordon Highlanders from 1926 to 1930, when he was made colonel. In November 1929 he attended the VC winners dinner hosted by the Prince of Wales at the House of Lords. From 1932 to 1934, when he retired, he became commander of 152nd Bde (Seaforth and Cameronians) Infantry Bde of the TA.

On 6 August 1927 he married Hilda, younger daughter of Sir Ralph Forster, at Christchurch, Sutton, Surrey. He retired in 1934 and went to live in Bourton-on-the-Water, some 15 miles from Cheltenham. He attended a couple of VC events and died at 'Chardwaw' on 5 August 1955. He was buried at in Section E1. Grave 717 of Cheltenham Borough Cemetery and is one of four VCs who are buried there. His widow Hilda died on 28 June 1976 and shares her husband's grave.

In March 2006 Forbes-Robertson's family lent his VC and other decorations to the Regimental Museum of the Border Regt in Carlisle. They included his DSO and Bar, MC, 1914–15 Star, BWM, VM, two Coronation Medals and a Defence Medal from the Second World War.

T.T. PRYCE

Near Vieux Berguin, France, 11–13 April

On 10 April 1918 the 4th Grenadier Guards 4th Guards Bde (31st Div.) were billeted in the village of Villers Brulin, when orders were received to move up to Strazeele Station via St Pol in buses. However, the transport was twelve hours late and the battalion didn't arrive at their destination until the following afternoon and the troops then marched southwards to positions in a field close to the village of Le Paradis which was also close to the Army Boundary.

Two battalions were to occupy the front line, with the 3rd Coldstreams to the right, the 4th Grenadier Guards to the left with the 2nd Irish Guards in reserve. The Guards moved off from Le Paradis at about 2.30 a.m. on the 12th but the companies dug in inadequately owing to a lack of entrenching tools. When daylight came the enemy swept them with field and machine-gun fire.

A/Capt. Thomas Pryce of the 4th Grenadier Guards (Special Reserve) won his VC at Vieux Berquin in the period 11 to 13 April 1918, the second to be won in Vieux Berquin within a 48 hour period when in command of No. 2 Coy when it made a successful advance to Pont Rondin to the south-east of Vieux Berguin. His official citation, published in the *London Gazette* of 22 May 1918 tells the story of a particularly gallant and ultimately very costly defence in human lives:

When in command of a flank to the left of the Grenadier Guards. Having been ordered to attack a village, he personally led forward two platoons, working from house to house, killing some thirty of the enemy, seven of whom he killed himself. The next day he was occupying a position with some thirty to forty men, the remainder of his company having become casualties. As early

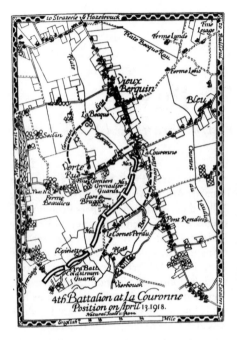

Vieux Berquin

as 8.15 a.m. his left flank was surrounded and the enemy was enfilading him. He was attacked no less than four times during the day, and each time beat off the hostile attack, killing many of the enemy. Meanwhile, the enemy brought up three field guns to within 300 yards of his line, and were firing over open sights and knocking his trench in. At 6.15 p.m. the enemy had worked to within 60 yards of his trench. He then called on his men, telling them to cheer, and charge the enemy and fight to the last. Led by Capt. Pryce, they left their trench and drove back the enemy with the bayonet some 100 yards. Half an hour later the enemy had again approached in stronger force. By this time Capt. Pryce had only 17 men left and every round of his ammunition had been fired. Determined that there should be no surrender, he once again led his men in a bayonet charge, and was last seen engaged in a fierce hand-to-hand struggle with overwhelming numbers of the enemy. With some forty men he had held back at least one enemy battalion for over ten hours. His company undoubtedly stopped the advance through the British line, and thus had great influence on the battle.

Of the deeds performed by Pryce his Commanding Officer, Lt Col W.S. Pilcher, wrote in the regimental *War Diary* (WO95/1226) in the entry of 16 April 1918 as follows:

I consider the heroic conduct of Captain Pryce and No. 2 Company to be beyond all praise, and think that the action of this Officer, who, with a small body of men, held the Germans for no less than 12 hours, on the 13th April – from about 8.15 a.m. when his left flank had been turned, to 6.15 p.m. when he made his final charge – to be difficult to surpass. More especially, as his company had carried out a determined attack the day before, and its left flank continuously since it came into the line had been in the air. How great the influence of this company's action on the general battle front has been remains to be seen; it may well have been the determining factor of the whole British line being completely driven in. The Officer who commanded this company had already been awarded the Military Cross and Bar for gallantry, and had taken part in seven attacks and raids upon the German trenches during the last three years.

Thomas Tannatt Pryce, youngest of four children, was born in Java Street, The Hague on 17 January 1886. He was the only son of a landowner, Thomas Pryce, and Rosalie Susannah Pryce of Pentreheylin Hall, Llandysilio, Montgomeryshire (now Powys), which was to the north-west of Four Crosses. Thomas senior was a tea and coffee merchant and had business interests in the city of London as well as in The Hague including extensive interests in the Dutch East Indies. He was also a local JP. The family rented the Hall which no longer exists but was where Thomas junior spent his boyhood. He also attended his first school at Mill Mead School, a small private school in the Sutton area of Shrewsbury where he was a pupil until 1900 when was 14 years old. He then continued his education at Shrewsbury Public School, in the Kingsland part of the town, before leaving to spend two terms at the Royal Agricultural College in Cirencester, and then leaving to go travelling.

On 11 March 1908 Thomas married Margaret Sybil Fordham at Ashwell in Hertfordshire and his wife was a daughter of a member of the brewing family, Mr E.S. Fordham, Metropolitan Magistrate, and Annie Fordham and the couple were to have three daughters; Rosalie, Violet and Pauline. From 1913. Thomas was a member of the Stock Exchange when he joined Henry Tudor & Son in London an for recreation he was fond of long-distance running, shooting and tennis. From 1912 the family home was at Craufurd Lodge, Gringer Hill , Maidenhead.

In 1914, three weeks after the war began, he joined the HAC as a private, and on 25 August left for France with them. On the 20th of the following month he was made lance corporal and nine months later, on 3 October, he was commissioned into the 6th Gloucesters and won the MC for gallantry on 25/26 November 1915 (*London Gazette*, 23 December 1915) at Gommecourt:

> When in charge of an assaulting column he succeeded in entering the German trenches unobserved, clearing them and bombing large parties of the enemy who were crowded in deep dug-outs. Although wounded himself, he subsequently extracted his men successfully in face of superior numbers.

After winning his first MC, Pryce was invalided home but later served in France again from May to September 1916. When 'leading a platoon in an assault at Fauquissart with great dash and determination' he won a bar to his MC (*London Gazette*, 19 July 1916):

> On 13 September 1916 Pryce was transferred to the 4th Grenadier Guards and made full Lieutenant on the following day and on 10 April 1918 promoted to Acting Captain. He was Mentioned in Despatches on 7 April 'for gallant and distinguished services in the field' but tragically six days later reported missing on 13 April 1918 at La Couronne. According to a witness, a Pte W.H.Warburton of the 4th Gren. Gds. He was 'shot through the head'.

Pryce was Mentioned in Despatches a second time on 22 May and after his death had been confirmed, his Colonel wrote the following tribute in a letter to Margaret Pryce: 'Your husband was perfectly splendid, and his record will be one of the finest episodes of the war.'

On 12 April 1919 Pryce's VC was presented to his widow by the King in the Ballroom of Buckingham Palace, she later married again, a friend of her late husband and became Mrs Waterall. In his will her first husband had left £19,281 Gross. The Guards Museum has a model which depicts Pryce winning the VC at La Couronne on 13 April and both *The Sphere* and the *Times History of the War* published a piece on him winning his VC.

His name is remembered in many ways: on Panel 1 of the Ploegsteert Memorial; the Maidenhead War Memorial in Berkshire; the Stock Exchange Memorial; and at Shrewsbury School with a Memorial Plaque. A wooden memorial board to the memory of Old Boys, displayed at Mill Mead School which included his name was moved to nearby St Giles Church after the school closed in 1966. He is also remembered at Llandysilio Church where his father, born in 1833, is also commemorated with a white marble cross and a stained glass window. His wife Rosalie, who died in 1915, is also remembered, as is one of the three daughters, Jane Esther (1884–1909), who died in The Hague. Thomas Junior is commemorated with a red marble wall plaque which was installed by his widow and one final link with the Pryce family in the church is a plaque on the organ which was presented by Mr and Mrs Pryce in 1897.

Thomas Pryce is also one of the names listed on a table in the church at Four Crosses, Llandysilio, between Welshpool and Oswestry, which is in the the same parish as Llandsilio, and on the War Memorial which was originally positioned at the crossroads of the village part of which was a busy trunk road. The noise of traffic often drowned out the words of the minister when remembrance services were being conducted. Recently a new bypass has been built to the north of the site and the decision was taken to move the memorial a hundred yards where it can be seen by motorists on the roundabout and will be also much safer for services. The whole operation took expert masons 11 months to complete and the new site was ready by 11 November 2011 however owing to poor weather and the Diamond Jubilee celebrations it was decided to delay the service of re-dedication until 24 June 2012 when it was organised by Llandysilio Community Council together with the local branch of the Royal British Legion.

Recently a new bypass has been built to the north of the site and the decision was taken to move the memorial 100 yards to where it can be seen by motorists on the roundabout. The whole operation took expert masons 11 months to complete and the new site was ready by 11 November 2011.Owing to poor weather and the Diamond Jubilee celebrations, it was decided to delay the service of re-dedication until 24 June 2012 when it was organised by Llandysilio Community Council together with the local branch of the Royal British Legion.

Capt. Pryce's VC and other decorations, including his MC and Bar, 1914–15 Star, BWM, VM and MID with Oakleaf are on loan to the Grenadier Guards.

J.J. CROWE

Neuve Eglise, Belgium, 14 April

2nd Lt/Acting Capt. John Crowe won his VC at Neuve Eglise when serving with the 2nd Worcestershire Regt on 14 April 1918, the same day as General Foch was appointed Allied Commander-in-Chief in France. The Worcesters were part of the 110th Bde of the 33rd Div. and the defence of Neuve Eglise was part of the Battle of Lys-Bailleul, with the town acting as a sort of sentinel in front of the more important town of Bailleul, 4 miles to the west, thus it would block an enemy advance.

The Worcesters had been in the village for three days and their commanding officer, Lt Col G.F.L. Stoney, was at his HQ at the local brewery when he was informed that the enemy was entering the village from the main and side streets. The battalion's C Coy managed to drive out the enemy while Stoney remained in the cellar of the brewery together with his Adjutant, Lt Crowe. Later in the afternoon he decided to move his HQ to the Mairie, a large building on the east side of the village commanding a better field of vision. At around 4.30 a.m. on the 14th there was a sudden outburst of rifle and machine-gun fire at close quarters which could only mean the enemy was at least on the outskirts of the village.

The defence of the village was thus directed from the Mairie, a windowless and almost roofless building, and Stoney and Crowe were accompanied by battalion runners. An aid-post was also established in the cellar set up by the Revd E.V. Tanner, the battalion chaplain.

By around 11.00 a.m. the men in the Mairie knew that the building was surrounded and that every conceivable exit point was covered by enemy machine guns. However, the beleaguered garrison was still

14th APRIL, 1918.

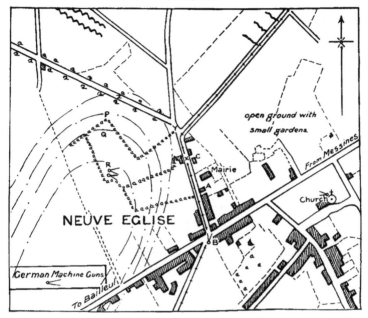

Neuve Eglise

answering fire with fire and the German machine guns were firing not only from the church but from high ground to the west, as well as from cross-roads at the end of the street. The defence included a Lewis gun which was set up at an upstairs window which proved too much for the enemy snipers, who ceased firing and temporarily withdrew. The Revd Tanner was continuing to tend the wounded and according to him, in discussing the desperate situation the besieged garrison were in that Crowe suggested to Stoney Colonel that he had a plan to get them out of their predicament. The Colonel allegedly said to Crowe: 'I am not going to order you to do it, but if you do you will be a very brave man.' Crowe together with seven volunteers left the rear of the building and first dealt with some of the enemy who were in a barn to the rear of the Mairie. Leaving five of his party on guard Crowe then took with him two NCOs and slowly moved up the hill, surprising an enemy machine-gun team which was concentrating its fire on the front of the Mairie. One of the NCOs was killed and the other wounded. Crowe then managed to recover one of the Worcesters' own guns which the Germans had been using against them then hurriedly returned to the Mairie. It was then reported that a group of the enemy was within a few hundred yards of the building. At about 1.30 p.m. Col Stoney then gave the order to retire, as the men in the Mairie decided that there was little more they could do to save themselves except to leave the building. This was to be done single-file, and one by one they rushed across the courtyard at the back of the building via the barn, their escape being covered by Pte F. Bough with his Lewis gun set up at an upstairs window. Not surprisingly the group's appearance surprised brigade HQ, who had given their colleagues up for dead. Somehow, thirty wounded men were also saved and only three of the more serious cases had to be left behind. The whole party made for the road to Dranoutre 3,000 yards away and were not pursued. Apart from Lt Crowe winning the VC and being promoted captain, Col Stoney won the DSO and Lt Charles Sargeant Jagger, later a distinguished sculptor won a MC on the far side of the village at La Trompe Cabaret.

The citation for Capt. John James Crowe's VC was published in the *London Gazette* of 28 June 1918 as follows:

For most conspicuous bravery, determination and skilful leading when the enemy, for the third time having attacked a post in a village [Neuve Eglise] ,broke past on to the high ground, and established a machine gun and snipers in the broken ground at the back of the village. Second Lieut. Crowe twice went forward with two N.C.O.'s and seven men to engage the enemy, both times in face of active machine-gun fire and sniping. His action was so daring that on each occasion the enemy withdrew from the high ground into the village, where Second Lieut. Crowe followed them, and himself opened fire upon the enemy as they collected in the doorways of the houses. On the second occasion, taking with him only two of his party, he attacked two enemy machine guns which were sweeping the post, killed both the gunners with his rifle, and prevented any others from reaching the guns and bringing them in action again. He then turned upon a party of the enemy who were lined up in front of him, killed several, and the remainder withdrew at once. He captured both guns, one of which was the battalion Lewis gun, which had been captured by the enemy the previous day. Throughout the seven days of operations Second Lieut. Crowe showed an utter disregard of danger and was recklessly brave. His personal example and cheerfulness contributed largely to the determination of the garrison of the post to hold out. It may be safely said that but for his coolness and skill at the last moment, when he personally placed the covering party in close proximity to the enemy, who were again closing round, and were also forming up in fours near by, the garrison of the post could never have effected its escape. The valour and zeal displayed by Second Lieut. Crowe were of the highest order.

John James Crowe was born in the Female Garrison Hospital, Devonport, Devon on 28 December 1876. He was the son of John James Crowe of County Wicklow, Ireland, who had served as a Private with the 36th Worcestershire Regt. When his Colonel retired he asked Crowe to help him run his estate in Baltinglas, Co. Wicklow. This was where John Crowe junior learnt to use a rifle to shoot rabbits and to fish. On 1 July 1897 he enlisted in Dublin with the Worcestershire Regt and served in the ranks for nearly eighteen years before becoming regimental sergeant major. He married Margaret Ellen Langran in Dublin on 3 February 1902 and his family lived in married quarters as he moved from post to post.

In 1914 Crowe's family set up home in Brighton at 120 Upper Lewes Road and later at Dudley House, Dudley, Brighton. During the war Crowe's parents lived at 28 Dorset Street, Reading, and each of their five sons served in the war.

On 13 August 1914 Crowe's battalion, the 3rd Worcestershires, with whom he had served for ten years, left Tidworth for France, reaching Rouen on 16 August. Until 1917 he was a Quarter-master Sergeant based at No 29 Infantry Base, B.E.F. Depot, near Rouen. He was always a keen vegetable grower and during the early part of the war he must having been growing them while stationed near Rouen. The French Government, duly impressed later awarded him with the Diploma d'Honneur de l' Encouragement.

In the final year of the war John Crowe was commissioned as a 2nd lieutenant on 1 April 1918 and on 14 April he transferred to the 2nd Worcestershire Bn. On 26 May 1918 Crowe became an acting captain and he received his VC from the King at 2nd Army Headquarters, Blendecques, 3 miles south of St Omer, on 6 August 1918. The painter Gilbert Holiday produced a picture of Crowe's VC action which appeared in the monumental history of the Worcestershire Regt in the Great War by H.V.Stacke.

Crowe finally left the Army in November 1920, having served for twenty-three years' service, but he did remain in the Reserve of Officers until 1927 when he was fifty years old. His penultimate job was Adjutant at the Folkestone disembarkation camp, which was followed by a spell of duty in Ireland. For recreation he was an all-round athlete, a particularly proficient fisherman and he won top prizes for shooting at Bisley. The last attribute was especially handy in battle conditions.

During his long service with the army he had served with the Worcestershire Regt and in three Regular battalions, the 2nd, 3rd and 4th. When he won the VC he was aged forty-one and a holder of the Long Service and Good Conduct Medals. On 23 August 1919 a Victory Parade was held in the city of Worcester when Crowe was one of four VC winners who guarded a temporary cenotaph in the cathedral grounds.

Returning to Brighton he held the position of school attendance officer for Brighton Corporation for twenty-two years and every November he often used to help sell poppies and one of his pitches was Victoria Station in London. In 1925 his wife sued him for desertion, as the couple had lived apart for at least two years and the *News of the World*, needless to say, wrote up the case with full detail.

From 1928 John Crowe's home was 16 McWilliam Road and in his later years he resumed his lifelong passion for gardening and also had an allotment. His wife predeceased him in 1960 and he had a son, Jack, who lived in Australia, and three daughters, all of whom were by now married. He was an active member of the Woodingdean over-60s club, the 'Happy Circle' for many years.

John Crowe, full of years, died at Brighton General Hospital on 27 February 1965 at the age of eighty-eight and his funeral was held at the Church of the Holy Cross, Woodingdean on 4 March but not all of his army colleagues were able to get to the church because of deep snow. Crowe's body was cremated at the Downs Crematorium, Brighton; the Revd E.V. Tanner MC assisted the vicar in conducting the service. Tanner was the battalion chaplain who had been one of Crowe's colleagues at Neuve Eglise. In addition to his VC, Crowe also received the French Croix de Guerre and during his life he regularly attended VC functions. His VC and seven medals were presented to the Worcestershire Regt in 1971 and are part of the collection in the City Art Gallery and Museum. The Woodingdean Community Centre has a seat dedicated to his memory and his name was listed on a wall plaque, which later went missing, and in the Book of Remembrance at Downs crematorium.

John Crowe was commemorated on 16 April 2011 with a memorial plaque unveiled by two of his granddaughters; Doreen Pannett and her sister Andrea Tingey. The plaque was close to the former hospice building in Nieuwerke and was unveiled some 93 years after the VC action. After a Vin d'Honneur, a tour of the village took place when the salient points of the actions in April 1918 were pointed out. Later on in the same day the family, there were thirty of them, also laid a wreath at the Menin Gate. Six days later a plaque was unveiled, again by Doreen Pannett at Dover Rifle Club where her grand father had been a member a century before between 1908 and 1911.

J.T. COUNTER
Near Boisleux St Marc, France, 16 April

94081 Pte Jack Counter was a member of the 1st Bn The King's (Liverpool Regt) 6th Bde, (2nd Div.) and won his VC near Boisleux St Marc on 16 April 1918.

Between Arras and Bapaume is a small village called Moyenneville. The 6th Bde had taken over a left sector of the line to the north-east where there was a sunken road which ran from Boyelles to Boisleux St Marc across no-man's-land. The King's Liverpool men were raided by the enemy, who had used the sunken road to cover their approach. At 9.00 a.m. the British front line trenches were heavily shelled, then after lifting the barrage the enemy began to concentrate on the support and reserve trenches. The King's Liverpool was thus enduring heavy casualties.

In spite of heavy artillery fire the enemy broke into the British lines at several points. Battalion HQ was starved of accurate information about the fighting and the only way to the front lines was down the sunken road and then across a forward slope of about 250 yards which was in full view of the enemy. A small party tried to get through, as did several runners, but they all became casualties.

It was at this time that Pte Counter volunteered to try and obtain the necessary information although he had already witnessed the deaths of men who had tried to cross the open landscape. However he succeeded in getting through and returned with the vital information on the number of the enemy who were in the British lines. A counter-attack was subsequently organised in the afternoon and the enemy began to dribble back to their own front line. By 6.30 p.m. the whole line had been restored and all the posts retaken. Counter's bravery had truly 'saved the day'. The King's was relieved by the 17th (S) Bn The Royal Fusiliers (Empire) and returned to Blairville.

The citation for Counter's VC was published in the *London Gazette* of 22 May 1918 as follows:

It was necessary for information to be obtained from the front line, in which the enemy had effected a lodgement. The only way was from the support line along a sunken road, and thence down a forward slop for about 250 yards with no cover, in full view of the enemy, and swept by their machine-gun and rifle fire. After a small party had tried unsuccessfully (the leader having been killed and another wounded before leaving the sunken road), it was thought that a single man had more chance of getting through. This was attempted five times, but on each occasion the runner was killed in full view of the position from which he had started. Private Counter, who was near his officer at the time, and had seen the five runners killed one after the other, volunteered to carry the message. He went out under terrific fire and succeeded in getting through. He then returned, carrying with him the vital information with regard to the estimated number of enemy in our line, the exact position of our flank, and the remaining strength of our troops. This information enabled his commanding officer to organise and launch the final counter-attack, which succeeded in regaining the whole of our position. Subsequently this man carried back five messages across the open under a heavy artillery barrage to company headquarters. Private Counter's extraordinary courage in facing almost certain death, because he knew that it was vital that the message should be carried, produced a most excellent impression on his young and untried companions.

Jack Thomas Counter, the son of Frank and Rosina Counter, was born in Blandford Forum, Dorset on 3 November 1898. He was educated at Blandford National School and apprenticed to the International Stores, but did not complete his apprenticeship before joining the Army in February 1917 as a Private; he was only nineteen when he won the VC. On 22 June 1918 he was presented with his award by the King at Buckingham Palace and then travelled to Blandford Forum, arriving in the early evening. He was met by the mayor and escorted to the station entrance where a large crowd waited to greet him. He was then ushered into a landau and taken in procession to the market place. The parade was headed by the town band and a large platform had been erected opposite the municipal buildings. Several speeches of congratulation were then made and the ceremonies ended with the playing of the national anthem. During the proceedings Counter was presented with £100 in War Savings Certificates together with a gold watch and chain as well as the Freedom of the Borough. He replied with a brief speech of thanks.

Cpl Counter visited Jersey with his regiment in 1919 and was demobilised in 1922, when he joined the Post Office in St Ouen as a postman. He transferred to Sunbury Common in 1925, where he lived in a council house, and returned to St Ouen on 24 November 1929, when he took over the town postal round. Counter had always been an active member of the British Legion and had joined the local branch in 1930 and was often the bearer of the King's and Queen's Standard on Legion parades. Counter and his wife lived at Conamar, Hansford Lane, First Tower, St Helier and remained on the island during the German occupation. After the war he took part in many of the VC commemorations. In 1959, when he was sixty, Counter retired from the Post Office, having made many friends in his work and on his rounds. He was a very cheerful and popular man and while he worked with the Post Office he was awarded the Imperial Service Medal.

However, after he retired he had not given up the idea of working and for a time held a position with G.D. Laurens, Queen Street and Bath Street, and then with R. Le Bail & Co. of Grenville Street. Laurens was a very old Jersey business and dealt in ships' chandlery and in general goods. Le Bail was a wholesaler of groceries and frozen foods opposite the former Forum Cinema.

In September 1970 when on a family visit to the mainland Counter was staying at Bristol with his sister and on 17 September he decided to visit his birthplace at Blandford Forum. It was when he was staying with his sister-in-law, Mrs Edith Counter in Dorset House, Dorset Street, when he collapsed and died when enjoying a cup of tea, shortly before he was due to catch a coach to take him back to Bristol. Counter was a widower of nine months and his only child, a daughter, had died in 1964. He was cremated at Bournemouth Crematorium on 24 September and his ashes were later taken to St Helier, Jersey. Blandford Corporation was represented at the service by the mayor, Alderman Mrs J.F. Lane. Other mourners present, apart from members of his family, were members of the King's Regt and British Legion of Blandford and of Jersey. A cushion in the design of a Victoria Cross was one of the wreaths placed at the local war memorial, as well as one from the British Legion. The cut flowers were later presented to the local hospital.

To mark the fiftieth anniversary of the British Legion, the Post Office issued a set of four commemorative stamps on 15 July 1971 and Counter's portrait was reproduced on the 7 ½p stamp. In 1972 there was a small controversy about the suitability of a memorial to Counter which took the form of an inscribed piece of oak 18 inches by 6 inches which was placed in St Andrew's Church, First Tower, St Helier, where Counter's ashes were buried in the family plot. It was placed as a gift from the Jersey Branch of the now Royal British Legion and was close to a plaque to the memory of the Old Contemptibles and dedicated on 20 August 1972. After the address at the service, the Last Post and Reveille were played by a member of the island band.

There is also a plaque to Counter's memory close to the war memorial at St Andrews and a Jack Counter Close at First Tower and also a Counter House in St Saviour's, Jersey.

In the 1970s Counter's VC and medals were sold to a Canadian buyer but in 1989 were purchased by a Jersey heritage group for between £12,000 and £15,000 and are now in the hands of the Société Jersiaise and on display in the Jersey Museum.

J.E. WOODALL

La Pannerie, France, 22 April

On 11 April the 1st Bn Rifle Bde (Prince Consort's Own) (11th Bde, 4th Div.) was rushed up in buses to a position on the La Bassée Canal in order to try and stem the German breakthrough on the Lys. Over the next eleven days it was involved in severe fighting in the area around Hinges and Robecq. On the 22nd, together with the 1st Hampshires of the same brigade, it took part in an attack which helped to secure the canal. It was during this fighting that L. Sgt Joseph Woodall won his VC on the far side of the canal at La Pannerie, near Hinges. To quote from Woodall's VC citation, he was:

> ... in command of a platoon, which, during the advance, was held up by a machine gun. On his own initiative he rushed forward, and, single handed, captured the gun and eight men. After the objective had been gained, heavy fire was encountered from a farmhouse some two hundred yards in front. Sergt. Woodall collected ten men, and with great dash and gallantry rushed the farm and took thirty prisoners. Shortly afterwards, when the officer in charge was killed, he took entire command, reorganised the two platoons, and disposed them most skilfully. Throughout the day in spite of intense shelling and machine-gun fire, this gallant N.C.O. was constantly on the move, encouraging the men and finding out and sending back invaluable information. The example set by Sergt. Woodall was simply magnificent, and had a marked effect on the troops. The success of the operation on this portion of the front is attributed almost entirely to his coolness, courage and utter disregard for his own personal safety.

❖ ❖ ❖

Joseph Edward Woodall was born in Robinson Street, off Regent Road, Salford, Manchester, on 1 June 1896, he was the eldest of ten children. His father worked for the London and North Western Railway Company as a train driver. Joseph attended St Ambrose Infants' School and when the family moved to Beech Street, Patricroft, Eccles, Manchester, he went to St Michael's Junior and Beech Street Schools. His family moved again in 1903 and settled at 39 Bridgewater Street, Winton, Eccles. When he ended his school days Joseph began working with a local newsagent and later had a job at Ermen and Roby's Mill in Cawdor Street, Patricroft; and afterwards at George Mort's Quilt Manufacturers, Leigh Street, where he was employed as a jobber. On 2 September 1914 he enlisted with the 1st Bn The Rifle Bde (Prince Consort's Own) with army number Z1030.

He was presented with his VC in the Ballroom at Buckingham Palace by the King on 23 November 1918. When he arrived back at Eccles he was met at the Town Hall by the mayor, who escorted him with a brass band to the Palladium Cinema, where he was presented with an illuminated address and some money from a locally organised public fund.

Woodall remained in the Army after the war ended and on 7 March 1919 became a 2nd lieutenant with one of the Service battalions of The Rifle Bde. Two years later he retired with the rank of captain on 1 September 1921. After he left the army Woodall was presented with a bicycle by George Mort, one of his former employers, although he was not offered his old job back. However, he was able to get a position with the Royton Mill in Oldham but had a severe setback when he lost part of his arm while working with an unfenced scutching machine. He was later retrained and given the job of a grey buyer for the United Turkey Red Company in Manchester. At some point he moved with his family to Bramhall in Cheshire and from there in 1955 he moved to Dun Laoghaire in Southern Ireland.

Woodall was married to Rosanna Leighton and they had two children, Patricia and David; the latter died on 14 April 1996. Woodall didn't attend the 1956 VC review, although he did attend a Festival of Remembrance in Dublin in November 1956, together with three other VC holders, – Adrian Carton de Wiart, John Moyney and James Duffy. The festival included a film of the 1956 Hyde Park review, and glimpses of the Queen and of Sir Winston Churchill were greeted with loud applause.

Joseph Woodall died at St Michael's Hospital, Dun Laoghaire on 2 January 1962 as a result of an accident at Newtownsmith. It appears that he had a seizure and perhaps fell into an open fire as when he was found by a neighbour, Joseph King, he was very badly burnt. He was buried in Dean's Grange Cemetery in the town in St Patrick's Plot H. 173.The Plot was purchased by his neighbour, Joseph King who is also buried in it. On 2 January 2010 a new headstone to Woodall's memory was unveiled in another part of the cemetery.

Woodall's name is included on the Rifle Brigade Memorial in Winchester Cathedral and his VC and medals; including the 1914–15 Star, BWM, VM and two Coronation Medals, are held by the Royal Green Jackets in the city. However at the time of writing his VC is on loan to the Imperial War Museum for display in their Victoria Cross Gallery.

C.W.K. SADLIER
Villers-Bretonneux, France, 24/25 April

Lt Clifford Sadlier of the 51st Bn, Australian Imperial Force (13th Australian Infantry Bde, 4th Australian Div.) won his VC during the second battle of Villers-Bretonneux on 24/25 April 1918. The military operations at this time were simply described as 'Actions of Villers-Bretonneux'.

On 24 April the Germans had occupied positions to the south-east of the village for nearly three weeks and decided to try and break out and make an attempt to reach the important city of Amiens, long one of their goals. They began a concerted attack at dawn in the fog and managed to capture Villers-Bretonneux, Abbey Wood to the west of the village and part of Hangard Wood to the south of it.

Towards evening an Allied counter-attack was planned which was to be made up of two pincer movements, with the 15th Bde to the north and the 13th Bde to the south. The latter was fired upon from the direction of Abbey Wood while they were assembling at 10.00 p.m. A British brigade was given the task of retaking Hangard Wood which was also to mop up in the wake of the Australians.

Lt Sadlier of the 51st Bn was instructed to capture Monument Wood south-east of the village and had collected men from his bombing section. Despite being wounded in the thigh he, together with Sgt C.A. Stokes, led them against machine guns. Casualties were very heavy and when Stokes, from the platoon next to Sadlier, asked him what he was going to do, he was told: 'Carry out the order – go straight to our objective.' 'You can't do it', said Stokes, 'you'll all be killed.' 'Well, what can we do?' 'Collect your bombers and go into the wood and bomb those guns out.'

It seemed certain death and no doubt the enemy was extremely surprised at the ferocity of the attack in the middle of the night. The attack was very bold and the Western Australians were not going to allow the enemy to recover from the surprise. Subsequently the machine-gun crews were killed and two guns captured. Not content with that, Sadlier on his own attacked a third machine gun, killed its crew and captured the gun.

Sadlier was then wounded a second time and was sent back to the rear. However, Stokes carried on and managed to put the guns along the wood out of action. The southern pincer was thus cleared to sweep forward and to join up with the northern pincer. So by dawn Villers-Bretonneux had been retaken.

Both Stokes and Sadlier were recommended for the VC but only Sadlier was awarded it, Stokes had to make do with a DCM.

The citation for Sadlier's VC was published as follows in the *London Gazette* of 11 July 1918 and he was presented with his award by the King at Buckingham Palace six days later.

> For most conspicuous bravery during a counter-attack by his battalion on strong enemy positions. Lieut. Sadlier's battalion, had to advance through a wood when a strong enemy machine-gun post caused casualties and prevented the platoon from advancing. Although himself wounded, he at once collected his bombing section, led them against the machine guns, and succeeded in killing the crews and capturing two of the guns. By this time Lieut. Sadlier's party were all casualties, and he alone attacked a third enemy machine gun with his revolver, killing the crew of four and taking the gun. In doing so, he was again wounded. The very gallant conduct of this officer was the means of clearing the flank and allowing the battalion to move forward, thereby saving a most critical situation. His coolness and utter disregard of danger inspired all.

Clifford William King Sadlier was born on 11 June 1892 in Camberwell, Victoria, Australia, the fourth child of Irish-born Thomas George Sadlier and his wife Mary Ann Sadlier (nee Roberts) who came from Adelaide. Clifford was educated at the University High School in Melbourne. The family moved to Perth in Western Australia and settled in Subiaco. As a young man Clifford became a commercial traveller before enlisting in the Army in Perth on 25 May 1915. He was 5 foot 9 inches tall and posted to 1st Australian General Hospital, Australian Army Medical Corps; he embarked to Egypt in June 1915 and served with the Australian General Hospital in Heliopolis. He returned briefly to Australia for convalescence in March 1916 before embarking for England on 9 November as a member of the 7th Reinforcements for the the the 51st Bn. His rank was acting sergeant but it reverted to the rank of private on 11 January 1917 and he was sent on an NCO course at Tidworth. He left for France, where he became a member of the 51st Bn of the 13th Bde on 13 May. Five days later he was promoted to Corporal and on 14 July 1917 he was appointed 2nd lieutenant and promoted to full lieutenant on 1 April 1918. As he was so badly wounded during his VC action that his active military career was at an end. He was invalided home to Australia on 24 October and his AIF appointment came to an end on 4 March 1919.

After the war he became state secretary of the Returned Soldiers League and was appointed its first president. On 23 August 1922 he married Maude Victoria Moore at St Mary's Anglican Church in Perth and for the rest of the 1920s worked as a manufacturer's agent, before briefly running his own agency in 1929. In 1930 he contested the state seat of Nedlands as a Nationalist but without success. In 1934 his marriage ended in divorce and on 17 July 1936 he married Alice Edith Smart at the Presbyterian manse, Subiaco, Perth. From 1949 he worked as a clerk in the repatriation department in Perth but was invalided out of public service jobs and moved to 151 Bussell Highway, Busselton, near Perth where in his retirement gardening became his chief hobby. In June 1956 he was a member of the Australian contingent to theVC review in London.

For ten years Sadlier had been suffering from emphysematic bronchitis and on 28 April 1964 he died in Busselton District Hospiital. A bearer party drawn from members of 22nd Construction Squadron Royal Australian Engineers took part in his funeral and he was cremated and his ashes were interred in Karrakatta Cemetery, Perth until 17 May 1990 when they were scattered in the Indian Ocean. His name is commemorated in the Crematorium on Row D in Wall 5. His decorations which apart from the VC include; the 1914–15 Star, VM, BWM and two Coronation medals are in St George's Cathedral, Perth, Western Australia. He is also remembered with Sadlier Place in Canberra, in the Australian War Memorial and in the Victoria Cross Memorial Park also in the city. Finally as with all Australian holders of the VC he is commemorated in the Victoria Cross Memorial in the Queen Victoria building in Sydney.

T.B. HARDY

Near Bucquoy and East of
Gommecourt, France, 25–27 April

Theodore Hardy won the VC after winning both the DSO and MC and became the most decorated non-combatant of the Great War. His VC was won in a series of acts of bravery on 5, 25, 26 and 27 April 1918. On the 5th, he was assisting the 8th (S) Bn The Lincolnshire Regt, who with the 8th (S) The Somerset Light Infantry, both of the 37th Div., were attempting to capture Rossignol Wood, east of Gommecourt, together with the enemy trenches to the west and south of it. The attack failed, leaving many wounded behind in the wood, and with the assistance of a Sergeant Hardy he was able to rescue one of the wounded from a position very close to a German pill box.

In the 1990s the wood was still full of shell holes; German trench lines, fallen trees and remains of the German pill box can still be seen in the wood, about 120 yards on the south-west side from the Bucquoy road. In addition in the spring there were masses of cowslips and the odd deer. Apart from Hardy's actions the wood also has links with Dick Travis VC and the German writer Ernst Jünger, author of *The Storm of Steel*.

Numerous tributes were made to Hardy's fearlessness and courage, and that he did not seem to want to be anywhere other than in a position close to the front line and therefore close to continuous danger. Even when ordered to return to his own lines he very often found some pretext for going out yet again to minister to the men on the battlefield.

The citation for his VC was published on 11 July 1918 as follows:

Although over fifty years of age, he has, by his fearlessness, devotion to men of his battalion, and quiet, unobtrusive manner, won the respect and admiration of the whole division. His marvelous energy and endurance would even be remarkable in a very much younger man, and his valour and devotion are exemplified in the following incidents: An infantry patrol had gone out to attack a previously located enemy post in the ruins of a village, the Rev. T.B.Hardy (C.F.) being then at company headquarters. Hearing firing, he followed the patrol, and about 400 yards beyond our front line of posts found an officer of the patrol dangerously wounded. He remained with the officer until he was able to get assistance to bring him in. During this time there was a great deal of firing, and an enemy patrol actually penetrated between the spot at which, the officer was lying and our front line and captured three of our men. On a second occasion, when an enemy shell exploded in the middle of one of our posts, the Rev. T.B.Hardy at once made his way to the spot, despite the shell and trench-mortar fire which was going on at the time, and set to work to extricate the buried men. He succeeded in getting out one man who had been completely buried. He then set to work to extricate a second man, who was found to be dead. During the whole of his time he was digging out the men the chaplain was in great danger, not only from shell fire, but also because of the dangerous condition of the wall of the building which had been hit by the shell which buried the men. On a third occasion he displayed the greatest devotion to duty when our infantry, after a successful attack, were gradually forced back to their starting trench. After it was believed that all our men had withdrawn from the wood, Chaplain Hardy came out of it, and on reaching an advanced post, asked the men to help him to get in a wounded man. Accompanied by a sergeant, he made his way to the spot where the man lay, within ten yards of a pill-box, which had been captured in the morning, but was subsequently recaptured and occupied by the enemy. The wounded man was too weak to stand, but between them the Chaplain and the sergeant eventually succeeded in getting him to our lines. Throughout the day the enemy's artillery, machine-gun fire and trench-mortar fire was continuous, and caused many casualties. Notwithstanding, this very gallant chaplain was seen moving quietly amongst the men and tending the wounded, absolutely regardless of his personal safety...

Theodore Bayley Hardy was born at Barnfield House, Southernhay, Exeter on 20 October 1863, the son of George and Sarah Richardson Hardy. Theodore had several half-brothers from his mother's two earlier marriages and one full brother, Ernest. George, who had been a commercial traveller, died three years after Theodore's birth. At first Theodore and Ernest were taught at home by their mother until they were nine or ten years old. They then went as boarders to the City of London School, and later Theodore went to London University, where he gained a BA in 1889.

On 13 September 1888 he married Florence Elisabeth Hastings in Belfast, the daughter of an architect. The couple had two children, William and Mary Elizabeth, but did not have much money with which to bring up their young family. In 1898, when Theodore was 35, he was ordained deacon in Southwell Minster and later to the curacy at Burton Joyce-with-Bulcote (1898–1902) and later the curacy of at St Augustine's, New Bagford (1902–7). In the sixteen years between 1891 and 1907 Hardy was a teacher at Nottingham High School and later became Head Master of Bentham Grammar School until 1913, when he was forced to resign because his wife had become seriously ill. He was then offered the living at Hutton Roof, a fairly bleak and remote hamlet near Kirkby Lonsdale, Westmoreland, as priest in charge. It was here in June that Florence died and was buried in Hutton Roof churchyard.

After the war began Hardy volunteered to serve with the Army but was rejected because of his age. However, he continued to volunteer and also took a course as a stretcher-bearer. Finally he was accepted as a Temporary Chaplain 4th Class on 16 September 1916. His two children were also to serve in the war: William, born in 1892, had become a doctor and served in the Mediterranean with the RAMC; Hardy's daughter, Mary Elizabeth, became a nurse and worked in Dunkirk at a Red Cross hospital for two years.

Hardy's first appointment as Temporary Chaplain was on attachment to the 8th (Service) Bn The Lincolnshire Regt (63rd Bde, 37th Div.) and prior to joining them he spent the last few months of 1916 at the vast British Camp at Etaples, to the south of Boulogne. In December he met Geoffrey Studdert-Kennedy, better known as 'Woodbine Willy'. This brief meeting was to have a very considerable influence on Hardy, who spent the greater part of the next two years helping to save lives and souls in the front line. He began by going to the part of the Front near Lens in December 1916, then south to the Arras sector at the end of March 1917.

Three months later he moved northwards again, this time to the Ypres Salient, and was awarded the DSO for gallantry carried out in on 18 October 1917 during the battle of Passchendaele, when he went out repeatedly with the stretcher-bearers to try and save lives. The citation for his DSO was published as follows in the *London Gazette* on 7 March 1918 as follows:

> He went out into the open to help bring in wounded; on discovering a man buried in mud, whom it was impossible to extricate, he remained under fire ministering to his spiritual and bodily comfort till he died.

Hardy was presented with the ribbons of the DSO at Arcques by Sir Henry Rawlinson in the winter of 1917/18 and his daughter Elizabeth was invited to the ceremony. This award was swiftly followed up in December (*London Gazette* 23 April 1918) with the MC for going out repeatedly with the stretcher-bearers during an attack in order to save lives. Hardy stayed in the Ypres sector until the end of March 1918 and then moved southwards to Gommecourt, a village to the north-west of Albert. He remained there until August and then took part in the last Allied offensive.

Elizabeth also attended the VC presentation ceremony. She left her nursing work at the Red Cross hospital in Dunkirk and travelled in a car provided for her by General Byng to Third Army HQ, the Château Frohen-le-Grand, Lucheux. She was able to spend an hour with her father. Elizabeth is clearly seen in the contemporary pictures of the VC presentation. The ceremony took place at 4.00 p.m.on 9 August. First the King spoke to each of his Generals in turn and on learning of Elizabeth's presence he asked for her to be presented to him and spoke to her about her father. At this presentation Hardy was the first person to receive an award and the reading of his citation and deeds took ten minutes. During this time Hardy looked like a scolded schoolboy and cameras were on him the whole time, although only a few seconds of the film that dealt with the ceremony survive. It was during this afternoon that Gregg and Beesley also received their VCs from the King. Later in the the salon of the château, a tea party took place with the King, about a dozen men and one woman, Elizabeth Hardy.

In September Hardy was appointed Honorary Chaplain to the King, and in October was severely wounded in the thigh when crossing a temporary bridge over the River Selle. He was taken to No. 2 Red Cross Hospital in Rouen. In addition to his wounds he was also suffering from extreme fatigue; pneumonia set in and he became slightly delirious and died at the hospital on 18 October 1918. He was buried at St Sever Cemetery, Extension Block S.Plot V. Row J. The cemetery, which is about 2 miles from the centre of Rouen, was begun in 1915 and was used in connection with the many hospitals in the area during the war. At the funeral six of the Rouen Chaplains acted as bearers. Once again his daughter was with her father and the Base Commandant, Gen. Phillips, showed her every sympathy and consideration. The King also showed great sympathy in remembering to send her and her brother William telegrams expressing his sorrow at their father's death.

Elizabeth, a graduate of London University, was herself to lead a remarkable life. After her father died she took up teaching and became headmistress of a girls' school in Rangoon. She narrowly escaped being captured by the Japanese in the Second World War and then took over a school in Bangalore before coming back to England and retiring to Cornwall.

A plaque to Hardy's memory was dedicated in August 1919 in the north aisle of Carlisle Cathedral. There is also a memorial plaque at Hutton Roof, Kirkby Lonsdale, which was also dedicated in August 1919 at a crowded service. A separate memorial was erected in the churchyard, made of limestone brought down from the crag. The inscription reads:

> Erected by the parishioners of Hutton Roof in memory of T.B. Hardy VC, DSO, MC, CF, Pte J.W. Thistlewaite, Pte J.W. Wilson, Pte C. Charnley who gave their lives for their King and Country in the cause of Justice and Right. 'They Shall Rise Again'. 1914–1918.

In 1965 his VC was presented on permanent loan by Miss P.H. Hardy, Hardy's granddaughter, to the Royal Army Chaplains' Department HQ at Bagshot Park, Surrey. The award is at present kept in the Museum of Army Chaplaincy in Amport, Hampshire. His other decorations apart from the DSO and MC include the BWM and VM and Oakleaf for MID.

In 1967 the artist Terence Cuneo painted a picture of the presentation at which Hardy received his VC from the King but when inspected alongside the original photograph of the ceremony it seems rather inaccurate. Hardy is wearing a helmet instead of an Army hat and the buildings show signs of shell damage which was not visible in the photograph. The painting is in the collection of the Royal Army Chaplains' Department. A copy of the Cuneo painting is also on display in the church at Hutton.

Theodore Hardy's birthplace, Barnfield House, narrowly being destroyed in the Exeter Blitz during the Second World War and is now an office building known as 25 Southernhay East, which is situated on the corner of Southernhay East and Barnfield Road. In 1940 it was occupied by the GPO Engineering Department and after 1951 the building was no longer used for residential purposes. On 27 June 2006 an oval green plaque to his memory was unveiled through the arrangements of the Exeter City Council together with The Devon Armed Charities. Hardy's name is also commemorated in the Garrison Church in Potsea, Hampshire. Nottingham High School Junior School has a schoolhouse named after him and there is a plaque to his memory in the Harrow Arts Centre in Pinner Middlesex, formerly the Royal Commercial Travellers School which he attended.

St John's Church, Hutton Roof is now part of the Rainbow Parish which is centered on Kirkby Lonsdale to the north-east of the village, and a thanksgiving service for Hardy's life is held every ten years with the most recent being on 19 October 2008. A film on Hardy's life has been made for the Museum of Army Chaplaincy and it was first shown in the Hutton Roof village hall on 29 January 2010.

J. HEWITSON
Near Givenchy, France, 16 April

James Hewitson (1/4th (TF) King's Own (Royal Lancaster Regt), 164th Bde, 55th Div.) won the VC on 26 April 1918. To paraphrase the Official History: 'At 2 p.m. an attempt was made to recapture part of the former front-line posts to the north-east and east of Givenchy, to the east of Béthune and close to La Bassée Canal. Two companies were employed in this task only and owing to German counter-attacks the attempts were unsuccessful although thirty prisoners were captured.'

According to Hewitson's VC citation (*London Gazette*, 28 June 1918):

> ... in a daylight attacks on a series of crater posts, L.-Corpl. Hewitson led his party to their objective with dash and vigour, clearing the enemy from both trench and dug-outs, killing in one dug-out six of the enemy who would not surrender. After capturing the final objective, he observed a hostile machine-gun team coming into action against his men. Working his way round the edge of the crater, he attacked the team, killing four and capturing one. Shortly afterwards he engaged a hostile bombing party which was attacking a Lewis-gun post. He routed the party, killing six of them. The extraordinary feats of daring performed by this gallant N.C.O. crushed the hostile opposition at this point.

It would appear that the citation puts a much better gloss on the incident than the Official History does.

Hewitson was wounded three times in the war, at Ypres, on the Somme and at Messines. He also served at Loos, Passchendaele and Armentières and at the war held the rank of corporal.

2nd Lt J. Collin, also of the 1/4 King's Own, also won the VC for gallantry at Givenchy on 9 April.

James Hewitson, (always known as Jimmy) was the son of Matthew and Mary Hewitson (née Hayton), and was born at Thwaite Farm, Coniston, Lancashire on 15 October 1892 which in the 1970s was to become part of the administrative county of Cumbria. His father worked in agriculture and at one time had been the last horse drawn coach driver in the Coniston area. James attended the local Church of England School and prior to the war helped on the family farm and also in other farms. Three months after the outbreak of war he enlisted on 17 November 1914 as a member of the 8th (Service) Bn King's Own and was later transferred to the 1/4 Bn (TF); his service number was 15833. He won his VC when a Lance Corporal and received the award from the King in France on 8 August 1918 and later, when he returned home, he was given a full civic welcome.

After the war, still suffering from war wounds, he married a local girl, Mary Elizabeth (née Dugdale) and worked as a local road repairer and in order to assist him in getting around he bought a motorbike, a Matchless 500 at a cost was £47, 17, 6. He was also fit enough to take part in regimental reunions. There is a story which cannot be verified or even dated that on one occasion he was approached by a former officer who thanked him for saving his life during the war and in a gesture of gratitude paid for the cost of Hewitson and his wife Mary to spend a few days in the south of England on holiday.

As with many other Great War holders of the VC Hewitson's life was blighted by his experiences in the war and after ten years he was forced to retire from working on the roads as he was suffering from neurasthenia and becoming mentally ill. He was taken to Stone House Mental Hospital in Dartford, Kent where he was placed under lock and key for sixteen-and-a-half years. His wife had therefore to continue to look after the family home without the help of her husband. At one point she lived in a whitewashed cottage on the mountainside which didn't even boast a bathroom and in order to subsidise her existence used to take in the squire's shirts (Major Hext's?) for washing and also sold garden produce in order to help to pay for her daughter Dorothy's clothing.

However it appears that Hewitson was well enough to return to Coniston in the early 1950s, but had to undergo an operation to remove shrapnel from his spine and in 1954 a further operation was performed to remove more shrapnel from his shoulder, however he was still fit enough to attend the 1956 VC centenary in London. At this period of his life he was also able to earn 2s 6d an hour for cutting hedges, cleaning out pigsties, laying out rose gardens and digging graves, but he was only able to do a few hours of this work in a week. The family moved home several times including living in Forge Cottage opposite the Ruskin museum.

At the age of 70 Hewitson died at Stanley Hospital, Ulverston, Lancashire, on 2 March 1963 and at his funeral four days later at Coniston six NCOs carried his coffin 200 yards from the village hall to the parish church of St Andrews. During the service the Last Post was played at the graveside which was sited very close to the village war memorial and Reveille was played at the end of the service. In June 1971, Mary Elizabeth Hewitson was buried in the same grave as her husband.

Hewitson is also remembered inside St Andrew Church, Coniston, with a memorial plaque and shield and he is also remembered on the local war memorial. In 1980 his VC and other decorations including; the 1914–15 Star, BWM, VM and two Coronation medals were in the hands of a Mr J. Derwent and at the present time they are still in private hands. By 1990 the Regimental Museum had at least managed to obtain Hewitson's tunic, cap and uniform as they were donated by Hewitson's daughter Dorothy by then Mrs Dodd and the uniform shows four overseas chevrons and four wound stripes. Mrs Dodd was to have four children who her father lived long enough to know.

In September 2012 an exhibit of the life and career of James Hewitson was set up in the excellent Ruskin Museum in Coniston which included his Matchless motorbike as part of the display.

G.B. McKean
Gavrelle Sector, France, 27/28 April

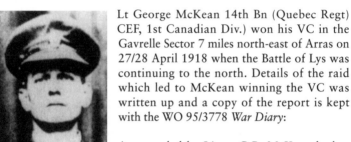

Lt George McKean 14th Bn (Quebec Regt) CEF, 1st Canadian Div.) won his VC in the Gavrelle Sector 7 miles north-east of Arras on 27/28 April 1918 when the Battle of Lys was continuing to the north. Details of the raid which led to McKean winning the VC was written up and a copy of the report is kept with the WO 95/3778 *War Diary*:

A group led by Lieut. G.B. McKean had the hardest task of all. The occupants of this trench, Hussar, were hemmed in by the barrage and had to fight or surrender. They decided to fight and so obstinately did they fight that Lieut. McKean was forced to send to the front line company for bombs. This exchange of bombs went on for several minutes and as there was considerable wire in front of the block things seemed shaky for a minute or so. Lieut. McKean set an example by making a flying dive over the block, landing 'Head on', striking the stomach of a Hun. The Hun was considerably startled – Lieut. McKean's revolver was in his hand ready for use when he dived – exit Hun. The rest of the group at once tumbled over and this block gave no further trouble. The second block fought for a few minutes and on being rushed the garrison ran to the dugout at H 5d 87.07. A mobile charge was thrown down by Sergeant Jones which exploded almost at once, not giving the Sergeant time to get clear and he was killed. A machine gun was destroyed with this dugout. Too much cannot be said of the excellent leadership and personal courage of Lieut. McKean.

His VC citation was published in the *London Gazette* of 28 June which tells the extraordinary story as follows:

... Lieut. McKean's party which was operating on the right flank, was held up in a block in the communication trench by most intense fire from hand grenades and machine guns. The block, which was too close to our trenches to have been engaged by the preliminary bombardment, was well protected by wire and covered by a well-protected machine gun thirty yards behind it. Realising if this block were not destroyed the success of the whole operation might be marred, he ran into the open to the right flank of the block, and with utter disregard of danger, leaped over the block head first on top of the enemy. Whilst lying on the ground on top of one of the enemy, another rushed at him with fixed bayonet. Lieut. McKean shot him through the body and then shot the enemy underneath him, who was struggling violently. This very gallant action enabled this position to be captured. Lieut. McKean's supply of bombs ran out at this time, and he sent back to our front line for a fresh supply. Whilst waiting for them, he engaged the enemy single-handed. When the bombs arrived, he fearlessly rushed the second block, killing two of the enemy, captured four others, and drove the remaining garrison, including a hostile machine-gun section, into a dug-out. The dug-out, with its occupants and machine gun, was destroyed. This officer's splendid bravery and dash undoubtedly saved many lives, for had not this position been captured the whole of the raiding party would have been exposed to dangerous enfilading fire during the withdrawal. His leadership at all times has been beyond praise.

A few months later, on 2 September, McKean won the MC at Cagnicourt, 11 miles south east of Arras during which time he was also severely wounded. The citation read:

As scout officer during two days' heavy fighting, he with his scouts led the battalion forward and sent in accurate reports and rallied men who had lost their officers. He was early wounded but pressed forward and entered Cagnicourt with three men, and observing a party of the enemy over 100 strong retiring from the village he dashed to a flank and headed them off and caused them all to surrender. Had these enemy troops been allowed to gain the high ground east of the village they would have inflicted heavy casualties on our troops. He continued to send in reports until exhausted by loss of blood. His conduct throughout was magnificent.

He was taken to the Red Cross Hospital at Le Treport and was soon invalided back to England and was unable to return to his regiment as during his convalescence he was also suffering from shell shock.

George Burdon McKean was the son of James McKean, a merchant, and his wife Jane Ann (née Henderson). He was born in Willington, Bishop Auckland, Co. Durham on 4 July 1888. He attended Bishop Barrington School, which had been endowed and erected in 1810 and it appears to have been a school for boys from poor homes who were bright enough to deserve a good education. The building was sited opposite the Town Hall in the Market Place but the school was later closed. At the time of writing part of the original building still exists though and is now occupied by a turf accountant. A new school was built elsewhere in the town and is called the Barrington Comprehensive. After leaving school McKean served an apprenticeship as a cabinet-maker with Messrs T. Thompson's Exors. of Newgate Street. However his future was elsewhere and he left Bishop Auckland in 1902 at the age of 14 in order to join his brother who was farming near Lethbridge, Alta in Canada, who had gone on ahead. On arrival in Canada George initially worked on a cattle ranch and later on a farm which was owned by his brother. In 1911 he entered Robertson College and later enrolled in the University of Alberta, when he took an arts course. His studies were interrupted when war was declared and during his time there he had also become a keen sportsman and football player and played for the college. He also found time to be scoutmaster of a troop attached to the Robertson Presbyterian Church in Edmonton and during the summers acted as a student missionary at Hardieville and Athabasca Landing (Athabasca)

McKean attempted to enlist in 1915 in Calgary and by coincidence the woman he was to soon marry was Isabel Hall who had a job as secretary to the Calgary military registrar. On his attestation papers McKean gave his job as school teacher but he had considerable difficulty in passing the medical examinations. Having been rejected (possibly owing to his small size, he was 5 ft 6 ins) on three occasions, he was finally successful on 23 Jan 1915.

He embarked for England on 18 April 1916 as a member of the 51st Infantry Bn and arrived in Liverpool ten days later. He was then transferred to the 14th Bn The Quebec Regt (CEF) and in early June sent to France as a private. On the 22nd he was promoted to corporal in the field, but at his own request reverted to being a private on 24 July. However his rank went back to Corporal on 11 October. He was wounded for the first time on 27 November and was in hospital until 3 December.

In the Spring of 1917 McKean won his first medal, the MM, at Bully Grenay, close to the town of Lens, and on 2 March was recommended for a commission and left for England in order to take an Officers Course. He passed and was made a temporary lieutenant on 28 April 1917, before being made a scout officer and later a full lieutenant.

After his VC citation was published in the *London Gazette* of 28 June he was honoured in his home town of Bishop Auckland in mid-July in a ceremony at King's Hal when he was presented with an illuminated address and a gold watch by Mr G.W. Jennings and Mrs Deans, members of the town council. Other council officials also took part in the ceremonies. McKean particularly appreciated the welcome from his old home town, as he had moved to Canada. On 31 July at an investiture he received his VC from the King in the Quadrangle of Buckingham Palace. He won the MC when taking part in a scout patrol at Cagnicourt in September 1918.

Capt. Mckean was released from hospital in February 1919 and placed in charge of the Bureua of Information in the Khaki University of Canada in London. It was an educational scheme ran by the YMCA of Canada with the aim of preparing soldiers for civilian life. In 1920, when still in the Army, he attended the VC reception at Buckingham Palace and served in Egypt until September 1925 and left the Army when working in the Corps of Military Accounts on 17 March 1926 with the rank of captain.

After the war McKean wrote up his experiences in a book called *Scouting Thrills* (Macmillan, 1919) and was also to write further books for boys in Canada.

He decided not to return to Canada and settled down in Brighton and in the mid 1920s he ran a sawmill in Cuffley, Hertfordshire whereon on 26 November 1926 he was severely injured in an accident when splitting logs. He was struck by pieces of a broken circular saw and died in Potters Bar Cottage Hospital without regaining consciousness. After an inquest in the hospital he was buried at Brighton Extra-Mural Cemetery, reference 41624. His gravestone is of the type used by the

Commonwealth War Graves Commission. However, his date of death is given as 16 November 1926, instead of 28 November and his age as being 37.

This dreadful accident left his widow in severe financial difficulties but even so it wasn't until 1979 that she sold her late husband's VC and medals, a decision which was not popular with some other members of the family. They were sold at Sothebys and purchased by Mr J.B. Hayward for £17, 000 ($40, 000). At the time the price was a record. Later they were acquired by the Canadian War Museum, Ottawa, where a painting of him by the Canadian war artist, Frederick Horsman Varley is also on display.

McKean is also commemorated in the Jasper National Park where he has a mount named after him and on 6 September 2003 a commemoration was unveiled in Cagnicourt near Arras in the presence of a group of members of his family, including his daughter Pat Stanley who wore her father's decorations. The Place, in front of the village church has been renamed 'Place du Lieutenant George Burdon McKean'. The village can be found slightly to the south of the D 939 Arras-Cambrai road and is where he won his MC on 2 September 1918.

W. BEESLEY

Bucquoy, France, 8 May

Pte William Beesley won his VC 12 miles south of Arras when serving with the 13th (S) (The Prince Consort's Own) Bn The Rifle Bde (111th Bde, 37th Div.) at Bucquoy on 8 May 1918 and forty-six years later in a copy of the *Sunday Mercury* of 2 August 1964 Beesley told the story of his exploits in his own words:

It was half-past two in the afternoon, I remember. A boiling hot day. Three trench mortars were the signal to go over and it was every man for himself. We had no artillery barrage, the Germans loosed every thing they had got.

I suppose it was about 400 to 500 yards to the top of that ridge, without a bit of cover. By the time we'd rushed to halfway, two out of every three men had been hit. I anchored down in a shell-hole to see what was happening and found I was the only man left out of my section of nine.

The platoon sergeant lay dead, all the section commanders had been killed. It looked as though the attack was a failure.

But Rifleman Beesley then leapt from his shell-hole, took command and rallied the remnants. Single-handed he rushed an enemy post and with his revolver killed two of the enemy manning a machine gun. An officer ran from a dug-out to take their place and Beesley killed him too. Three more officers tumbled out and one tried to destroy a map, but Beesley's bullet got him before he could tear the sheet to pieces. Six more Germans emerged with cries of 'Kamerad!' and were taken prisoner.

Just at that moment a young soldier got through with a Lewis machine gun. 'He was a lad called Douglas, and he had dropped his shovel in the support trenches when he saw the way things were going and dashed up the ridge.'

With the Lewis-Gun, Pte Beesley cut the retreating enemy to pieces and for four hours the two men held the position under heavy machine gun and rifle fire. 'We stuck it out, me and this kid. I don't know whether we were scared or not.'

Then the Germans counter-attacked when Douglas was wounded but Beesley held the position alone against all comers until 10.00 p.m., long after the posts on his right and left had been wiped out.

'It was mainly due to his action that the enemy were prevented from rushing the position and that the remnants of his company when compelled to withdraw, were able to do so without further loss', an official report recounted later.

Under cover of darkness, Beesley got back to his own lines, bringing the Lewis gun and his wounded mate with him. Then he set up the gun again and gave the Germans some more. Pte Beesley was to the left of Sgt Gregg at Bucquoy.

The citation for Beesley's VC was published in the *London Gazette* of 28 June as follows:

The young soldier, realising the situation, at once, took command and led the assault. Single-handed, he rushed a post, and with his revolver killed two of the enemy at a machine gun. He then shot dead an officer who ran across from a dugout to take their place at the machine gun. Three more officers appeared from the dug-out. These he called on to surrender; seeing one of them trying to get rid of a map, he shot him and obtained the map. He took four more prisoners from a dug-out and two others from a shelter close by, disarmed them and sent them back to our lines. At this moment his Lewis gun was brought up by a comrade who was acting as a carrier. Private Beesley at once brought it into action, and used it with great effect against the enemy as they bolted towards their support line, inflicting many casualties. For four hours Private Beesley and his comrade held on to the position under very heavy machine-gun fire and rifle fire. The enemy then advanced to counter-attack and the other soldier was wounded. Private Beesley carried on by himself and actually maintained his position until 10 p.m. Long after the posts on his right and left had been practically wiped out and the survivors had fallen back. It was mainly due to his action that the enemy was prevented from rushing the position, and that the remnants of his company, when compelled to withdraw, were able to do so without further loss.

When darkness set in, Private Beesley made his way back to the original line from which the attack had started, bringing with him the wounded carrier and the Lewis gun. He at once mounted the Lewis gun in the trench and remained in action until things quietened down. The indomitable pluck, skilful shooting and good judgment in economising ammunition displayed by Private Beesley stamp the incident as one of the most brilliant actions in recent operations.

William Beesley was born in Gresley, a sub-district of Burton-on-Trent, Staffordshire on 5 October 1895. He went to school at Ansley village school near Nuneaton and later moved to Galley Common. Prior to the war he worked in the mines, at Haunchwood and Tunnel Collieries.

2nd Lt Cecil Knox VC also lived in Nuneaton and was a director of the Haunchwood Colliery, where Beesley used to work. Beesley enlisted at Nuneaton Police Station and at first his application was rejected but he queued up a second time and gave his age as twenty instead of nineteen, as it actually was. His first action in the war was with the 9th King's Royal Rifle Corps on the Ypres sector in June 1915 and in July he was wounded in the shoulder by a piece of shrapnel and in November he was wounded a second time, this time in the legs when taking some supplies up to the St Julian road. After a time spent in hospital he was back on the Western Front in time for the Somme offensive of 1916. By this time he was a member of a machine-gun section with the 13th Rifle Bde. His Army number was B.203174.

Beesley was promoted to Corporal on 28 June 1918, the same day as his VC was published in the *London Gazette*. In France after he won his VC but before he received it from the King Beesley was pulled out of the trenches on one occasion and invited to tea with his commanding officer; on another he lunched with the divisional general who gave him a box of chocolates. His colleagues in the ranks also clubbed together and gave him gifts. He served with Sgt Gregg, also of the 13th Rifle Bde, and won the VC on the same day and the two men were presented with the award at the château at Frohen-le-Grand on 9 August at the same ceremony, together with the Revd Theodore Hardy. After he won his VC Beesley returned to Nuneaton on leave and during this time was presented with £700 in War Bonds by the local townspeople. He was also given the Freedom of the Borough on the same day as Cecil Knox, who had won his VC on 22 March 1918. Beesley was, therefore, Nuneaton's second VC of the war.

Beesley was demobilised in 1919 and returned to coalmining for a time. In 1920 he married Mary Ada Wilson at Stockingford Church, Nuneaton and the four bridesmaids wore miniature VCs. The wedding reception was held at the Royal Oak pub in Hartshill. The couple later had a daughter and settled in Coventry. In the Second World War Beesley served in the Royal Artillery and left the Army in 1941 owing to his age. His duties had been to do with 'instructing youngsters', probably cadets.

In 1947 Beesley moved to 24 Brooklyn Road, Foleshill, Coventry and joined the Coventry Gauge and Tool Co. as a commissionaire and later as a progress chaser, retiring in 1960. During his life Beesley attended several of the VC functions, including the 1956 centenary in Hyde Park.

In 1966 he went on holiday with his wife to Abergavenny, Monmouthshire in south Wales, where he was taken ill and died in a local hospital on 23 September. His funeral was at Holy Trinity Church, Coventry on 29 September and was attended by a large congregation including the Lady Mayoress of Coventry, the Mayor of Nuneaton and members of his former regiment. Henry Tandey, another winner of the VC in 1918 who lived in the area, also attended the service. The Rifle Brigade provided two buglers to play the Last Post in the church. Beesley was buried at St Paul's Cemetery, Harbrook Lane, Coventry. At his service the vicar described him as 'a brave and kindly man' and he was much loved for his quiet kindness and great personal charm. At a Nuneaton Borough Council meeting members stood in silence for a few moments in Beesley's memory.

Beesley used to keep his medals in a brown paper bag in a drawer, and in addition to his VC he also earned eight other medals including the 1914–15 Star, BWM, VM, Defence Medal, War Medal, George VI Coronation, Queen Elizabeth Coronation Medal and Médaille Militaire. All these are with the Royal Green Jackets Museum at Winchester. To commemorate his name there is a William Beesley Crescent at Bramcote Barracks, in Nuneaton. His name is also included on the Rifle Brigade Memorial in Winchester Cathedral.

At some point Beesley must have remarried, as he is buried with Elizabeth May Beesley, who was born in 1896 and died in 1975, nine years after her husband.

Beesley' s life was also commemorated in a special service held in Lichfield Cathedral on 10 June 2007 to the memory of several memory local VC holders who had links with either Coventry or Warwickshire. It was 150 years since Queen Victoria invested the very first VC in 1856. Relatives of the local VC recipients including Cecil Knox and Henry Tandey were present.

W. GREGG

Bucquoy, France, 8 May

Sgt William Gregg of the 13th (S) Bn The Rifle Bde (111th Bde, 37th Div.) won his VC at the same time as Pte Beesley, who also served with the 13th (S) Bn The Rifle Bde (The Prince Consort's Own), and in Bucquoy – the same village – on 8 May. The attack in which Gregg won his VC began in the afternoon when the right company of the 13th Rifle Bde ran into difficulties from machine-gun fire from the village cemetery and crucifix. As a consequence many casualties were suffered by the battalion and two parties were organised to try and capture a machine gun set up in the cemetery. It was discovered there were at least thirty of the enemy in the cemetery, of whom eleven were then taken prisoner and the remainder killed. As Gregg's officer, 2nd Lt G.D. Fraser, was wounded, the Sergeant took charge with the parties moving on to the crucifix which they then captured as well as some posts to the north of the position. However the Germans re-organised themselves and began a counter-attack which forced the battalion back to the cemetery position. Here they were assisted by a support company and were then able to bomb the enemy back to his earlier positions. The Riflemen remained in their positions until 5.40 p.m., having by then lost half of their men.

Gregg's VC was gazetted on 28 June 1918 and the citation was as follows:

> Two companies of his unit attacked the enemy's outpost position without artillery preparation. Sergt. Gregg was with the right company, which came under heavy fire from the right flank as it advanced. All the officers with the company were hit. He at

once took command of the attack. He rushed an enemy post and personally killed an entire machine-gun team, and capture the gun and four men in a dug-out nearby. He then rushed another post, killed two men and captured another. In spite of heavy casualties, he reached his objective, and started consolidating the position. By his prompt and effective action this gallant N.C.O. saved the situation at a critical time and ensured the success of the attack. Later Sergt. Gregg's party was driven back by an enemy counter-attack but reinforcements coming up, he led a charge, personally bombed a hostile machine gun, killed the crew and captured the gun. Once again he was driven back. He led a successful attack, and hung on to the position until ordered by his company commander to withdraw. Although under very heavy rifle and machine-gun fire for several hours, Sergt. Gregg displayed througout the greatest coolness and contempt on danger, walking about encouraging his men and setting a magnificent example.'

In the same month when he was home on leave Gregg was presented with an illuminated address and £200 in War Savings Certificates by his home town. He was demobilised as a sergeant in 1919 and returned to the mines to work.

William Gregg was the son of Mr and Mrs William Gregg of 97 Yorke Street, Mansfield Woodhouse, Derbyshire. He was born at Heanor, Derbyshire on 27 January 1890 and attended school at Heanor Mundy Street School. After leaving school he worked as a miner in the Shipley Colliery. On 25 June 1910 he married Sarah Hardy, the daughter of Mr and Mrs William Hardy, at Heanor Church and the couple lived in Midland Road for the rest of their married life. On 24 November 1914 Gregg enlisted in the Army as a private in the Rifle Brigade and in 1916 was wounded during the Somme offensive and on 4 February 1917 was awarded the MM, for his role in a daylight patrol in securing identifications from a dead German whose body was lying in a crater. Later in the year, on 30 November, he also won a DCM for his work in '. . . carrying messages across a road swept by machine-gun fire, being cut off from his company; he led a counter-attack, killing and driving off the enemy.' He was made acting corporal on 7 January 1917, full corporal on 2 March and on 5 June 1917 was made acting sergeant.

On 4 October Gregg's battalion was resting at Zillibeke Camp and two days later they moved into the support lines in the Mount Sorrel sector where they stayed for four days. They then returned to a position named Dead Dog Farm for a further four days. Next they moved to positions between Locre and Dranoutre at a position called Locrehof Farm. They trained there until 2 November and then moved by bus to St Jean, where they worked at road repairs for a week before going back to the Strazeele area. Training was resumed and Gregg won a cross-country race, beating 400 other officers and men to the tape. A barrel of beer was won by A Coy. On 8 November the 13th Rifle Bde moved into hutments at Kemmel Shelters and Gregg was made a full Sergeant on 12 December.

Gregg played for the local football team, Heanor Athletic FC, as a full-back and helped to train youngsters and a football cup was named after him known as the Gregg Cup. In the Second World War he served with the Sherwood Foresters, National Defence Company, but left them in 1941 when he had reached the upper age limit. He still took an active part in the war though and worked on the ferries and helped to bring back survivors from the Dieppe Raid in 1942. After the war he returned to Shipley Colliery where he worked until 1959 but eventually was forced to retire through ill health. The colliery ceased producing coal in the 1960s and all that remains are the headstocks to the Woodside Colliery; the site of the mine itself is now the Shipley Country Park and the American Adventure Theme Park.

During his life Gregg attended several of the VC celebrations including the 1956 centenary at Hyde Park and back home he took a keen interest in local affairs.

Aged 79 William Gregg died on 9 August 1969 in Heanor Memorial Hospital and his funeral, with full military honours was held in the Heanor Free Church, Midland Road, the road he had lived in for 59 years. He was later cremated in Heanor Crematorium and his ashes scattered on the smaller section of the Garden of Remembrance at Heanor Cemetery.

Gregg and his wife Sarah had celebrated their golden wedding in June 1960 but Sarah not only outlived her husband but also reached the milestone of a hundred years old. On her birthday in January 1992 she was visited by members of the Royal Green Jackets who brought her late husband's medals to show her.

After his death a swimming bath in Heanor was named after Gregg (now part of the Heanor Leisure Centre) and in 1964 a street in the town was also named after him. He was one of a small group of eight men to win the VC, DCM, (*London Gazette*, 6 February 1918) and

MM (*London Gazette*, 26 March 1917) in the Great War. His name is on the Rifle Brigade Memorial in Winchester Cathedral. Apart from his VC he won seven other medals: 1914–15 Star, BWM, VM, 1939–45 Star, War Medal, George VI Coronation, and Queen Elizabeth Coronation and these are in the collection of the Royal Green Jackets in Winchester.

W. RUTHVEN
Ville-sur-Ancre, France, 19 May

Sgt William Ruthven of the 22nd Bn (Victoria) 6th Bde of the 2nd Australian Div. won his VC near the village of Ville-sur-Ancre on 19 May 1918. The battalion objective was the high ground to the south which overlooked the village of Morlancourt which was in German hands, and to force the enemy to evacuate the village. Most of the Australian battalion was involved in the attack, which was on a frontage of about three-quarters of a mile, and which had the same distance in depth. The plan was also for companies of the 21st and 23rd battalions to clear the village.

The objective included two strongly held sunken roads named 'Little Caterpillar' and 'Big Caterpillar', which were guarded by a series of outposts and defended by machine guns. After these objectives were taken the battalion was meant to meet up with a company of the 24th Bn to the east of the village which would then allow the other two battalions to mop up. An intensive creeping barrage began at about 2.00 a.m. was directed on to the enemy lines. The Australians initially had surprise on their side and were able to penetrate the German outposts before the enemy could properly reorganise itself. On the outskirts of the village was a cemetery and crucifix which were strongly held and which were opposite the battalion's left flank and these two positions were taken immediately.

It was at this point that Sgt Ruthven, whose company commander, Capt. W.R. Hunter, had been wounded, took his place and took command of the company. Getting the men in order he took the company to the 'Big Caterpillar', where a machine-gun, opening fire about 30 to 40 yards ahead was preventing the advance. Bitter hand-to-hand fighting then took place as the German defenders, with their superior numbers, put up a stout defence. Soon the enemy began to inflict heavy casualties, mostly with machine guns.

Ruthven ran forward to within bombing range and threw a bomb which exploded close to the German machine gun which was doing the most damage. After bayoneting one of the crew he captured the rest, together with their gun. By this time other Germans were beginning to leave the sunken road. Ruthven then shot two of the parting men and when his colleagues caught up with him they found that he had captured six more of the enemy together with two German machine guns. In all he collected about thirty prisoners. Further down the 'Big Caterpillar' another German machine gunner was at work on the top edge of the bank but he and his gun were dealt with by Lt P.J. Abercrombie, a well-known cricketer, who threw a bomb which hit the gunner on the side of the head. Although the gunner was not injured, it seems that the bomb damaged the gun. For his actions and others later on the same day Ruthven was awarded the VC.

Within half an hour of the attack starting, success was claimed except in one area, which, owing to the barrage falling short. Soon, though, the whole battalion was able to dig in on the top of the hill overlooking Morlancourt and by the morning more than 200 prisoners had been captured, along with many German machine guns. The other battalions also did well and the total number of prisoners taken by the brigade during the day came to 300. Enemy artillery fire had been significant by its absence.

Ruthven' s VC Citation was published in the *London Gazette* of 11 July 1918 as follows:

> During the advance Sergt. Ruthven's company suffered numerous casualties, and his company commander was severely wounded. He thereupon assumed command of this portion of assault, took charge of the company headquarters, and rallied the section in his vicinity. As the leading wave approached its objective, it was subjected to heavy fire from an enemy machine-gun at close range. Without hesitation he at once sprang out, threw a bomb which landed beside the post, and rushed the position, bayoneting one of the of the crew and capturing the gun. He then encountered some of the enemy coming out of a shelter. He wounded two, captured six others in the same position and handed them over to an escort from the leading wave, which had now reached the objective. Sergt. Ruthven then reorganised the men in his vicinity and established a post in the second objective. Observing enemy

movement in a sunken road near by, he, without hesitation and armed only with a revolver, went over the open alone and rushed the position, shooting two enemy who refused to come out of their dug-outs. He then, single-handed, mopped up this post and captured the whole of the garrison, amounting in all to thirty-two, and kept them to assistance arrived to escort them back to our lines. During the remainder of the day this gallant non-commissioned officer set a splendid example of leadership, moving up and down his position under fire, supervising consolidation and encouraging his men. Throughout the whole operation he showed the most courage and determination, inspiring everyone by his fine fighting spirit, his remarkable courage and his dashing action.

William Ruthven was born in Collingwood, Melbourne, Victoria, Australia on 21 May 1893. He was the son of a carpenter, Peter Ruthven, and his wife Catharine Charlotte (née Bedwell), both of Victoria. Ruthven attended Vere Street State School, Collingwood and after leaving school trained as a mechanical engineer and when the war began he was working in the timber industry.

On 16 April 1915 he enlisted in the 22nd Bn (Victoria) Australian Imperial Force and left for Gallipoli in August with other reinforcements, arriving there in October, a short while before the peninsula was evacuated. In March 1916 the battalion sailed for France and Ruthven's first tour of duty on the Western Front in April was in the area of Fleurbaix in Flanders and during this period he was wounded and out of action for four months. He rejoined his battalion in August and was promoted Lance Corporal during the battle of the Somme and on 26 January 1917 became a Sergeant. After he won his VC on 19 May 1918, the only one awarded to a member of his regiment, he was wounded again on 11 June near Méricourt. On 1 July 1918 he was commissioned as 2nd lieutenant.

His VC was gazetted on 11 July 1918 and in the same month he was presented with his VC ribbon by General Sir John Monash during a review of the 2nd Australian Div.. On 16 August, he was decorated by the King at Buckingham Palace in a private ceremony.

Before the war ended he was made a full lieutenant in October in the month when he returned to Australia and assisted in recruiting together with other holders of the VC and on 11 December his service with the

AIF ended. After the war Ruthven returned to engineering and on 20 December 1919 married Irene May White at St Philip's, Abbotsford and the couple were to have two children, a boy and a girl.

The Ruthvens left Melbourne in 1923 when he took up an 800-acre soldier settlement at Werrimull in the Victorian Mallee but sadly this land scheme never thrived, partly owing to poor seasons and he returned to Collingwood in 1931, where he began to work as a master carrier and later worked with the State Rivers and Water Supply Commission.

In 1938 Ruthven saved the lives of two boys who were calling for help in a lift in Russell Street which had broken down when he grabbed the lift cable, which was moving so fast that it burnt the flesh off his hands, and their lives were saved. During the Second World War Ruthven served in several garrisons including those centred on Murchison, Victoria's largest POW camp. When he ceased full-time duty in August 1944 it was with the rank of Temporary Major. He then became a member of Collingwood Council and in 1945 the Mayor of Collingwood. He was a member of the Australian Labour Party and became a well-known figure in politics and was also a member of the Victoria Legislative Assembly from 1945 to 1961 and from 1954 to 1955 was Labour member for Preston. In February 1954 he was presented to the Queen in a ceremony at the Melbourne Cricket Ground and in 1956 he was part of the Australian contingent in London for the VC centenary.

Ruthven kept close links with other holders of the VC and other ex-servicemen and in 1932 had been one of the pall bearers at Albert Jacka's funeral. On 25 April 1965 he visited Anzac Cove in Gallipoli as part of an Australian pilgrimage and during this visit Ruthven, together with seventy-seven former veterans, met up with thirty-four Turkish veterans from fifty years before. New Zealand and Newfoundland were also represented by visitors and surviving veterans but there was no British contingent present owing to the cost of the trip and the Foreign Office's lame excuse was that ' no public funds could be made available'. Ruthven was president of the Werrimull and Collingwood Returned Sailors' and Soldiers' Imperial League of Australia sub-branches; a life member of the Preston sub-branch and a Trustee of Melbourne's Shrine of Remembrance and the St Kilda Memorial Hill. 'Rusty', as he was often known, was also timekeeper for the Collingwood Football Club and a founder member of its social club. In 1969 he was living at Namur Street, East Kew and died in the following year in the Heidelberg Repatriation Hospital in Victoria on 12 January 1970 he had suffered from his war injuries for much of his life.

William Ruthven was cremated with full military honours at the Fawker Crematorium, New Melbourne Cemetery, Victoria and his ashes are in the Garden of Remembrance and there is also a plaque to his memory in the Crematorium. In addition his name is remembered with the Ruthven Soldiers' Club which was was opened at Broad Meadows in 1959 and a new railway station was named after him in 1963 at NERA Reservoir. As with all Australian VCs he is also remembered in the Victoria Cross Memorial in the Queen Victoria Building, Sydney and in the Victoria Cross Memorial Park in Canberra and his decorations including his VC; 1914–15 Star, BWM, VM, two medals from the Second World War and two Coronation medals are on display in the Hall of Valour of the Australian War Memorial, Canberra, together with a portrait of him by George Bell.

G.W.St G. Grogan

River Aisne, France, 27 May

At about 6.00 am on 27 May 1918, the opening day of the Battle of the Aisne, T/Brig. Gen. George Grogan of the (23rd Bde) was given instructions by Maj. Gen. Heneker (8th Div.) of IX Corps to take command of all the men in the Vesle area for about a mile to either side of Jonchery and to organise the defence of the south bank. The village is about 18 miles south-east of Soissons and British troops were sandwiched in a section of the battlefield between two sections of the French Army.

The outlook on the morning of the 27th looked grim and Grogan could see the enemy coming over the ridge and that some men of the 8th, 25th and 50th divisions were retreating. His first job therefore was to round up these stragglers, which he quickly did. During the afternoon Grogan's troops were being outflanked continuously on their west side and were forced to move back a mile to the high ground between the Rivers Ardre and Vesle. The position was north of Montazin Farm and astride the Jonchery-Savigny road and on the right flank the French Army was in support. This new position was visible from the enemy side as they were only about 250 yards distant and so Grogan gave orders to move the line of the position even further back, which was managed before darkness fell. The 8th Div. remained in the area of Montazin Farm until 2 June.

Grogan was to be awarded the VC for his very fine leadership on the 27th and the details were published in the *London Gazette* two months later on 25 July 1918 and read as follows:

> For most conspicuous bravery and leadership throughout three days of intense fighting. Brigadier-General Grogan was, except for a few hours, in command of the remnants of the infantry of

a Division and various attached troops. His actions during the whole battle can only be described as magnificent. The utter disregard for his personal safety, combined with sound practical ability, which he displayed, materially helped to stay the onward thrust of the enemy masses. Throughout the third day of operations, a most critical day, he spent his time under artillery, trench mortar, rifle and machine-gun fire, riding up and down the front line encouraging his troops, reorganising those who had fallen into disorder, leading back into the line those who were beginning to retire, and setting such a wonderful example that he inspired with his enthusiasm not only his own men, but also the Allied troops who were alongside. As a result the line held and repeated enemy attacks were repulsed. He had one horse shot under him, but nevertheless continued on foot to encourage his men until another horse was brought. He displayed throughout the highest valour, powers of command and leadership.

Today Jonchery, former HQ of the IX Corps, finds itself in a section between the N31 to the north and the A4 to the south.

George William St George Grogan, the eldest of five sons of Brig. Gen. E.G. Grogan CB, CBE, was born in St Andrews, Fifeshire on 1 September 1875. George's father was in charge of developing the dockyard at Devonport. The Grogan family were of Irish descent and George's mother died in 1881, when he was only six years old. He was educated at United Services College, Westwood Ho and RMC Sandhurst and was gazetted as 2nd lieutenant in the West India Regt on 5 September 1896. He was made a full lieutenant on 22 December 1897 and during the following year served in Sierra Leone (Medal and Clasp) and in West Africa in 1898–9 (Clasp). He was promoted to captain and worked with the Egyptian Army from 9 May 1902 to 10 May 1907. Meanwhile he was transferred to the King's Own Yorkshire Light Infantry on 27 March 1907 and later to the Worcestershire Regt on 18 January 1908.

When the war began Grogan was in Egypt with the 1st Worcestershires, who returned to Britain and joined the newly formed 8th Div.. He was quickly promoted to Major, on 28 September 1914, and went to France to join the 2nd Bn of the 2nd Div.. He took over command in December 1914 but on 6 January was wounded. He rejoined the 1st Worcestershires and on 22 March 1915 was made temporary lieutenant colonel in command after the Battle of Neuve Chapelle. He was also Mentioned in Despatches. In 1916 he was created CMG on 14 January and fought on the Somme. He won the DSO in March 1917 as a result of a successful attack to the east of Bouchavesnes. The award was for 'bold and capable leadership' and was gazetted on 11 May 1917. He became commander of the 23rd Bde, 8th Div. in June.

He led his brigade at Bellewaarde Ridge on the first day of Third Ypres on 31 July 1917 and it was at this time that Capt. F.C. Roberts was Grogan's brigade major. Roberts was also destined to win a VC in 1918. In March 1918 Grogan was back on the Somme with his brigade taking part in the severe fighting and in the retreat from the river line. At the end of March, at Moreuil, Grogan was in command of the 24th and 23rd Bdes. of the 8th Div. during the enemy advance during the defence of Amiens. For his service during this very difficult period he was awarded a bar to his DSO. After being involved in the fighting on 24 April at Villers-Bretonneux close to the Monument the brigade moved to the Chemin des Dames where on 27 May he won the VC. (The Monument was often called Monument Wood and is a commemoration of the French dead from 1870.)

In the advance to the Armistice he led the 23rd Bde towards Douai and in October, when to the east of Arras, he captured Greenland Hill, which made it possible for leading troops to cross the Scarpe. He was decorated by the King in France at First Army Headquarters at Ranchicourt in early August. Grogan won many medals, a testimony to his skill as commander and leader as well as to his extreme bravery and cheerfulness. After the Armistice he was given the command of the 1st Bde of the Russian Relief Force under Lord Rawlinson whose mission was to evacuate the fronts at Archangel and Murmansk. Such was the demand from members of the British Army to go to Russia that in many cases officers volunteered to go as Privates.

Other winners of the VC who went to Russia included Col Douglas, Lt Col Sherwood-Kelly, Lt Moore and Capt. Toye. In 1919 Grogan was awarded the CB and in 1920 he married Ethel Gladys Elger, daughter of Mr and Mrs John Elger, and when the couple left Holy Trinity Church in Sloane Street, an arch of bayonets held by a group of NCOs was waiting for them as a tribute. The couple were to have two sons.

Grogan was unable to attend the 1920 VC celebrations as he was in Russia and in April of the same year he became an ADC to the King and received another brevet. He was lieutenant colonel with the 3rd Worcestershires from February 1920 to 1923 and was responsible for bringing the battalion home from India prior to their disbandment. In

October 1923 he reached the substantive rank of Colonel and went to Aldershot to command 5th Infantry Bde of the 2nd Div.. In 1926 he retired from the army as an honorary Brigadier-General and was a member of the Reserve of Officers until 1930, when he reached the age limit of fifty-five. He was invited to unveil the War Memorial at St Jude's Cemetery, Egham on 11 November 1929.

In November 1933 Grogan became a member of the King's Bodyguard of the Hon. Corps of Gentlemen of Arms, a position he held until 1945. Between 1938 and 1945 he was colonel of the Worcestershire Regt and retired again from the Army on 28 August. During his whole army service he was always known as 'Grogy' and if someone upset him in any way then they would receive the full force of his temper, – a sign of trouble in store was when Grogan was seen to scratch the back of his neck!

In 1956 he attended the VC centenary review in Hyde Park.

Grogan's favourite hobbies were playing golf and reading and he was a member of the United Services Club. At the age of 83 he was involved in a minor car accident near his home and was treated for slight injuries at Chertsey Hospital. He died at Silverdene, Sunningdale, on 3 January 1962 at the age of eighty-six and had a private funeral at Woking Crematorium on 8 January. The commemorative reference is 51565 and his ashes were scattered in the Tennyson Lake Garden of Remembrance. Grogan's wife died nearly seven years later on 1 December 1968 at the age of 83.

Grogan's decorations apart from the VC include the CB, CMG, DSO & bar, 1914 Star, BWM, VM (MiD Oakleaf). Defence Medal (from the Second World War), the 1935 Silver Jubilee Medal, and two Coronation Medals. He was also awarded medals linked with his service in Africa at the end of the 19th Century and the complete collection is on loan from his family to the Imperial War Museum.

J. HALLIWELL
Muscourt, France, 27 May

The 11th (S) Lancashire Fusiliers (74th Bde, 25th Div.) were at Kemmel at the beginning of May and then after being relieved marched to Esquelbecq, where they spent two days in training. On the 8th they entrained for the Aisne area and found themselves 15 miles to the south-south-east of Soissons at Fère-en-Tardenois, in the middle of the zone of the French Army. The French had relieved the British in this area in October 1914 and now the 25th Div. was one of the units which had been exchanged for a French one, which had been sent to Flanders. The 25th Div. was now supposed to be in a quiet and restful sector. The battalion then spent at least the next ten days in training, 6 miles to the east of Fère-en-Tardenois and this was when Lt Col G.P. Pollitt DSO, Royal Engineers, assumed command. Training was then continued 10 miles north-west of Rheims at Montigny-sur-Vesle, where the battalion moved on the 23rd. Three days later the French Army captured two Germans who stated that a formidable attack was to be delivered the following day. The French were disinclined to accept this information but the British, who had additional evidence of an impending attack, thought differently.

The 11th Lancashire Fusiliers were subsequently ordered to 'stand to' at 7.30 p.m. on the 26th and to be ready to move at ten minutes' notice. Two-and-a-half hours later they moved off to billets in the village of Muscourt, a mile to the south of the Aisne river and canal and 4 miles to the north-east of Fismes. As a prelude the start of the Battle of the Aisne a huge enemy bombardment began at about 1.00 a.m. and two hours later the battalion reached Muscourt. At 5.00 a.m. SOS flares were seen to go up and soon afterwards the forward positions were overrun by large numbers of the enemy. Communication immediately broke down and it was soon clear that the original front line was broken, so reserves were moved to secondary positions with the purpose of trying to stem any further advance. At 9.00 a.m. the battalion occupied a frontage of 400 yards on high ground to the south of the Aisne. Nearly two hours later the enemy came into contact and soon afterwards the 9th Loyal North Lancashire Regt also of the 74th Bde, to the left of the 11th Lancashire Fusiliers, engaged them.The Germans had crossed both the Aisne and the canal by 1.30 p.m. using the bridge at Maizy, to the north-west, and were moving quickly along the valley towards Muscourt. However the Lancashire Fusiliers had some success in slowing the attackers on the road to Concevreux but soon the enemy was entering Muscourt. The battalion's left flank was then turned as it was forced to retreat to a ridge near Meurival, to the south-east. It was not able to hold on there for very long owing either to the heavy concentration of shelling. It was here that L.Cpl Halliwell won his VC during the next few hours, on the same day that T/Brig. Gen. Grogan won his on the Aisne. At the time Halliwell was holding Lt Col Pollitt's horse when he realised that there were several wounded men who were in severe danger of either being killed or taken prisoner. He then left the Colonel, caught a stray German horse, and under very heavy shell and machine-gun fire brought back to safety no fewer than nine men as well as one officer. For each man he made sure that the stretcher-bearers and medical staff provided adequate and proper medical attention. Halliwell tried three times to save an eleventh man but as the enemy was then so close to him he was unable to achieve this final deed.

Not surprisingly, the battalion was shelled off the ridge and forced to move to a new position 500 yards to the south. During the next twenty-four hours the enemy was able to get the upper hand by turning flanks at other points in the battlefield and the battalion suffered heavy losses. Lt Col Pollitt was captured, and 13 officers and 319 other ranks were listed as missing. In addition to Halliwell winning the VC, Pollitt was awarded a bar to his DSO.

Halliwell's VC was published in the *London Gazette* of 25 July 1918, the same date as Grogan's and read:

> For most conspicuous bravery and determination displayed during the withdrawal of the remnants of the battalion, when closely engaged with the enemy. L.-Corpl. Halliwell, having captured a stray enemy horse, rode out under heavy rifle and machine-gun fire and rescued a man from No Man's Land. He repeated this performance several times, and succeeded in rescuing one officer and nine other ranks. He made another effort to reach a wounded man,but was driven back by very close

advance of the enemy. His conduct was magnificent throughout, and it was a splendid and inspiring example to all who saw him.

Joel Halliwell, the eldest of four children, was born at 3 Parkfield, Middleton, near Manchester on 29 December 1873 and was educated at Parkfield Church of England School, where he was keen on football. When he left school he became a foreman in the Middleton Cotton Mill and when war broke out joined the 11th Lancashire Fusiliers and served in France with the service number 9860. During 1916 his younger brother Tom was killed.

When Halliwell was due home on leave on 7 September 1918 word got round the town that he was to arrive at Middleton railway station. When he arrived several thousand people were waiting to greet him, having left their work at the mills or elsewhere. He was welcomed by the Mayor and Mayoress and was then driven in the mayor's carriage to his home. In addition he was welcomed by the local council and by the children of his old school. He was presented with an illuminated address, a large number of War Bonds and a gold watch by the townspeople of Middleton and was also presented with a chain by the Middleton Licensed Victuallers' Association. A few days later, on 11 September 1918, he was decorated with his VC by the King at Buckingham Palace.

In 1918 Halliwell married Sarah Greaves and they had three daughters, the first born in 1923. In 1919 he was discharged from the army with the rank of Lance Corporal.

Halliwell attended the Coronation of King George VI in 1937 and of Queen Elizabeth II in 1953, and a number of VC functions including the 1956 centenary in Hyde Park. He tried his hand at keeping the New Inn public house at Long Street between 1930 and 1940 and later began working with the local Highways Department. Although he was already fifty-seven when the Second World War began, he tried to enlist but was rejected because of poor eyesight and a wounded left leg from the previous war. He continued to live at 24 Manchester New Road, Middleton, a terraced house, and was working for a firm of dyers when he was taken ill in 1957, suffering from the effects of thrombosis. He died in hospital in Middleton after an eight-month illness on 14 June 1958 and after his death was announced flags in Middleton were flown at half-mast along the route of the funeral cortège. Prior to the interment a funeral service was conducted at Holy Trinity Parkfield Church when his decorations were placed on a purple cushion on the coffin, which was draped with the Union Jack. The Mayor of Middleton and many other local dignitaries attended the service and he was buried in Boarshaw New Cemetery, Middleton, section 10 Grave 106. Men of the Lancashire Fusiliers acted as bearers and one of their buglers played the Last Post and Reveille. At this point Lt W.D. Johnson of the Lancashire Fusiliers Depot stepped forward and placed a wreath on the open graveside. Members of the detachment then gave a final salute. A plaque in his memory has been erected on the side of the cemetery chapel which quotes 25 July 1918 as the date of his winning the VC. This was the date of his citation published in the *London Gazette*; the actual date of the deed was 27 May 1918.

After his death the British Legion, of which he had been a prominent member, gave financial support to his widow, who died ten years after her husband, in 1968. Halliwell's decorations which include the BWM, VM and two Coronation medals remain with his family although his VC is on loan for display in the Fusiliers' Museum in Bury.

J. KAEBLE
Neuville-Vitasse, France, 8/9 June

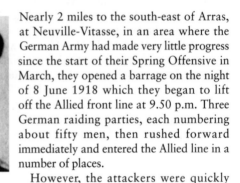

Nearly 2 miles to the south-east of Arras, at Neuville-Vitasse, in an area where the German Army had made very little progress since the start of their Spring Offensive in March, they opened a barrage on the night of 8 June 1918 which they began to lift off the Allied front line at 9.50 p.m. Three German raiding parties, each numbering about fifty men, then rushed forward immediately and entered the Allied line in a number of places.

However, the attackers were quickly repulsed before they reached the line of the 22nd Bn Quebec Regt (5th Bde) 2nd Canadian Div. (CEF) and the Canadians turned the tables on their foe by rushing forward, using bombs and Lewis guns and capturing a German prisoner. A few Germans from their attacking party managed to reach the Canadian parapet but were then immediately repulsed. Cpl Joseph Kaeble was in charge of one of the Lewis gun sections and at this point was largely responsible for keeping the enemy raiders at bay. In spite of being mortally wounded he continued operating his Lewis gun, until through total exhaustion he fell back down into the trench. He had suffered compound fractures of both legs and other wounds and died the following day at Neuville-Vitasse and was buried 7 miles west of Arras in Wanquertin Cemetery (Plot II. Row 8. Grave 8). Three months later became the first French Canadian to win the VC when he was awarded a posthumous one. (*London Gazette)* 16 September 1918) and the citation reads:

For most conspicuous bravery and extraordinary devotion to duty when in charge of a Lewis-gun section in the front-line trenches, on which a strong enemy raid was attempted. During an intense bombardment Corpl. Kaeble remained at the parapet with his Lewis gun shouldered ready for action, the field of fire being very short. As soon as the barrage lifted from the front line, about fifty of the enemy advanced towards his post. By this time the whole of his section except one had become casualties. Corpl. Kaeble jumped over the parapet, and holding his Lewis gun at the hip, emptied one magazine after another into the advancing enemy, and, although wounded several times by fragments of shells and bombs, he continued to fire, and entirely blocked the enemy by his determined stand. Finally, firing all the time, he fell backwards into the trench, mortally wounded. While lying on his back in the trench he fired his last cartridges over the parapet at the retreating Germans, and before losing consciousness shouted to the wounded about him 'Keep it up, boys; do not let them get through! We must stop them!' The complete repulse of the enemy attack at this point was due to the remarkable personal bravery and self-sacrifice of this gallant non-commissioned officer, who died of his wounds shortly afterwards.

Joseph Kaeble was born in St Moise, Mantane County, Quebec, Canada, on 5 May 1892 and was the son of a farmer, Joseph Kaeble and his wife Marie Ducas. Joseph junior was one of three children as well as a half-brother and after their father died the family moved to the village of Sayabec. When Joseph left school he trained to be a mechanic and worked at a local sawmill.

In March 1914 he was one of ten volunteers who enlisted in Sayabec and he spent six months in training in Valcartier before leaving for England on 27 September. He had been allocated the service number of 889958. At first he was assigned to the 69th Bn (CEF) but at the end of · the Battle of the Somme was transferred to the 22nd Bn Quebec Regt (CEF) the only French Canadian battalion to serve on the Western Front. At the time the battalion was being reorganised to the north-west of Lens at Bully–Grenay. The battalion were to remain there for much of the winter before taking part in the capture of Vimy Ridge in the battle of Arras in April 1917. During the fighting Kaeble was wounded in the right shoulder and was out of action for 25 days during which time he was in hospital however he was soon back with his unit on 25 May and was once more made a machine gunner. During 1917 the battalion took part in the fighting for Hill 70 in August and then in the autumn during the struggle for the possession of Passchendaele

Ridge in Belgium. At the end of March 1918 the battalion moved to the Neuville-Vitasse sector and on 23rd Kaeble was promoted to Corporal.

Six months after he won a VC the posthumous award was presented to his mother by the Duke of Devonshire, Governor General of Canada, in Rimouski, Quebec, on 16 December. His decorations including a MM together with a plaque are in the care of the Royal 22e Regimental Museum, The Citadel, Quebec.

Kaeble's name is remembered in Sayabec Parish Church in Quebec and in recent times he has been commemorated in a number of ways including being honoured at the Canadian Forces Base Valcartier with a Mount Kaeble east of Vimy Camp; also on the camp is a street named after him and an NCO's club as well. The base, sixteen months north of Quebec City, has been used for military purposes since 1914 and at that time the 22nd Canadian Bn trained there.

On 5 November 2006 the Governor-General unveiled the Valiants Memorial in Ottawa which included a series of five busts and nine statues which commemorate some of Canada's heroes and which include a bust of Joseph Kaeble.

In February 2011 the Department of Fisheries and Oceans announced that nine new Mid shore patrol boats (Hero Class) would be built and the first one would be named after a Passchendaele VC, Private James Robertson which has already been launched. Kaeble's boat is due to be ready in 2013.

P. DAVEY

Merris, France, 28 June

On 28 June 1918 the 10th (South Australia) Bn was holding the line to the north-west of Merris, 5 miles east of Hazebrouck. The battalion had two companies in the line. Major Rumball was in command of the southern company and Lt W.R. Jenkins of the northern one. Davey won his VC in the late morning in what was later described as a Minor Operation (*War Diary* WO 95/3249). The citation for Davey's VC published in the *London Gazette* (17 August) tells the story of his actions in a much more detailed way:

In a daylight operation against the enemy position his platoon advanced 200 yards, capturing part of the enemy line, and whilst the platoon was consolidating the enemy pushed a machine gun forward under cover of a hedge and opened fire from close range, inflicting heavy casualties and hampering work. Alone Corpl. Davey moved forward in the face of fierce point-blank fire, and attacked the gun with hand grenades, putting half the crew out of action. Having used all available grenades he returned to the original jumping-off trench, secured a further supply, and again attacked the gun, the crew of which had, in the meantime, been reinforced. He killed the crew, eight in all, and captured the gun. This very gallant N.C.O. then mounted the gun in the new post, and used it in repelling a determined counter-attack, during which he was severely wounded. By his determination Corpl. Davey saved the platoon from annihilation, and made it possible to consolidate and hold a position of vital importance to the success of the whole operation.

❖ ❖ ❖

Phillip Davey was born in Unley, Goodwood, South Australia on 10 October 1896, one of at least three sons of William George Davey, a carpenter, and Elizabeth Davey (née O'Neil). He went to school at Flinders Street Model School and then Goodwood Public School.

Before the war Davey was a horse-driver and he enlisted in the AIF with the number 1327 at Morphettville on 22 December 1914. After initial training, he left Melbourne on 2 February 1915 with the 10th Bn 2nd reinforcements who were bound for Egypt and Lemnos prior to the attack on the Gallipoli Peninsula. Davey was involved in the initial landing on 25 April 1915 and took part in the following four days' heavy fighting. Later he was evacuated from the peninsula with enteric fever and was treated in Egypt at the 1st Australian General Hospital in Heliopolis. By January 1916 Davey was back in Australia and five months later on 27 June he embarked for England, this time with the 10th Bn's 18th reinforcements. In September he joined his battalion in France just before it moved into the Ypres sector close to the infamous Hill 60. On 15 March 1917 he was wounded and on 3 October gassed.

On 3 January 1918, at Warneton, Belgium, Davey won the MM for crawling out into no-man's-land to rescue a comrade, when all the time under very heavy fire. His brother Claude had received the same medal the previous year for a similar act of bravery before he was later killed. A third brother, Richard, also won the same medal.

On 24 April Davey was promoted Corporal and took part in an attack against enemy positions at Merris in France on 28 June during which time he was severely wounded but also earned a Victoria Cross. He was sent to England, where he was cared for in a hospital in Weymouth, Dorset. Ten weeks later he received the VC from the King at Buckingham Palace on 11 September 1918 and on 19 October left for Australia. He was discharged from the AIF on 24 February 1919.

Between the two wars Davey worked with the South Australian Railways as a labourer and linesman during three different periods: 27 April 1926 to 4 October 1938, 6 March 1939 to 12 February 1942 and 17 December 1943 to 22 February 1946.

He married Eugene Agnes Tomlinson on 25 August 1928 but he was never really fit and suffered from emphysema and bronchitis for many years. At the early age of fifty-six he died at the Repatriation General Hospital in Springbank, South Australia on 21 December 1953 with the cause of death being a coronary occlusion. He was buried with full military honours in the AIF Garden of Memorial Cemetery, West Terrace, Adelaide, and two other holders of the VC, Arthur Blackburn and Reginald Inwood, attended the his funeral.

In his will Davey bequeathed his VC to his cousin, Mrs J. Whisson of Seaton Park, South Australia, and apart from his VC, his medals include the MM, 1914–15 Star, BWM, VM and two Coronation medals and they are held by the Australian War Memorial in Canberra, A.C.T. As with all Australian holders of the VC he is commemorated in the Victoria Cross Memorial Park also in Canberra and in Sydney in the Victoria Cross Memorial at the Queen Victoria Building.

T.L. AXFORD

Vaire and Hamel Woods, France, 4 July

Cpl Thomas Axford won the VC on 4 July 1918 in the battle of Hamel close to Vaire and Hamel Woods, north-east of Villers Betonneux. His battalion, the 16th, was part of the Australian 4th Bde and was positioned in the centre of the planned attack to capture both Vaire and Hamel Woods. At 3.10 a.m. an Allied barrage opened falling on the German lines but just missed hitting the German-held Pear Trench, whose occupants were later to put up a stiff resistance. After four minutes the barrage lifted and the Australians kept as close to it as possible advancing up a slope but they then encountered heavy fire from the German front along the terraces in front of Vaire Wood. The enemy artillery had only made a weak response to the Australian batteries and the Allied tanks were to do splendid work, moving up and down and firing at enemy machine-gun points as well as other enemy strong points, although they were hampered by trees in the woods.

As a result of this progress the enemy front line was soon taken, together with many prisoners, but Pear Trench, at the top of the slope, continued to be troublesome, although the wire was cut as well as being passable. An enemy machine gun killed Capt. F.F. Woods as well as Sergeant, CSM H.G. Blinman, and the rest of their Lewis gun team. At this point in the struggles for Pear Trench L. Cpl Axford took direct action on reaching it and his platoon moved through gaps in the wire. The adjoining platoon was seen to be held up by uncut wire and were losing many casualties to an enemy machine gun. Axford decided to help them out; dashing over to the flank he threw bombs down amongst the German machine-gun crew and then jumped into the trench and began to use his bayonet. In all he killed ten Germans and took six prisoners. He then picked up the machine guns and tossed them over the parapet and urged on the delayed platoon. For this and work later in the day he was deservedly awarded the VC.

At 6.00 a.m. Vaire and Hamel Woods had both been cleared by the 16th Bn and all trenches and dug-outs had been mopped up. Many prisoners had been captured in a large communication trench in Vaire Wood. In their role as observers for the artillery the Flying Corps performed poorly, which probably led to many of the Australian casualties being caused by their own artillery firing short. However, despite this setback the Battle of Hamel has been described as a textbook battle which further enhanced the reputation of the Australian General, Sir John Monash. As a coincidence Henry Dalziel also won a VC on the same day, during the fighting in Hamel Wood when serving with the 15th Bn of the AIF.

On 11 July the 16th Bn moved to Bussy-les-Daours when they were relieved by the 39th Bn and the following day they moved to dug-outs near Querrieu remaining there until 1 August. On the 17th of the month the citation for Axford's VC was published in the *London Gazette* as follows:

When the barrage lifted and the infantry advance commenced,his platoon was able to reach the first enemy defences through gaps which had been cut in the wire. The adjoining platoon being delayed in uncut wire, enemy machine guns got into action and inflicted many casualties, including the company commander, L.-Corpl. Axford, with great initiative and magnificent courage, at once dashed to the flank, threw his bombs amongst the machine-gun crews, jumped into the trench, and charged with his bayonet. Unaided he killed ten of the enemy and killed six prisoners; he threw the machine guns over the parapet, and called out to the delayed platoon to come on. He then rejoined his own platoon, and fought with it during the remainder of the operations. Prior to the incidents above mentioned, he had assisted in the laying out of tapes for the jumping-off position, which was within 100 yards of the enemy. When the tapes were laid he remained out as a special patrol to ensure that the enemy did not discover any unusual movement on our side. His initiative and gallantry undoubtedly saved many casualties, materially assisted towards the complete success of his company in the task assigned to it.

Thomas Leslie Axford (Jack) was born in Carrieton, South Australia on 18 June 1894, the son of Walter Richard, an auctioneer and Margaret Anne Axford (née McQuillan). In the mid 1880s the family moved to Coolgardie in Western Australia and Jack attended the local state school. He later worked on a farm and moved to Kalgoorlie, working as a labourer in the Boulder Brewery. He served in the Militia from 1912 and enlisted on 19 July 1915 with the service number 3399 and was allocated to the 11th Reinforcements of the 16th AIF in Egypt and France. Prior to this service he had served for three years with the 84th Infantry Regt in the militia.

Axford was allocated to the 11th reinforcements of the 16th Bn and embarked on 1 November 1915 on board HMAT *Benalla* and taken on the strength on 7 March 1916 at Tel el Kebir, Egypt. He was wounded and shell shocked on 9 August 1916 when taking part in the attacks towards Mouquet Farm on the Somme in France and in August 1917 was kept out of action until January 1918 owing to being wounded by shrapnel on his left knee in action at Gapaard Farm in Belgium.

In January he took a course in gas training and was made a Lance Corporal in February and in March-April helped to stop the German Spring Offensive at Hébuterne on the Somme. He was awarded the MM in May (*London Gazette* 13 September) and promoted to Corporal on 14 July 1918, the month in which he also won his VC ten days earlier. In September he was sent back to England, where, where on the 26th he received the decoration from the King in the Quadrangle of Buckingham Palace. At the end of 1918, when he was on furlough in Australia, the Armistice was signed, and he was discharged from the Army in Perth on 6 February, the following year.

Axford then returned to farming near Perth, and worked as a clerk for the H.V. McKay Sunshine Harvester Company. On 27 November 1926 at St Mary 's Catholic Cathedral, Sydney he married a shop assistant, Lily (Maud), daughter of W.J. Foster, and the couple settled down at 12 Harrow Street, Mount Hawthorn, a suburb of Perth, where they reared five children – two sons and three daughters.

Nearly two years after the Second World War began Axford enlisted on 25 June 1941 with the AMF, and after serving with the Western Australian Echelon and Records Office and six years later he was discharged with the rank of Sergeant on 14 April 1947. He was part of the Australian contingent at the 1956 VC centenary in Hyde Park and in early October 1983 travelled to London for a VC–GC reunion. It was on his way back to Perth that he died between Dubai and Hong Kong on 11 October 1983.

His funeral with full military honours, took place on 21 October in a service which was preceded by a Requiem Mass, the coffin was placed on a flag-draped gun carriage and bore a digger's hat. Axford's medals were also displayed on a cushion supported by a soldier. Axford is commemorated at the Garden of Remembrance, Ground Niche, Karrakatta Crematorium, Hollywood, Perth, where his ashes were interred in Portion M. Row C. Niche 1 and later a plaque to his memory was placed on the Remembrance Wall-19. Row A. Two other holders of the VC attended his funeral, Jim Gordon and Keith Payne together with many of his former comrades, some on crutches. Axford's wife, Maud, predeceased him by three months.

Apart from the VC his decorations included the MM, 1914–15 Star, BWM, VM and two awards for his service in the Second World War: the War Medal (1939–45) and the Australia Service Medal 1939–45. He was also awarded Coronation medals, for 1937 and 1953 and the Queen Elizabeth II Silver Jubilee Medal 1977. All these are held by the Australian War Memorial in Canberra, A.C.T. having been presented in 1985.

In the same city he is commemorated with Axford Place and in the Victoria Cross Memorial Park, and in Sydney at the Victoria Cross Memorial at the Queen Victoria Building.

H. DALZIEL
Hamel Wood, France, 4 July

On the same day that L. Cpl Thomas Axford (16th Bn, AIF) won his VC near Vaire and Hamel Woods, Pte Henry Dalziel of the 15th (Queensland & Tasmanian) Bn AIF (4th Bde, 4th Div.) was winning his at Hamel Wood in the battle for the possession of Hamel and Vaire Woods, to the north-east of Villers-Bretonneux on 4 July 1918.

Pear Trench to the south-west of the village of Hamel was one of three main, known obstacles and fire was coming from it. To assist the 15th Bn three tanks had been allocated to the left of the battalion. The infantry was lying down and waiting for the tanks to move over the obstacle. However, there was no sign of the tanks and the infantry had to cope without their assistance. Though the companies on the flanks were enfiladed by machine guns they could still work forward. Each platoon had two Lewis guns and it was found that by firing over tall crops from the hip these guns could silence the enemy. Both of Capt. E.K. Carter's legs were broken, but his gunners silenced two German machine guns and his men rushed forward to capture the guns. However, a third machine gun on the left opened up. Dalziel, one of the few men still unwounded, clapped an extra drum of ammunition to his colleague's gun and then drawing his revolver rushed the German machine-gun post, captured it, shot two men and took the remainder prisoner. One German fought so bravely that Dalziel took him prisoner rather than shooting him. Dalziel was wounded in the hand, losing his trigger finger. He was ordered back but continued fighting before being ordered back a second time. When bringing back some ammunition which had been dropped by parachute he was shot in the head.

The citation for his VC won during the battle of Hamel, was published three weeks later in the *London Gazette* of 17 August as follows:

For most conspicuous bravery and devotion to duty when in action with a Lewis gun section. His company met with determined resistance from a strong point which was strongly garrisoned, manned by numerous machine-guns, and undamaged by our artillery fire, also protected by strong wire entanglements. A heavy concentration of machine-gun fire caused many casualties, and held up our advance. His Lewis gun having come into action and silenced enemy guns in one direction, an enemy gun opened fire from another direction. Private Dalziel dashed at it, and with his revolver killed or captured the entire crew and gun, and allowed our advance to continue. He was severely wounded in the hand, but carried on and took part in the capture of the final objective. He twice went over open ground under heavy enemy artillery and machine-gun fire to secure ammunition, and though suffering from considerable loss of blood, he filled magazines and served his guns until severely wounded through the head. His magnificent bravery and devotion to duty was an inspiring example to all his comrades, and his dash and unselfish courage at a lost critical time undoubtedly saved many lives and turned what would have been a severe check into a splendid success.

Henry Dalziel was born in Irvinebank, North Queensland, Australia on 18 February 1893 and was the son of a miner, James and his wife, Eliza Maggie Dalziel (née McMillan). Henry was educated at various state schools in Queensland including Irvinebank. After leaving school he got a job as a fireman with the Queensland Government Railways on the scenic line between Cairns on the coast and Atherton, where the family had also moved.

On 16 January 1915 Dalziel enlisted in Cairns and was allocated the number of 1936 and after training he embarked from Brisbane on 16 April as a reinforcement for the 15th Bn, joining them in July on the Gallipoli Peninsula. He took part in the battle of Sari Bair in the following month and serving with the machine-gun section he became known as 'Two Gun Harry'. On 28 August he was evacuated to Hospital in Egypt with rheumatism and was sent to England where he was a patient in the 3rd London General Hospital from 15 September.

Having been declared fit he left for France on 14 August where he served on the Somme with the 15th Bn. He took part in the actions at Mouquet Farm, Pozières, Flers and Gueudecourt, by which time he had been appointed driver. At the beginning of February 1917 he took part in the attacks on Stormy Trench, north-east of Gueudecourt and later in the spring fought at Bullecourt and in June in the capture of Messines Ridge. On 16 October he was wounded by shrapnel at Polygon Wood and sent to hospital in England at the end of the month. He was back in France at the end of May 1918, when he rejoined the 15th Bn as a gunner, and during the Battle of Hamel in July he became the thousandth winner of the Victoria Cross. He had been wounded again and after surgery in Rouen he was returned to England where he was in hospital for three or four months. All told during the war Dalziel was said to have been wounded thirty-two times and on the last occasion his skull was smashed in and his brain exposed. Skilful medical treatment in England saved his life, and despite his wounds he lived for another forty-seven years, a shock of black hair hiding the scars on his head.

Discharged from hospital Dalziel left England for Australia on 5 January 1919 and once back in his country on 7 March 1919 he was soon receiving further medical treatment but at the same time he was receiveing a hero's welcome at every station from Townsville to Atherton, where his home was. On his return he was made a great fuss off and much entertained and feted as the story of his dashing deeds were widely published. In May 1919 he was the guest of honour at a dinner given by the members of the Atherton sub-branch of the Sailors' and Soldiers' Imperial League of Australia at Markham's BV Hotel and during the evening was presented with cheques totaling £35.

In June 1919 he was discharged from the army at Brisbane and in 1920, when a patient at the 17th Australian General Hospital at South Brisbane, Dalziel met a nurse named Ida Maud (née Ramsay) and the couple married in 1921. He found that he was unable to cope with his former job on the railways and instead returned to Atherton where he tended a small orchard which was close to the railway station. The couple then took part in a land settlement scheme and acquired a block of land which they called 'Zenith'. However, because of his injuries Dalziel's wife did most of the work involved in running a small mixed farm. The couple suffered hardship during the years of depression and Dalziel even went as far as Sydney in order to try and get work, leaving his wife to look after the smallholding. He worked at one point in a Sydney factory in the late 1920s and tried his hand at gold prospecting at Bathurst but the serious illness of his wife led to his return to Queensland. In 1933 he settled in Brisbane for a time but was unemployed. He did qualify for a war pension and developed an interest in writing songs, some of which were published in Britain. In the early 1930s he and his wife separated and he joined the Citizen Military Forces 9th/15th Bn becoming a Sergeant in 1933 and then became the first holder of the VC to be a member of the Guard of Honour at the opening of the Queensland Parliament, when he was a member of the King's Colour escort.

On 15 December 1935 he married Elsie Kanowski and the couple were to have three children, two sons and one daughter. After the Second World War broke out he rejoined the Army and in June 1940 became a Pioneer Sergeant and on the occasion of Anzac ceremonies used to carry the 15th Bn Colour. In June 1956 he attended the VC centenary at Hyde Park as a member of the Australian contingent and on the same trip laid a wreath on the memorial at Hamel in France. While there he attempted to discover the area where he won his VC but owing to the lush agricultural growth was unable to find any trace.

At the time of his death his home address was 157 Ardyne Road, Oxley, Queensland; and he died from a stroke in Greenslope Repatriation Hospital, Brisbane on 24 July 1965 and was cremated with full military honours with about fifty troops present when his coffin was laid on a gun-carriage. The service took place at Mount Thompson Crematorium, Brisbane on 27 July 1965 and his ashes scattered in the Garden of Remembrance. There is also a plaque to him at the crematorium Wall 12. Section 16. No 106.

Dalziel's name is commemorated in a number of different ways including the name of the Officer's Club in the Brisbane army barracks at Enoggera (Brisbane) and on three roads, one at Enoggerra barracks, another in New South Wales in Singleton and a third north of Brisbane in Nundah. He was also commemorated at the Athetrton RSL Club and with a bar and with an artillery piece in a nearby park. He is also remembered with a display at the Australian War Memorial in Canberra A.C.T. and in the same city in the Victoria Cross Memorial Park and in Sydney with the Victoria Cross Memorial at the Queen Victoria Building. On 28 August 2003 a dialysis centre was opened in his name in Greenslopes Private Hospital in Brisbane.

His decorations apart from the VC included the 1914–15 Star, BWM, VM, two Coronation medals, the Australian War Medal 1939/45 and Australian Service medal, were in private hands until 2010 when they were offered for sale by Noble Numismatics of Sydney on 25 November and fetched $525, 000 (£326,665). They were presented by the purchaser to the Australian War Museum.

W.E. BROWN

Villers-Bretonneux, France, 6 July

On 5 July, the day after the Australian success at the Battle of Hamel it was obvious the enemy was thoroughly disorganised and that it would be a good time to push forward as far as possible. Cpl Walter Brown was a member of the 20th Bn (5th Australian Bde, 2nd Australian Div.) and was to win a VC north of the Roman road which ran between Villers-Bretonneux and Warfusée Abancourt.

The 6th (Victoria) Bde was due for relief and the next day Cpl Brown, a member of one of the incoming battalions, was told that some German snipers 'over there' and were being troublesome. After waiting half an hour for the enemy to reveal themselves he decided to go and see the situation for himself. The trench that he was using soon became shallow and therefore he had 70 yards of open line to cross before seeing a mound from where a shot rang out. Hearing that it had been decided to rush this post, Brown on his own initiative decided to take matters into his own hands. He dropped his rifle, picked up two Mills bombs and ran towards the mound, throwing a bomb as he did so, which unfortunately fell short of the enemy position. He then dropped down into some broken ground and waited for several minutes before moving on and jumping down into a German trench. With only one bomb left he then stood at the door of a dug-out calling on the occupants to surrender. One of the occupants came out and after a scuffle Brown knocked him to the ground. Soon shouts of surrender were heard and one officer together with eleven men emerged from the dug-out. Brown 'encouraged' the thirteen Germans to go back to the Australian lines where they were 'taken care of' by the 21st Bn. As they moved across the open ground they were machine gunned from their own lines.

The party captured had been holding support posts on the day of the Hamel battle and after the German defeat these posts became part of the German front line.

Not surprisingly, news of Brown's extraordinary exploit spread like wildfire and Lt C.E. Cameron, Brown's company commander, asked him 'What the devil have you been doing up there?' General Monash too heard of it and included the incident in a divisional order.

Six weeks later the citation for Brown's VC was published in the *London Gazette* on 17 August 1918 as follows:

> For most conspicuous bravery and determination when with an advance party from his battalion which was going into the line in relief. The company to which he was attached carried out during the night a minor operation resulting in the capture of a small system of enemy trench. Early on the following morning an enemy strong post about seventy yards distant caused the occupants of the newly captured trench great inconvenience by persistent sniping. Hearing that it had been decided to rush this post, Corpl. Brown, on his own initiative, crept out along the trench and made a dash towards the post. An enemy machine gun opened from another trench, and forced him to take cover. Later he again dashed forward and reached his objective. With a Mills grenade in his hand he stood at the door of a dug-out and called on the occupants to surrender. One of the enemy rushed out, a scuffle ensued, and Corpl. Brown knocked him down with his fist. Loud cries of ' Kamerad!' were then heard, and from the dug-out an officer and eleven other ranks appeared. This party Corpl. Brwn brought back as prisoners to our line, the enemy meanwhile from other positions bringing heavy machine-gun fire to bear on the party.

Walter Ernest Brown (known as Wally) was born in New Norfolk, Tasmania on 3 July 1885, the son of a miller, Sidney Francis Brown and his wife Agnes Mary, (née Carney). After leaving school he became a grocer in Hobart the Tasmanian capital but later moved to Petersham in New South Wales, where he enlisted in the infantry with the service number 1689A on 11 July 1915. On 4 October he left for Egypt and joined the 1st Light Horse on 14 January 1916, later transferring to the Imperial Camel Corps. He wished to get to France and in July 1916 transferred to the 20th Bn reinforcements and his wish was fulfilled when he served briefly with the 55th Bn in Flers. Having experience as a butcher he then changed to the 1st and 2nd Australian Field Butcheries for six months and in St. Omer joined the 20th Bn in July 1917. By now he had formed a great friendship with another private called Hughes, who was subsequently killed. The two men had often carried out 'stunts' together and were inseparable cobbers. The Third Battle of Ypres began on 31 July and Brown won the DCM in Passchendaele in October 1917 for:

> ... most self-sacrificing devotion to duty, attending to the wounded of his company under heavy shell-fire. Later in the action he took charge of his section, after its sergeant had become a casualty, and showed a fine example of courage and leadership to the men.

He was promoted to lance corporal on 19 October and wounded on 3 November. In January 1918, when he was due for some leave, Brown applied for permission to search for the body of Hughes, his dead friend and succeeded in finding his remains and carved a wooden cross which he then erected on the grave.

Brown was promoted to corporal on 7 April 1918 and after he won his VC in early July he was wounded again on 11 August and promoted to Sergeant on 13 September.

On 6 October he was awarded his VC at York Cottage, Sandringham, Norfolk, together with Lt Borella. He was discharged from the Army on 15 February 1919 and later lived in Sydney and got a job as a brass finisher in Victoria.

On 4 June 1932 Brown married Miss Maud Dillon from Ireland in Bexley, New South Wales and at the ceremony eight VC holders provided a guard of honour. The couple had two children – a son who did not reach adulthood and a daughter. Brown's home address was 38 Arthur Street, Allawah, New South Wales and from 1931 to 1940 he worked for the Murrumbidges Irrigation Company as a channel attendant (water-bailiff) and during this time was posted to Leeton.

After the Second World War broke out in September 1939 Brown enlisted in the 2nd AIF on 21 June 1940 and was posted to the 2nd/15th Field Regt (2nd AIF) as a Sergeant. On the application form he stated that he had no previous military experience, as that way he thought he stood a better chance of getting back into the army. Although he was already in his mid-50s, he lied too about his date of birth, which he gave as July 1900, making him fifteen years younger than he really was. In the camp at Wagga Wagga, however, his cover was blown and his identity revealed and the Australian press took it up, but the military authorities took no action. At this stage he decided to revert in rank to gunner.

Brown set out for Malaya with his battalion on 28 June 1941 and was in the thick of the fighting with the Japanese invaders on Singapore Island. During the fierce fighting he was to be seen walking with a bagful of grenades towards the enemy lines, shouting 'No surrender for me' and was never seen again. His comrades who survived this fighting became POWs on 15 February 1942, when Singapore disastrously fell to the Japanese invaders. However, in *The Reveille* of 1 March 1968 a former officer, Lt Frederick Turner, was quoted as having met Brown ten days after he was allegedly last seen and the sighting was in Sumatra! This seems to be a genuine report but it only delays Brown's death by about ten days. Turner was also a First World War veteran.

Walter Brown is commemorated at the Kranji Memorial, Singapore, column 115 and his VC and medals are with the Australian War Memorial, Canberra and apart from the VC, he won the DCM and bar, 1914–15 Star, BWM, VM, 1939–45 Star, Pacific Star, and Coronation Medal 1937. Brown's portrait by Sir John Longstaff is also at Canberra, as well as the enemy machine gun which he captured during his VC exploit. In the same city he is commemorated in the Victoria Cross Memorial Park and also commemorated with Brown Street. There is also a plaque at the Leeton Soldiers' Club in New South Wales. In Sydney he is remembered at the Victoria Cross Memorial at the Queen Victoria Building.

Walter Brown's VC deed was written up in the *Victor* comic, with the Second World War element included but with no updating of uniform. Despite this exaggerated fiction Wally Brown certainly seems to have been a man of his time and a Digger in the best sense, he was a loyal, cheerful and very brave man.

A.C. BORELLA

Villers-Bretonneux, France, 17/18 July

On 17 July the 26th Bn (Queensland & Tasmaina) (7th Bde) 2nd Australian Div. advanced from the Monument Farm area east of Villers-Bretonneux to a position just short of the German line which straddled a railway line. The 26th Bn attacked to the south and the 25th (Queensland) Bn of the same brigade, to the north. The men attacking in the south had 500 yards to cover before reaching the first German trench and they started off from an orchard. Lt Borella was in charge of a raid in the direction of a trench called Jaffa and while leading his platoon he noticed an enemy machine gun firing through the Australian barrage, which was planned to last for six minutes. He ran out in front of his men and into the barrage and shot the gunners with his revolver and captured the gun. He then led his small party of ten men and two Lewis guns against Jaffa Trench, a western branch of the German support line which turned out to be full of Germans. The Queenslanders threw bombs into the trench and a Lewis gunner firing from the hip sprayed bullets at the enemy. A few bombs were also rolled down the steps of two large dug-outs and thirty prisoners captured. In fact the trench that Borella had seized was a trench 200 yards beyond Borella's objective. As soon as the enemy had vacated their positions a fire suddenly broke out as a result of the Germans' destruction of maps and documents. Borella, who as has been noted, was too far forward, and he therefore decided to withdraw to a position on the edge of the trench; where if enemy reserves came up they would be quickly spotted.

Towards dawn Borella was able to see further activity in the German-reoccupied Jaffa Trench, where the enemy appeared to be passing stick bombs from hand to hand. A counter-attack was clearly in the offing and Borella took his men further back and out of bombing range. At the same time he sent an SOS for artillery support, a request which was also repeated by the 25th Bn to the north. Unfortunately, the artillery caught some of Borella's men by accident as they were still too far ahead. Borella's 'cool determination inspired his men to resist heroically, and the enemy were repulsed with very heavy loss'. Although on 18 July the enemy continued to move forward for short periods, no further counter-attacks took place. However, the enemy artillery continued shelling throughout the day and by mid-evening further reserves were being sent up in large numbers. A second counter-attack was now expected and when about 500 Germans were in their front line positions, their artillery increased in intensity. Borella's party could see a large German group advancing with three machine guns which were turned on his position. Again the Allied artillery was called up by Borella but this time he made sure that they themselves were not going to be caught up in it. The artillery responded immediately and Australian rifle and machine-gun fire concentrated on the attackers at point blank range. Allied airmen also assisted by flying overhead and using their guns to good effect. The second counter-attack also failed, and seventy men, including two officers, had been captured in the fighting.

Lt Borella had earned a very well deserved VC and the citation for it was published eight weeks later in the *London Gazette* of 16 September 1918 as follows:

Whilst leading his platoon with the first wave, Lieut. Borella marked and enemy machine gun firing through our barrage. He ran out ahead of his men into the barrage, shot two German machine gunners with his revolver, and captured the gun. He then led his party, now reduced to ten men and two Lewis guns, against a very strongly-held trench, using his revolver and later a rifle, with great effect, causing many enemy casualties. His leading and splendid example resulted in the garrison being quickly shot or captured. Two large dugouts were also bombed and thirty prisoners taken. Subsequently the enemy twice counter-attacked in strong force, on the second occasion outnumbering Lieut. Borella's platoon by ten to one, but his cool determination inspired his men to resist heroically, and the enemy were repulsed with very heavy loss.

Albert Chalmers Borella was born in Borung, to the north-west of Bendigo, Victoria, Australia on 7 August 1881, the son of a farmer, Louis Borella, and his wife, Annie, (née Chalmers) of Thyra. Annie died when Albert was only four years old and his father remarried. The boy was educated in Borung and Wychitella state schools. He later farmed in the Borung and Echuca district and served with a local volunteer infantry company of Victoria Rangers for eighteen months. He then moved to Melbourne and joined the Metropolitan Fire Brigade in April 1910. In January 1913 he resigned from this post and tried his hand at farming again, taking up a pastoral lease on the River Daly in the Northern Territory. With the assistance of aboriginal boys he erected a house and built a fence for his property before spiraling costs caused him to abandon the project.

The war therefore came at a good time for him and solved his immediate career problems, but he had to travel to Queensland as recruits weren't being taken in in the Northern Territories and his destination was Townsville in Queensland, where he enlisted on 15 March 1915. He was then posted to B Coy of the 26th Bn on 24 May. The full name of his battalion was the 26th Bn (Queensland and Tasmania), which was part of the 7th Australian Bde, 2nd Australian Div.. After training in Egypt his battalion landed on Gallipoli on 12 September 1915, and there he was made a Corporal. He was wounded in November and evacuated with jaundice to England.

On 5 February 1916 Borella rejoined his battalion in France and was wounded a second time at Pozières on the Somme on 29 July 1916. He was then evacuated for four months and in January 1917 was promoted to Sergeant. In March he was awarded the MM for bravery at Malt Trench, Warlencourt and on 7 April he was commissioned as a 2nd lieutenant and Mentioned in Despatches. In August he returned to England for officer training and in November was made a full lieutenant.

Early in 1918 his battalion held the line at Dernancourt near Albert and during this time he took part in patrols and raids. He was also involved in the fighting at Morlancourt and Hamel. On 17/18 July he won the VC at Villers-Bretonneux and was decorated with the award at York Cottage, Sandringham on 6 October 1918, on the same occasion as Cpl Walter Brown was.

After winning the VC and returning to England Borella embarked for Australia, where he arrived on 6 November 1918 and in the following February he was demobilised and was transferred to the Reserve of Officers. He then went to Hamilton in Victoria to take up farming again, at a soldier settlement block and a few years later in

1924 he became the National Party Candidate for Dundas and was
only narrowly beaten in the Legislative Assembly election.

On 16 August 1928 Borella married Elsie Jane Love, the daughter
of Mr G. Love, at Wesley Church, Hamilton and the couple were to
have four sons, of whom two survived infancy. In September 1939
Borella changed his name to Chalmers-Borella by deed-poll and soon
after the Second World War began he was appointed from the Reserve
of Officers to serve in the 12th Australian Garrison Bn. In 1941 he
was transferred to the POW group at Rushworth, where he remained
until 16 March 1943. On 1 September 1942 he had been promoted
to captain and served with the 51st Garrison Coy at Myrtleford until
1945.

When the Second World War finished Capt. Borella became an
inspector of dangerous cargoes for the Commonwealth Department
of Supply and Shipping and remained in this job until 1956, when he
moved to Albury, New South Wales.

Also in 1956 he was a member of the Australian contingent at
the VC centenary celebrations at Hyde Park, London and in 1967 he
was awarded the Anzac Medallion as a Gallipoli veteran. His address
in Albury was at 958 Sylvania Avenue, North Albury and for the last
four years of his life he was in poor health and died at the age of
86 on 7 February 1968. Two days later he was given a full military
funeral with a gun carriage for his coffin; band, eight pall-bearers
and a fourteen-man firing party. His funeral took place in St David's
Presbyterian Church in Olive Street and the Mayor Albury gave the
address. Afterwards Borella was buried in the Presbyterian Cemetery.

Albert Borella, a big tough-looking bloke, was survived by his wife and
his two remaining sons. He is commemorated in a number of ways apart
from having a display at the AWM in Canberra; he has a park in the Jingili
a suburb in Darwin, Northern Territory, opened in 1980 named after him
where there was already a Borella Circuit. There is also a Borella Club
at 31 Supply Bn, Wodonga, New South Wales and a road and plaque
named after him in Albury. Finally there is also a street in Canberra
named after him and he is also one of the VC winners remembered in the
in the Victoria Cross Memorial in Canberra and at the Queen Victoria
Building in Sydney. A Borella Commemorative display is in Albury and
his original Albury Street plaque was unveiled on 17 July 1978 at the
east end of Borella Road but in July 2007 it was moved owing to road
changes and is now at the base of Borella Road Bridge.

Borella's VC and medals include the MM, 1914–15 Star, BWM,
VM, Australian Service Medal for service in the Second World War,

two Coronation medals, a Gallipoli Medalion, a Battle of the Somme Medal, Federation of Veterans of King Albert I (Cross) 1909–34, and Front-Line Service Medal. The group is not publically held.

J. MEIKLE

Near Marfaux, France, 20 July

Sgt John Meikle 1/4th Bn Seaforth Highlanders (Rossshire Buffs) Territorial Force (154 Bde, 51st (Highland) Div.) was with No. 2 Coy in the valley of the River Ardre, a tributary of the River Vesle, south-west of Rheims on 19 July 1918 when the enemy was aiming to cross the River Marne; converge on Rheims from east and west and seize Paris. In the evening the battalion left the village of Champillon in order to enter the line at 8.00 the following morning. Unfortunately the company mistook Marfaux for Chaumuzy and therefore found itself too far over to the right. Other companies also suffered from a degree of confusion in the morning, and to add to the confusion the 62nd Div. to the right of the Highland Div. had been given the incorrect jumping-off position and therefore had to retire to its left.

In the early afternoon the leading companies of the 1/7th Bn The Argyll & Sutherland Highlanders (TF) also of 154 Bde came up and by 2.00 p.m. were heavily engaged alongside the 4th Seaforth Highlanders. Machine guns severely hampered progress and in the centre a small group from the Seaforths, which had been holding on to a crest of the ridge, withdrew for a short time but re-established its position later. At 4.30 p.m. the enemy counter-attacked and was repelled; and two hours later a fierce bombardment took place around Rectangle Wood however the brigade failed to reach its objective and suffered heavy casualties. It had been thought that the enemy would be making a determined defence instead of fighting a rearguard action.

It was when No. 2 Coy was held up by machine-gun fire that Sgt Meikle advanced over 150 yards alone and rushed one of the machine-gun nests single-handed, firing his revolver at the gun crews and putting the remainder out of action with a heavy stick. After this he waved his company forward. Later in the day, the company was again held up by an enemy machine gun and by this time most of Meikle's platoon had become casualties. On this occasion he seized a rifle and bayonet from a fallen colleague and again rushed forward at the gun crew. This time he was killed when almost at the gun position, but two other men who had followed him put the gun out of action.

Two days later the line reached from the southern edge of the Bois d'Aulnay to the western side of the very large wood called the Bois de Courton which lay behind Marfaux village. The 4th Seaforths withdrew into reserve to a wood 500 yards to the south-east of Bullin Farm and the fighting in this area continued until 6 August, when the Marne district was finally liberated and the German rout completed.

Meikle is buried in the Marfaux British Cemetery, Plot VIII, Row C, Grave 1. Marfaux is a village and commune in the département of the Marne on the north-east bank of the small River Ardre. It is 11½ miles from Rheims and the village had been captured by the Germans in May 1918. The cemetery was made after the Armistice by the concentration of graves in the area of the Marne. It is possible that Meikle's first grave was at Bois d'Aulnay British Cemetery, Chaumuzy, across the River Ardre. It was mainly men from the 51st (Highland) Div. who were buried in this cemetery before they were gathered into one cemetery.

For his selfless bravery Meikle was awarded a posthumous VC which was published in the *London Gazette* of 16 September 1918. It read as follows:

> ... when his company, having been held up by machine-gun fire, he rushed single-handed a machine-gun next. He emptied his revolver into the crews of two guns, and put the remainder out of action with a heavy stick. Then, standing up, he waved his comrades on. Very shortly afterwards another hostile machine gun checked progress and threatened also the success of the company on the right. Most of his platoon having become casualties, Sergt. Meikle seized the rifle and bayonet of a fallen comrade, and again rushed forward against the gun crew, but was killed almost on the gun position. His bravery allowed two other men who followed him to put this gun out of action. This gallant non-commissioned officer's valour, devotion to duty and utter disregard for his personal safety was an inspiring example to all.

John Meikle was one of eleven children, of whom eight survived into adulthood, and he was born on 11 September 1898 at 34 Freeland Place, Kirkintilloch, Dunbartonshire, Scotland. His father was also named John and from 1901 John senior worked at Messrs Perry & Hope as a section charge hand at their chemical works on the nearby canal bank. John Junior was educated at Levern Public School, Nitshill, where he became very keen on football and ran errands in connection with the local soccer team, Nitshill Victoria Football Club. By then the growing family had moved to a new home at 1 Office Row, Nitshill.

After leaving school Meikle joined the railways and worked for the Glasgow, Barrhead and Kilmarnock Railway Company at Nitshill station, as a clerk at the salary of 7s 6d a week. He enlisted from there in February 1915 with the Seaforth Highlanders at the age of sixteen with the service number 200854. He had made previous attempts to enter the Army but on this occasion he lied about his age; he had been asking his mother to make him porridge in order that his chest should expand! He reported to the Maryhill Barracks, Glasgow and was drafted into the 4th Bn Seaforth Highlanders (Rossshire Buffs) Territorial Force, which later became part of the 154 Bde, 51st (Highland) Div. Meikle was then given training on the Lewis gun, at which he became extremely proficien and remained in Scotland as he was still under age for service abroad. In July 1916 he joined his battalion in France and was promptly made a Corporal. During his first month of fighting he was wounded by a bayonet and was out of front-line duties for a period before rejoining his company.

During the Arras battle in April 1917 the 4th Seaforths did particularly well, capturing a number of German trenches and taking many prisoners. For bravery and leadership in the Third Battle of Ypres Meikle was awarded the MM. The fighting moved on slowly and the Menin Road Ridge was the next feature to be captured.

After going home for a short leave Meikle was presented with a gold watch by the people of Nitshill at The Hurlet and Nitshill Public Hall. He always carried a heavy walking stick during his exploits on the battlefield and on returning from leave on one occasion he realised that he had left the stick at home, but fortunately one of his sisters saw that it had been left behind and ran with it to the station. Soon after his leave Meikle was promoted Sergeant for his qualities of leadership and his skill with the Lewis gun. At the beginning of 1918 he returned to France when his battalion was once again heavily involved in the fighting: their stand to the east of Beaumetz helped to save the 51st (Highland) Div.

At the end of May the right bank of the River Marne from Dormons to Château-Thiérry fell to the Germans and there was a lull in the fighting until mid-July.

When Meikle was killed he had been in the army for three years but was still only nineteen years of age. His captain, C.H. Harris, wrote to his mother a letter which gave a very handsome assessment of his character and abilities as a soldier and Lewis gunner in particular. On his death his mother gave some of the money which John had been sending to her to two local churches. John Meikle senior was presented with his son's VC at Maryhill Barracks by General Sir F.W.N. McCracken KCB, DSO on 28 October 1918. After his death the VC became the property of one of Meikle's brother.

The first public memorial to Meikle took the form of a large photograph of him which was unveiled at Levern Public School, Nitshill. In 1920 his mother was invited to the Buckingham Palace VC garden party and in 1956 two members of the family were invited to the centenary celebrations at Hyde Park. In the following year Levern Primary School decided to incorporate the design of the Victoria Cross into their school cap and blazer. After the war a 7 foot high memorial to Sgt Meikle was erected by his railway colleagues at St Enoch's, station, Nitshill, Glasgow, made out of rough-hewn granite, which was unveiled in 1920 by Lady Lorimer. Owing to the risk of vandalism it was decided to take down the memorial in 1971 and the 4th Seaforth Club in Dingwall arranged for it to re-erected in the town on a safer site infront of Dingwell Station. A large crowd attended the unveiling ceremony and Col H.A.C. Mackenzie, who conducted it, introduced Mr Simon Calder, who had fought alongside Meikle fifty-three years before, and asked him to unveil the memorial. Meikle's brother and sister also attended the ceremony. The Last Post and Reveille as well as 'The Flowers of the Forest' were played during the service. The memorial was officially handed over to the care of the 4th Battalion Seaforth Club by the British Rail Commercial Officer of the Highland Area.

In an act of generosity Perry & Hope, paid for a memorial plaque to be set up in Nitshill Public Hall, where Meilkle had been presented with a gold watch in 1917. The plaque was later taken down for safe-keeping-keeping and ended up in the new Levern Primary School. In

November 1972 Meikle's decorations including the VC, MM, BWM and VM were presented to the 4th Battalion Seaforth Club, Dingwall by his family and are on display at the Military Room at the Dingwall Museum.

In addition to his commemoration at St Enoch's railway station in Glasgow and in Station Square, Dingwell, Meikle's name is remembered on the war memorial in Edinburgh Castle; the roll of honour at the Methodist Church, Pollockshaws; the United Free Church, Nitshill, the local war memorial and the Nitshill Rechabite Society.

R.C. TRAVIS

North of Hébuterne, France, 24 July

In mid-September 1916 Sgt Travis was in the thick of the fighting in the renewed attempts to capture High Wood on the Somme. In 1917 he was in the Ypres Salient with his battalion and was in charge of sniping and observation activities. At the time he was already being described as 'the greatest raiding sergeant on the Western Front'. He gathered about him a very experienced team of scouts who were sometimes called 'Dick and his scouts' or 'Dick Travis and his gang', or even as 'cut-throats'. These men were carefully chosen, and very closely associated with Travis in many of his exploits.

By the end of 1917 Travis's fame had increased even more and in the confusion of the German advance in March 1918 he was in his element, successfully identifying those enemy units which were opposite the New Zealanders' lines.

After the March Spring Offensive the enemy was unable to progress in the area of Rossignol Wood, a position close to the villages of Gommecourt and Bucquoy.

The day before he was killed, Travis wrote the following report, which turned out to be the last from a man whose work as scout leader was without parallel on the Western Front and also covered the incident which won him the VC. The action was described in a New Zealand newspaper account as follows:

> A few seconds before 5 p.m. several Stokes bombs thrown in enemy entanglements in front of blocks. At 5 p.m. our trench mortars put up a perfect barrage on enemy's forward posts for one minute. Our bombing parties rushed the trench and found the enemy very much shaken, some ran down some com. trenches,

while remainder were killed except those who were sent to the rear. Fifteen bodies counted and two M-gs captured in forward positions.

On several occasions enemy tried to hold c.t.s. with bombing parties, but the ground was gained yard by yard. We reached objective about two minutes after 5 p.m., but our bombing party and several scouts bombed up Hawk trench for about 250 yards.

As we were running short of bombs we had to establish a temporary block and hold the enemy until we put permanent blocks across saps. Huns tried to cut us off from the left of Hawk trench, but were beaten off with their own bombs.

Very heavy casualties inflicted on enemy in Hawk trench. Total for day about 50 killed (including two officers) and 6 M-gs captured. Had our party had enough bombs they could have gone to Berlin.

Tragically Travis was killed within his own lines by a shell splinter during a morning bombardment between 8.00 and 9.00 a.m. close to Hawk Trench, Rossignol Wood, on 25 July 1918. A very impressive funeral took place the following day. The cortège was attended by all ranks, from the divisional commander downwards, and slowly wound its way uphill from Coigneux in the valley of Couin to the top of the hill at the Couin New British Cemetery, 10 miles north-west of Albert. As the procession went by some British soldiers who were 'bivied' on the hillside stood to attention, the officers saluting, as the cortège passed. The cemetery is on the north-west side of the Souastre road and was used from January 1917 onwards. Travis was buried with full military honours at 8.00 p.m. in Row 9, Grave 5. 2nd Lt C.A. Kerse, who was killed with him, was buried at the same time. Brig. Gen. Young of the 2nd Bde attended the funeral, along with men of the division. When the 2nd Otago returned from the cemetery down the hill in quick time after the funeral was over, the same British soldiers who had stood to salute Travis now cheered lustily for the battalion and for the memory of Sgt Dick Travis. To quote the battalion *War Diary*:

The death of Sergeant Travis cast a gloom over the whole battalion. Only those who have been with us for any length of time can realise what a loss his death means to us. His name will live in the records of the battalion as a glorious example of heroism and devotion to duty.

The citation for Travis's posthumous VC was published in the *London*

Gazette of 27 September 1918 as follows:

> During surprise operations it was necessary to destroy an impassable wire block. Sergt. Travis, regardless of all personal danger, volunteered for this duty. Before zero hour, in broad daylight, and in close proximity to enemy posts, he crawled out and successfully destroyed the block with bombs, thus enabling the attacking parties to pass through. A few minutes later a bombing party on the right of the attack was held up by two enemy machine guns, and the success of the operation was in danger. Perceiving this, Sergt. Travis with great gallantry and utter disregard of danger, rushed the position, and killed the crew and captured the guns. An enemy officer and three men immediately rushed at him from a bend in the trench and attempted to retake the guns. These four he killed single-handed, thus allowing the bombing party, on which much depended, to advance. The success of the operation was almost entirely due to the heroic work of this gallant N.C.O., and to the vigour with which he made and used opportunities for inflicting casualties on the enemy. He was killed twenty-four hours later when, under a most intense bombardment prior to an enemy counter-attack, he was going from post to post encouraging the men.

Richard Charles Travis was born on 6 April 1884 at Otara, Opotiki, Southland, Auckland, New Zealand. His real name was Dickson Cornelius Savage and he was a son and fifth child of nine of James Savage an Irish immigrant and his wife Frances Theresa (née O'Keefe from Sydney, Australia. The couple had married in 1875. James became a member of the New Zealand Armed Constabulary and took up farming. Richard's education at the Opotiki and Otara schools was reduced to four years as his assistance was required to help out on the farm. He became a useful farmhand and shepherd drover and was especially good as a horse breaker. He grew into a short and stocky young man but in the year of his majority in 1905 he fell out with his father and quit the family home. For a time he lived in Gisborne again working in farming before moving to Winton in 1910 where he carried on with similar work. On 20 August 1914, two weeks after the war broke out he enlisted in Ryal Bush, Southland under the name of Richard Charles Travis, joining the 7th (Southland) Squadron of the Otago Mounted Rifles in Invercargill with the regimental number 9/523.

He travelled to Egypt for training arriving in December and although his regiment landed on the Gallipoli Peninsula as part of the Anzac Force in April 1915 it didn't take part in the initial landings on the 25th, neither did Travis join them until December 1915, a month before the Allied evacuation. However and unofficially he did serve briefly on the Peninsula at an earlier date before being discovered when he was returned to Egypt where he served fourteen days' detention. Leaving Egypt he arrived in France in April 1916; he served with the New Zealand Div. and learnt his craft east of Houplines in the Pont Ballon sector. He then took part in the Battle of the Somme where he won the DCM on 15 September after an attack made by the 2nd Otago Bn on a German pillbox which was holding up an Allied advance. After this deed his rank was made up to sergeant and placed in command of a newly set up observation and sniper section known as 'Travis's Gang'. On 27 March he transferred to the 8th (Southland) Coy of the 2nd Bn Otago Infantry Regt. On 15 February 1918 he was awarded the Croix de Guerre (Belgium) and in May earned the MM

During the war Travis found his true vocation as a soldier and man of action and appeared to be in his element developing into a very fine soldier. What he lacked for in education he more than made up for in his ability of handling men supremely well and at the same time becoming a first class scout and expert with infantry weapons. He was often to be seen carrying a sniper's rifle about with him and one of his favorite trophies was a pair of Zeiss binoculars-cum-periscope which he had acquired from a German officer who no longer had use for them.

According to the *New Zealand Divisional History* it was in 1916 that notice was first taken of Dick Travis who:

> … began to win a name for marked resourcefulness and initiative. Not satisfied with night, he repeatedly led daylight patrols close up to the enemy's wire. For 40 nights in succession from dusk to daylight, he spent the whole time in No Man's Land.

Travis's VC gazetted on 27 September 1918 and sent by mail by the War Office to his Excellency Viscount Jellicoe, Governor General of New Zealand, for presentation to Miss E.L. Murray of Ryal Bush, Southland. Later, all Travis's medals, which included the VC, DCM, MM and Croix de Guerre (Belgium) , were left to Mrs John Wilson as his next of kin. Her husband, John Wilson, later sold or gave the medals to the Invercargill Museum. Otago New Zealand. At the moment they are part of the Southland Museum Collection in Invercargill. Travis was also commemorated at the RSA HQ in Dunedin.

On Anzac Day in 1965, a special ceremony was held in the village of Couin on the Somme attended by the New Zealand Ambassador to France. He also attended other Anzac ceremonies at this time in France and Belgium. Despite the day being overcast and chilly, the party were surprised when they found that the residents of Couin and Hébuterne had turned out in large numbers to greet them. A wreath, which had come from Travis's birthplace, was presented to the Mayor of Couin to lay at the grave. Other wreaths were laid and as a special reciprocal goodwill gesture the New Zealanders laid a wreath at the village memorial. This final ceremony was followed by a *vin d'honneur* at the *Mairie*. The French *tricouleur* used at the graveside was presented by the Mayor of Hébuterne to the New Zealand party to take home with them.

Other commemorations of Travis include a memorial in Ryal Bush, Southland and a plaque in Queens Gardens, Dunedin. In 1965 a biography, Travis VC, by James Gasson was published.

Throughout his life neither discipline nor conformity were ever Travis's strong suit but his military prowess and skill in adapting perfectly to the conditions of a serving soldier on the Western Front more than made up for any deficiencies. He achieved a unique group of decorations aside from the VC including the DCM; MM, 1914–15 Star, BWM, VM and a Croix de Guerre (Belgium). He really was the *King of No Man's Land*.

SOURCES

The sources used in the preparation of this book include the following:
The Lummis VC files at the National Army Museum, London
The Victoria Cross files at the Imperial War Museum, London
The National Archives, Kew, Surrey
Regimental Museums and Archives
The *London Gazette* 1914–1920 (HMSO)
Stand To! and *Bulletin* are journals published by the Western Front
  Association.The Victoria Cross Society also publish a regular
  journal.

C. G. Robertson
Surrey Advertiser
TNA WO 95/2522

E. F. Beal
The Green Howards' Gazette, vol. XXVI, no. 302
TNA WO 95/2616
TNA WO 339/111250

J. C. Buchan
Clackmannan District Council
The Alloa Advertiser
John M. Cameron

E. de Wind
Newtownards Chronicle
Keith Haines
Lester Morrow
TNA WO 339/9643

W. Elstob
The Army Quarterly
Philip Guest
TNA WO 95/2339
TNA WO 339/9643
TNA WO 339/56791

R. F. J. Hayward
Philip Guest
TNA WO 95/2245

M. A. James
Sothebys
Roger Pritchard
TNA WO 95/2085

A. E. Ker
Buchan Dix and Wood (Auctioneers)
Scottish United Services Museum

J. W. Sayer
Stand To! No. 80 September 2007 pages 9–13 by David Baker.
TNA WO 95/2208

C. E. Stone
Royal Artillery Historical Trust
Stand To! Spring 1989, number 25, p. 24–26
Victoria Cross Society, volume 12, p. 35–37
TNA WO 95/2025

J. S. Collings-Wells
David Baines
Bedfordshire Record Office
Luton News
Terry Oliver
TNA WO 95/3118
TNA WO 339/43614

H. G. Columbine

East Essex Gazette
Derek Johnson
Town Council of Frinton and Walton

H. Jackson

Sothebys
Bulletin 52 Oct 1998 Pages 10
TNA WO 95/2003

C. L. Knox

Nuneaton Library
Terry Reeves
TNA WO 95/2497

F. C. Roberts

Burton Daily Mail
TNA WO 95/1721 and 1723

C. Bushell

R. Cude MM
Sidney Lindsay
Donald Sykes
Victoria Cross Society Vol 3 pages 7 to 8.
TNA WO 95/2051

J. R. Gribble

Norah Gribble
Burton Bradstock Online
TNA WO 339/38999

A. C. Herring

Medals International
TNA WO 95/2044
TNA WO 339/76527

J. T. Davies

Sidney Lindsay
TNA WO 95/2323

W. H. Anderson
The Covenanter
The Outpost
Victoria Cross Society Vol 8 page 27
TNA WO 339/21674

A. H. Cross
Stephen Snelling

A. M. Toye
The Aldershot News
Sothebys
TNA WO 95/1713

T. Young
Jack Cavanagh
TNA WO 95/3077

A. Mountain
The White Rose, Regt Journal, April 1967
TNA WO 95/2361

B. A. Horsfall
Spinks
TNA WO 95/2358

B. M. Cassidy
TNA WO 95/1507

S.R. McDougall
Australian Dictionary of Biography – Online Edition

G. M. Flowerdew
Eastern Daily Press
Framlingham College
The Framlinghamian
Dictionary of Canadian Biography – Online Edition

P. F. Storkey
Australian Dictionary of Biography – Online Edition
Napier Daily Telegraph
Reveille
TNA WO/95/3318

R. G. Masters
Sidney Lindsay

E. S. Dougall
Glendinings
Sidney Lindsay
Pembroke Gazette
Spinks
Tonbridge School and the Great War of 1914–1919: A Record of
the Services of Tonbridgians in the Great War of 1914 to 1919 Pages
103–105
TNA WO 339/55092

A. Poulter
Denis Poulter
Yorkshire Evening Post
Bulletin 54 June 1999 Page 19
Daily Telegraph 11 Sept 1999

J. Forbes-Robertson
Cheltenham Chronicle
Glo'shire Graphic
Graham Sacker
TNA WO 95/2305

T. T. Pryce
The Grenadier
Carol Davies
Peter Francis
Michael Pryce May
TNA WO 95/1226
TNA WO 339/95298

J. J. Crowe
Keith Chambers
Doreen and Robin Pannett
Bulletin 90 2011 page 16
Bulletin 92 2012 page 11
TNA WO 95/2430

J. T. Counter
Jersey Evening Post
Sidney Lindsay
Bernard Mann
TNA WO 95/1371

J. E. Woodall
TNA WO 95/1497

C. W. K. Sadlier
Australian Dictionary of Biography – Online Edition
TNA WO 95/3523

T. B. Hardy
Keith Chambers
Andrew and Eleanor Fisher
David Raw

J. Hewitson
Margaret Dickinson
The Ruskin Museum, Coniston
Andrew and Eleanor Fisher
The Lion and the Dragon
Scottish Daily Mail
The Westmorland Gazette
TNA WO 95/1506

G. B. McKean
Jack Cavanagh
County Chronicle
Canadian War Museum, Ottawa
TNA WO 95/3778

W. Beesley

The Coventry Evening Telegraph
Nuneaton Library
Rifle Brigade Association Journal
TNA WO 95/2534

W. Gregg

John Tunstall

W. Ruthven

TNA WO 95/3331
Australian Dictionary of Biography – Online Edition
The Herald
Reveille
Murray Sayle, 'Anzacs "Invade" Gallipoli Again', *Sunday Times*,
  25 April 1965
Stand To! 87 January 2010 page 40

J. Kaeble

Dictionary of Canadian Biography – Online Edition
TNA WO 95/3822

P. Davey

Australian Dictionary of Biography – Online Edition
TNA WO 95/3249

T. L. Axford

Australian Dictionary of Biography – Online Edition

H. Dalziel

Australian Dictionary of Biography – Online Edition
Victoria Cross Society Volume 12 Pages 32–34 (Harry Willey 2002)

W. E. Brown

Australian Dictionary of Biography – Online Edition
The Bulletin
Reveille

A. Borella

Australian Dictionary of Biography – Online Edition
TNA WO 95/3341

J. Meikle

J.M. Cameron
Portrait of a Soldier
Dingwell Museum Trust
Local Studies No. 4
The Royal British Legion (Scotland)

R. C. Travis

Christchurch Star (NZ)
The Otago Daily Times
Stand To! No 28. Spring 1990 pp. 12–13
Fox, Aaron: Travis, Richard Charles 1884–1918: Horse-breaker,
    soldier. (Te Ara Encyclopedia of New Zealand)
TNA WO 95/3703

BIBLIOGRAPHY

Arthur, M., *Symbol of Courage: Men Behind the Medal* (Pan 2005)

Ashcroft, M., *Victoria Cross Heroes* (Revised edition Headline/ Review, 2007)

Australian Dictionary of Biography

Bailey, Roderick, *Forgotten Voices of the Victoria Cross* (Ebury Press, 2010)

Bancroft, J. W., *Devotion to Duty-Tributes to a Region's VC* (Aim High Publications, Manchester, 1990)

Bancroft, J. W., *The Victoria Cross Roll of Honour.* (Aim High Productions, Manchester 1989)

Bean, C. E. W., *The Official History of Australia in the War of 1914–1918, Volume VI, The A. I. F. in France during the Allied Offensive, 1918* (Angus & Robertson, 1942)

Brazier, K., *The Complete Victoria Cross: A Full Chronological Record of all Holders of Britain's Highest Award for Gallantry* (Pen & Sword, Barnsley, 2010)

Canadian War Records, Thirty Canadian VCs, 1918 (Skeffington, Canada, 1919)

Chapman, R., *Beyond Their Duty: Heroes of the Green Howards* (The Green Howards Museum, Richmond, Yorkshire, 2001)

Clark, B., *The Victoria Cross: a Register of Awards to Irish-born Officers and men* (The Irish Sword, 1986)

Deeds that Thrilled the Empire: True Stories of the Most Glorious Acts of Heroism of the Empire's Soldiers and Sailors during the Great War (Hutchinson, London, no date)

De la Billiere, P., *Supreme Courage: Heroic Stories from 150 Years of the VC* (Abacus 2005)

Doherty, R. and Truesdale, D., *Irish Winners of the Victoria Cross* (Four Courts Press, Dublin. 2000)

Edmonds, Sir J. E. (ed.), *Military Operations France and Belgium* (Macmillan/HMSO 1922–1949

Falls, C., *The History of the 36th (Ulster) Division* (McCaw, Stevenson & Orr, Belfast, 1922)

Gliddon, G. (ed.), *VCs Handbook:* The Western Front 1914–1918 (Sutton Publishing, Stroud, 2005)

Gough, General Sir Hubert, *The Fifth Army* (Hodder & Stoughton, 1931)

Grieve, W. Grant and Newman, B., *Tunnellers: The Story of the Tunnelling Companies, Royal Engineers, during the World War* (Herbert Jenkins, 1936)

Harvey, D., *Monuments to Courage: Victoria Cross Headstones & Memorials* (D. Harvey 1999)

James, E. A., *British Regiments 1914–1918* (Samson Books, 1978)

Kelleher, J.P. (comp.), *Elegant Extracts: The Royal Fusiliers Recipients of The Victoria Cross* 'For Valour' (The Royal Fusiliers Association, London, 2010)

The King's Regiment 8th, 63rd, 96th: For Valour (Fleur de Lys Publishing, Cheshire, no date)

Kirkby, H. L. and Walsh, R. R., *The Seven VCs of Stonyhurst College* (THCL Books, Blackburn, 1987)

Lindsay, Sidney, ' *Merseyside Heroes'* (unpublished manuscript)

Lovell, N., *VCs of Bromsgrove School: The Stories of Five Victoria Crosses won by old Bromsgrovians* (Bromsgrove School, no date)

Middlebrook, M., *The Kaiser's Battle, 21 March 1918: The First Day of the German Spring Offensive* (Allen Lane, 1978)

Montell, H. A., *Chaplain's War: The Story of Noel Mellish VC, MC* (Serendipity, 2002)

Murphy, James, *Liverpool VCs* (Pen & Sword Military, Barnsley, 2008)

Napier, G., *The Sapper VCs: The Story of Valour in the Royal Engineers and its Associated Corps* (The Stationery Office, London, 1998)

Nicholson, G. W. L. N., *Canadian Expeditionary Force 1914–1919* (Queen's Printer, Ottawa, 1962)

O' Moore, General Sir Creagh and Humphris, E. M., *The VC and DSO, Vol 1* (1924)

Pannett, R. J. and Pannett, D. A., *Captain J.J. Crowe VC. A Short Biography* (unpublished)

Pillinger, D. and Staunton, A., *Victoria Cross Presentations and Locations* (D. Pillinger & A. Staunton, Maidenhead, 2000)

Raw, D., *'It's Only Me': A life of The Reverend Theodore Bayley Hardy VC, DSO, MC, 1863–1918* (Frank Peters, Kendal, 1988)

The Register of the Victoria Cross (This England Books, 1988)

Scott, Brough, 'Galloper Jack: The remarkable story of the man who rode the real war horse' (Racing Post, 2012)

Seaton, D., *A Tiger and a Fusilier: Leicestershire' s VC Heroes* (Author, 2001)

Seeley, J.E.B., *Adventure* (Heinemann, 1931)

Shannon, S. D., *Beyond Praise: The Durham Light Infantrymen Who Were Awarded the Victoria Cross* (County Durham Books, Durham, 1998)

Smith, M., *Award for Valour: A History of the Victoria Cross and the Evolution of British Heroism* (Palgrave Macmillan, 2008)

Smyth, J., *The Story of the Victoria Cross* (Muller, 1963)

Shaw Sparrow, W., *The Fifth Army in March 1918* (Allen Lane, The Bodley Head, 1921)

Staunton, A., *VICTORIA CROSS: Australia's Finest and the Battles they Fought* (Hardie Grant Books, Victoria, 2005)

Times History of the War

Who's Who. (A. & C. Black) various editions

Wigmore, L. and Harding, B., *They Dared Mightily* (Second Edition revised by Williams, J. & Staunton, S., Australian War Memorial, Canberra 1986)

Williams, W. Alister, *Heart of a Dragon: The VCs of Wales and the Welsh Regiments, 1914–1982* (New Edition Bridge Books, Wrexham, 2008)

Divisional, Regimental and Battalion histories have all been consulted where appropriate but unfortunately are too numerous to list here.

INDEX

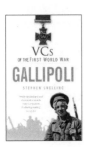
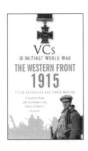